The Integrated
Reporting Movement

The Wiley Corporate F&A series provides information, tools, and insights to corporate professionals responsible for issues affecting the profitability of their company, from accounting and finance to internal controls and performance management.

Founded in 1807, John Wiley & Sons is the oldest independent publishing company in the United States. With offices in North America, Europe, Asia, and Australia, Wiley is globally committed to developing and marketing print and electronic products and services for our customers' professional and personal knowledge and understanding.

The Integrated Reporting Movement

Meaning, Momentum, Motives, and Materiality

ROBERT G. ECCLES
MICHAEL P. KRZUS
with
SYDNEY RIBOT

WILEY

Cover Design: Wiley
Cover Illustration: ©iStock.com/patilankur

Published by John Wiley & Sons, Inc., Hoboken, New Jersey.
Published simultaneously in Canada.

Limit of Liability/Disclaimer of Warranty: While the publisher and author have used their best efforts in preparing this book, they make no representations or warranties with respect to the accuracy or completeness of the contents of this book and specifically disclaim any implied warranties of merchantability or fitness for a particular purpose. No warranty may be created or extended by sales representatives or written sales materials. The advice and strategies contained herein may not be suitable for your situation. You should consult with a professional where appropriate. Neither the publisher nor author shall be liable for any loss of profit or any other commercial damages, including but not limited to special, incidental, consequential, or other damages.

For general information on our other products and services or for technical support, please contact our Customer Care Department within the United States at (800) 762-2974, outside the United States at (317) 572-3993 or fax (317) 572-4002.

Wiley publishes in a variety of print and electronic formats and by print-on-demand. Some material included with standard print versions of this book may not be included in e-books or in print-on-demand. If this book refers to media such as a CD or DVD that is not included in the version you purchased, you may download this material at http://booksupport.wiley.com. For more information about Wiley products, visit www.wiley.com.

Library of Congress Cataloging-in-Publication Data:

Eccles, Robert G.
 The integrated reporting movement : meaning, momentum, motives, and materiality / Robert G. Eccles, Michael P. Krzus, with Sydney Ribot.
   1 online resource. – (Wiley corporate F&A series)
 Includes bibliographical references and index.
 Description based on print version record and CIP data provided by publisher; resource not viewed.
 ISBN 978-1-118-99373-6 (ebk); ISBN 978-1-118-99374-3 (ebk); ISBN 978-1-118-64698-4 (hardcover) 1. Corporation reports. 2. Corporation reports–South Africa–Case studies. 3. Social responsibility of business. 4. Sustainability. I. Krzus, Michael P. II. Title.
 HG4028.B2
 658.15'12–dc23   2014029756

Printed in the United States of America

10   9   8   7   6   5   4   3   2   1

Contents

Chapter 8: Reporting Websites 225

Appendix 8A: Methodology for Website Coding 253

Chapter 9: Information Technology 261

Chapter 10: Four Recommendations 281

Foreword

TRUE LEADERS AIM TO TAKE people to a place they have never been, and they have a plan to get them there.

For those among us who dream of leading our companies toward economic, environmental, and social sustainability, "integrated reporting" is a key part of the plan to get us where we need to go.

This is why Robert Eccles's and Mike Krzus's *The Integrated Reporting Movement* is such an important book; it arms today's leaders with reasons to continue the movement's momentum.

More than a trend, a public relations (PR) incentive, or just "the right thing to do," sustainability is about growth and innovation. It's about winning the war for talent and winning in the marketplace. It recognizes that, today, people care as much about a company's purpose, values, and global impact as they do about its products, packaging, and prices. Integrated reporting is a big idea because, as a methodology, it helps create the strategies, the business models, the cultures, and the thinking that lead to a more sustainable business—and a more sustainable world.

From my own front-row seat as a chief executive officer (CEO), I've been a proud champion of the movement that Professor Eccles and Mike Krzus so thoroughly describe and enthusiastically support. SAP is a global technology company with 66,000 employees and more than 260,000 customers. As we went from having a stand-alone sustainability strategy to creating a corporate strategy that is sustainable (a huge difference), we began presenting our financial and nonfinancial results in a single report. This bold shift is helping us achieve several goals:

First, it enhances transparency and accountability at a time when customers, shareholders, and business partners are demanding more of each.

Second, it allows us to more fully live up to SAP's core vision—to help the world run better and improve people's lives—as well as fulfill our responsibilities as a global corporation by ensuring we substantially address serious issues, such as the threat of climate change.

Third, it lets us tell one, more unified story.

Fourth, integrated reporting helps tackle another big, budding movement: the desire to run simple.

One of the most intractable problems of our time, especially for CEOs, is complexity. I hear it every day. Businesses large and small are under siege. The demand for more insight into how companies do business is overwhelming. Meanwhile, doing business is more complicated than ever due to the explosion of data, multiple channels of communication, paralyzing layers of management, and the choke of sprawling technical infrastructures. Amid all this complexity is a craving to simplify everything.

When it comes to sustainability, one choice is simple: Combining financial and nonfinancial reporting in one place beats back complexity by reducing redundancy and increasing efficiency. In today's economy, less means more.

Integrated reporting also unleashes a new competitive advantage. No company can help its customers navigate the changing world unless it does so itself. Early adopters of integrated reporting are better positioned to serve their clients than those that ignore or resist the movement. At SAP, lessons learned as we go down this path combine with the power of information technology to help our customers track their own energy consumption and greenhouse gas emissions as SAP does—companywide, averaged per employee—as well as begin to link that data to revenue and profit margins.

In that way, sustainability is not solely about reporting. More exciting is the fact that economic, environmental, and social actions are linked, and their connections have the potential to create amazing value. The challenge for today's leaders is not just to operate, but to innovate by identifying how actions in one area can affect another.

At SAP, we believe that social investing—employee volunteering, financial gifts, technology donations—links to greater employee engagement, productivity, and the ability to acquire new customers, especially in emerging markets. Reducing our greenhouse gas footprint with renewable energy sources or reducing our employees' travel, for instance, is not only good for the environment: we believe it can positively affect our people's overall health, our ranking as a top employer, and our customers' loyalty, as well as grow revenue as more companies require this of their suppliers.

Looking ahead, the integrated reporting movement is poised to speed up, fueled by innovation. It will be easier to execute and embrace as cloud computing, analytics, and in-memory technologies simplify companies' ability to track, assess, compare, and share data. As always, the best companies will change before they absolutely have to.

I've always believed that the only way to achieve audacious outcomes is to set audacious goals. And audacity is at the heart of sustainability. As leaders, we are our records. Our leadership will be defined by the people we touch and what we leave behind. So as you read this important book, reflect on what it means for your legacy, your people, your company, and our world.

Bill McDermott,
Chief Executive Officer, SAP

Preface

MANY EXCITING DEVELOPMENTS have taken place since we published the first book on integrated reporting (*One Report: Integrated Reporting for a Sustainable Strategy*) four years ago. The International Integrated Reporting Council (IIRC) was formed in 2010 and the Sustainability Accounting Standards Board (SASB) in 2011. Global Reporting Initiative (GRI) released its G4 Guidelines in 2013, the same year the Climate Disclosure Standards Board (CDSB) updated its Reporting Framework and announced plans to expand the scope of its Framework to include other natural resources and the IIRC published "The International <IR> Framework" (<IR> Framework). Other important events include the launch of the UN-sponsored Sustainable Stock Exchanges Initiative (SSE) in 2009 and the Corporate Sustainability Reporting Coalition (CSRC), sponsored by Aviva Investors, in 2011.

For these and many other reasons, we decided that now was the time to take stock of the integrated reporting movement. We very consciously use the term "movement" to describe what is happening with integrated reporting today. Its members include companies, investors, supporting organizations and initiatives, and firms that supply products and services to help companies produce an integrated report. With the exception of South Africa, no country has made any kind of regulatory intervention in support of integrated reporting. The bulk of adoption today is being accomplished through a social movement. The people and organizations involved see integrated reporting as an essential, but certainly not sufficient, mechanism to help companies create more sustainable strategies to support investors making longer-term investment decisions that, together, will support the creation of a sustainable society. Just as financial reporting played a critical role in creating the capital markets we have today, integrated reporting, supported by sustainability reporting, will help create the capital markets and society we need for tomorrow.

Chapter 1 is a case study on the emergence of integrated reporting in South Africa. Members of the movement are well aware of the country's leadership here, but they may not know the full story of how this country became the first and only one so far to require integrated reporting on an "apply or explain" basis. Chapters 2 through 4 review the state of the integrated reporting movement today. Although the topics in these chapters will be familiar to those involved in the promotion of integrated reporting, we examine them through the lens of a movement. Chapter 2 posits four overlapping phases for how meaning has evolved, starting with company experimentation, through early commentary, up to codification, and ending with the recent start of institutionalization. Chapter 3 examines the movement's momentum in terms of adoption, acceleration, and awareness, and Chapter 4 analyzes the motives of the different types of actors involved.

Chapter 5 focuses on materiality—a core, albeit elusive, concept in integrated reporting and reporting in general. Chapter 6 looks at efforts companies have made to operationalize it through a "materiality matrix." To the extent that this book attempts to break new conceptual ground, this is the work of Chapter 5, where we introduce the idea of an annual board "Statement of Significant Audiences and Materiality" (Statement) and 6, where we describe the "Sustainable Value Matrix" (SVM) as a tool for translating this statement into management decisions. Through the Statement, the company makes clear its purpose vis-à-vis providers of financial capital and other stakeholders. The SVM provides guidance to management on reporting, stakeholder engagement, resource commitments, and opportunities for innovation.

In Chapter 7, we assess the quality of integrated reporting prior to the publication of the International <IR> Framework through a careful analysis of the self-declared integrated reports of 124 companies. In Chapter 8, we do the same for the corporate reporting websites of the largest 500 companies in the world. These two chapters set the stage for Chapter 9, which discusses the role of information technology (IT) in integrated reporting and how it can be used to promote integrated thinking. We believe that the movement needs to be more cognizant of the importance of IT, and this chapter seeks to place this topic at the center of the conversation.

In our final chapter, we make four recommendations for what needs to be done to ensure the success of the movement. The first concerns the role the IIRC can play in certifying the quality of integrated reports. The second describes how best to marshal market and regulatory forces to spur the adoption of integrated reporting, and our last two recommendations focus on organizations, clarifying the role of accounting firms and professional accounting associations and emphasizing the need for the major NGOs supporting the movement (CDP, GRI, and the SASB) to collaborate as much as possible.

As we submit this book to our publisher in May of 2014, how do we feel about the integrated reporting movement? Cautiously optimistic. That said, the future is not predetermined. It is there to be shaped. We will continue to do everything we can to support the movement in our own modest way, and we encourage all who care about creating a sustainable society to do the same.

Acknowledgments

WE COULD NOT HAVE WRITTEN this book without the help of many other members of the integrated reporting movement, starting with Sydney Ribot. A research associate at the Harvard Business School who is also working on a narrative web TV series about globalization in Istanbul, she contributed to every chapter and appendix in this book through research, writing, critiquing, editing, and the final polishing before the book could be called done. Sydney also took the lead on Chapter 1, "South Africa," where we would also like to thank Leigh Roberts for making sure we told the South African story accurately. As someone deeply involved in the movement in South Africa and on a global basis as well, Leigh was well positioned to do that for us.

There were other chapters where we depended upon extensive contributions by others, starting with Tim Youmans, an independent researcher, and Andy Knauer, a research associate, both at the Harvard Business School. Tim and Andy had joint responsibility for Chapter 5, "Materiality," and 6, "The Sustainable Value Matrix." Tim had the lead on the former and gets credit for having the insight that materiality should be linked to corporate governance by making its determination a responsibility of a company's board of directors. Tim also gave us excellent feedback on the many drafts of the other chapters. Andy conducted a thorough analysis of the materiality matrices of 91 companies that served as the data backbone for this chapter, no doubt making him one of the world's experts on this topic. He also helped with all of the other quantitative analysis described in the book. Without his technical skills, we would not have been able to garner the insights we did from the data he and others worked so hard to gather.

Chapter 7, "Report Quality," simply would not have been possible without the extraordinary efforts of David Colgren (President and CEO at Colcomgroup), Brad Monterio (Managing Director at Colcomgroup), and Liv Watson (Director of New Markets at Workiva, formerly WebFilings). In spite of demanding day jobs, they managed to spend hundreds of hours collectively gathering and analyzing data based on the integrated reports of 124 companies. They were also instrumental in producing Chapter 9, "Information Technology." Neither of us has the expertise to have written this chapter on our own. We are also grateful to Jyoti Banerjee of the International Integrated Reporting Council (IIRC) and Peter Graf and Thomas Odenwald of SAP for their feedback on a draft we thought was pretty close to done. We were wrong, and they set us on the right path. Jyoti called the chapter "not ready for prime time," and when we challenged him to help us get it ready, he readily agreed to do so. Without his involvement, this chapter could very well have ended up on the cutting room floor. Instead, it survived and gave us the opportunity to introduce his idea of "contextual reporting."

Chapter 8, "Reporting Websites," would not have been possible without the indefatigable efforts of Barbara Esty of the Harvard Business School's Baker Library. She singlehandedly coded up the corporate websites of 500 companies—a daunting task. In doing so, Barbara probably became the world's expert on reporting websites and we relied heavily on her for help in interpreting the data she gathered.

Steve Waygood and Louise Haigh of Aviva Investors and Aviva, respectively, are important players in the integrated reporting movement, and we relied upon them for their insights in many areas, especially public policy initiatives and nongovernmental organization (NGO) campaigns important to integrated reporting. We have and continue to learn a great deal from them about such initiatives. In our view, Steve is one of the most important people today supporting the movement from a regulatory and campaign perspective. A "thinker" as well as a "doer," Steve has also made contributions to the integrated reporting movement through his own writing. We look forward to working with him, Louise, and their colleagues at Aviva Investors and Aviva in the years ahead in support of the movement.

Our book describes five "supporting organizations," and we are grateful to representatives of each for their feedback on our descriptions of their organizations and their role in the movement. Thus, we would like to thank Nigel Topping of CDP, Allen White of the Global Initiative on Sustainability Ratings (GISR), Nelmara Arbex and Ernst Ligteringen of Global Reporting Initiative (GRI), Paul Druckman and Lisa French of the IIRC, and Amanda Medress and Jean Rogers of the Sustainability Accounting Standards Board (SASB). We look forward to working with all of them in the years ahead, including Ernst. We suspect that even though he is retiring as CEO of GRI, he will remain an important member of the movement. We would also like to thank him for the great contributions he has made to sustainability and integrated reporting and wish him well in his new endeavors.

We interviewed a number of people for this book, all of whom contributed important insights. For this we would like to thank Nelmara Arbex, Jyoti Banerjee, Aron Cramer, Peter DeSimone, Alexandra Dobkowski-Joy, Jane Diplock, Paul Druckman, Louise Haigh, Bob Herz, Yan Hui, Anthony Miller, Jeanne Chi Yun Ng, Kathee Rebernak, Richard Sexton, Yoshiko Shibasaka, Susanne Stormer, Nigel Topping, Mike Wallace, Steve Waygood, Allen White, Christy Wood, and Ying Zhang. In terms of data, we got help from Satu Brandt and Ian van der Vlugt of GRI for data on the number of sustainability and integrated reporting companies as discussed in Chapter 3 "Momentum" and from Christina Salomone, Scott Dill, and Susanne Stormer of Novo Nordisk for data on their website usage. We would also like to thank Pippa Armbrester for quick and careful copyediting and Pranay Bose for a careful analysis of reporting by some large pharmaceutical companies, which analysis we now want to use in a separate publication, and Eric Hermann of Workiva, formerly WebFilings, for his graphical expertise that was much needed for some of the figures. Stacey Rivera, our development editor, provided just the right mix of discipline and support to ensure the timely delivery of a book that met her quality standards.

We appreciate financial support from the Harvard Business School for some of the research on which this book is based. We would also like to thank fellow movement member Professor George Serafeim, also of the Harvard Business School, for his intellectual contributions and moral support in so many ways. He too is someone we look forward to working with in the years ahead in terms of both ideas and actions.

Finally, words alone cannot express the gratitude we have to our wives Anne Laurin Eccles and Marilyn Mueller Krzus for their love, encouragement, and moral support. Since this is our second book, they knew full well what lay ahead for them until the book was done. Now that it is, we look forward to giving them back at least some of the time they gave to us.

CHAPTER ONE

South Africa

I N 2011, SOUTH AFRICA became the first country to require integrated reporting on an "apply or explain" basis.[1] In 2014, it remains the only country to have done so. Since the Johannesburg Stock Exchange (JSE) added King III to its listing requirements—which as of 2011 have included integrated reporting—some 450[2] South African companies have been filing reports that present both financial and nonfinancial information[3] in a meaningful way. While a variety of proposals related to sustainability and integrated reporting have been submitted in countries of the European Union,[4] and while an initiative by the World Federation of Exchanges slated for discussion in 2014[5] would require some form of nonfinancial reporting,[6] no other country has shown signs of implementing such a far-reaching requirement.

Those not deeply entrenched in the topics of corporate governance and reporting are often surprised to learn that South Africa is the first country where integrated reporting was given a widespread mandate. Indeed, in 20 years the country's corporate governance code went from being undeveloped to regarded as an international vanguard. The governance principles that would launch South Africa's integrated reporting journey coincided with the country's first multiracial elections in 1994. In codifying values of stakeholder inclusivity—the idea that nonshareholder interests and expectations should be taken into account during strategic decision-making—those principles testified to a burgeoning democracy's effort to create structural and corporate transparency where, previously, corruption had prevailed. Because integrated reporting's meaning in South Africa—for companies, investors, and the country as a whole—must be seen in the context of its evolution from corporate governance principles, and because the movement has gathered more momentum in South Africa than any other geography, we will describe the motives of the key individuals and groups that led to this recommendation, ultimately reviewing the results of this country's experience.

THE UNIQUENESS OF SOUTH AFRICA

The particularity of South Africa's circumstances begs the question of how much momentum the country's decision has created for the adoption of integrated reporting on a global basis. One might suppose the adoption of integrated reporting by a midsized country (population of 51 million in 2012)[7] with a divisive history says little about the integrated reporting movement's prospects for the rest of the world. It is unlikely that a developed country would be motivated by the same set of reasons to improve its corporate governance.

As the increased trust thought to accompany integrated reporting could signify easier entry into foreign markets directly, through joint ventures, or through acquisitions, however, other developing countries may have similar incentives to attract foreign investors and make their large companies credible players on a global stage.[8] Although this suggests integrated reporting can play a role in establishing the legitimacy of the State and its economy in times of turmoil and change, it certainly does not mean that it always will. In countries where the legitimacy of the State and its business community are more secure, companies and countries may see fewer benefits of integrated reporting—particularly when taking into account its costs and risks.

Yet, while South Africa's unique circumstances may have led it to be the first country to adopt integrated reporting, one could argue, as South Africans Mervyn King and Leigh Roberts have in *Integrate: Doing Business in the 21st Century*,[9] that the underlying forces that put integrated reporting on the agenda are the same worldwide. Central to the development of South Africa's code of corporate governance, King now occupies a similar role on the global integrated reporting stage as Chairman of the International Integrated Reporting Council (IIRC). As a member of the Integrated Reporting Committee of South Africa (IRC of SA) and the Technical Task Force of the IIRC, Roberts was deeply involved in the development of integrated reporting in South Africa.

They see integrated reporting as one of "four corporate tools" to manage companies in a changing business environment. "Integrated thinking" is suggested as the most important, with the other two being stakeholder relationships and good corporate governance.[10] We will discuss the relationship between integrated reporting and integrated thinking in detail in the next chapter, "Meaning."

While the analysis of King and Roberts would suggest that integrated reporting is as relevant elsewhere as in South Africa, exactly how its adoption might best be aided remains unclear. The authors' four tools, much like the five forces they cite as changing the investor environment, are useful to companies all over the world even as their strength varies by country.[11] The nine problems with corporate reporting they identify are similarly applicable.[12] The remaining instrumentalist questions are concerned with scope and strategy. Should the focus be on improving corporate reporting *per se*, which is how it is largely being defined in other countries? Or should integrated reporting be part of a larger context, such as a code of corporate governance, as it was in South Africa? What is the right combination of market and regulatory forces? The South African strategy was what might be called "soft regulation" due to the "apply or explain" basis and the central role of the JSE, in contrast to the hard regulation of a pure mandate supported by the country's securities commission. These questions will be addressed in our final chapter. Here, we present South Africa's particular journey in order to glean what can be learned from the only country in which integrated reporting is mandatory.

 ## SOUTH AFRICA'S JOURNEY TO INTEGRATED REPORTING

In 1990, the Republic of South Africa emerged from the shadow of 42 years of apartheid into an uncertain future. The ruling white-controlled National Party began negotiations to dismantle the system of racial segregation that had allowed it to enforce white supremacy and Afrikaner minority rule at the expense of a black majority since 1948.[13] Nelson Mandela, a Xhosa attorney and organizer of resistance against that system, was released from prison and his political party, the African National Congress (ANC), was legalized by the last State President of apartheid-era South Africa, F.W. de Klerk. While the path to democracy seemed secure by the mid-1990s, South Africa's social triumph was projected onto a backdrop of fiscal unknowns.

By 1989, 155 American educational institutions had fully or partially divested from South Africa and 22 countries, 26 states, and more than

90 cities had taken binding economic action against companies doing business there.[14] Between 1985 and 1988, the United States, Japan, Great Britain, Israel, and a number of European countries enacted legislation or initiated trade restrictions with South Africa.[15] Around the same period, the country—the world's largest gold producer—saw a precipitous drop in the price of gold from $850/oz. in 1980 to $340/oz. by 1992. Coupled with political unrest and sanctions, this drop resulted in South Africa's withdrawal of its last gold reserves from the International Monetary Fund in 1986, just as pressure from the sanctions intensified.[16] Net capital movement out of the country between 1985 and 1988, the most intense years of divestment political pressure and sanctions, totaled over R23.9 billion, causing a dramatic decline in the international exchange rate of the South African rand and, consequently, a rise in the price of imports. Inflation was rising at a rate of 12–15% per year.[17]

Even measures like the 1973 Companies Act,[18] which the South African government adopted in its eagerness to attract foreign investment, did not prevent the extensive flight of private capital that occurred as a result of anti-apartheid pressure.[19] Foreign direct investment, at 34% of gross domestic product (GDP) in 1956, had dropped to 9% by 1990 (Figure 1.1), and the

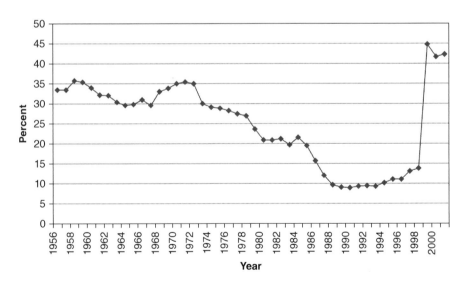

FIGURE 1.1   Foreign Direct Investment in South Africa as a Percent of GDP

Source: Fedderke, J.W., and Romm, A., 2006, Growth Impact and Determinants of Foreign Direct Investment into South Africa, 1956–2003, Economic Modelling, 23, 738–60.

depleted South African economy cast corporate accountability deficiencies into sharp relief.[20] What remained were a few large companies—often, family corporations operating in a culture of cronyism and impunity.[21] While the language of reconciliation spoken by politicians like Nelson Mandela lent the postapartheid state moral credence, the basic unreliability of the South African business environment and economy posed a critical challenge to the new government's legitimacy.[22]

King I

Based on the Companies Act of 1973, corporations were allowed to withhold information from their auditors on the basis of "national interest."[23] Such opaque business standards, when combined with the political turmoil of the early 1990s, fostered an atmosphere of uncertainty for foreign investors. While Great Britain lifted the first economic sanction against South Africa in 1990, the last would remain until 1994. Meanwhile, the new government had difficulty attracting foreign capital, likely due to lack of experience,[24] as repugnance to a fairly stable apartheid system was replaced with nervousness about the State's political and economic solvency. To mitigate some of this uncertainty, the Institute of Directors in Southern Africa (IoDSA)[25] resolved to reinterpret business practices to prepare the South African economy for exposure to international markets by establishing the King Committee in 1992. Named after Mervyn King, a former corporate lawyer and Supreme Court judge selected as its chair, the King Committee sought to develop corporate governance standards that adequately reflected the values of postapartheid South Africa.[26]

Published in 1994, the first King Code of Corporate Governance Principles (King I) went beyond the reigning standard of corporate governance, the U.K.'s Cadbury Report,[27] to advocate total transparency. Key topics included who should be on a company's board, the role of nonexecutive directors, and the categories of people who should fill this role—none of which had ever been addressed in South African business history. "King I" also advocated for disclosure of executive and nonexecutive directors' remuneration, set guidelines for effective auditing, and encouraged companies to implement a Code of Ethics to demand "the highest standards of behavior."[28] King I did not, however, call for sustainability reporting.

Mervyn King explained this approach to corporate governance as a way to understand a company's worth in a more comprehensive manner, saying, "The board should take account of the needs, interests, and expectations of the stakeholders . . . their duty being the best interests of the company for the total maximization of the total economic value of the company, not just book value."[29] South Africa began to address the "shareholder vs. stakeholder" polemic debated so vigorously around the world today. In his quote, King makes clear that the duty of the board is to the company, not to its investors or any particular stakeholder group. While this is true in many parts of the world, there is a common perception, especially in the United States—and in spite of the law's lack of affirmation on this point—that directors are responsible for putting shareholder interests first.[30]

Although the report advocated a principles-based approach,[31] the JSE made elements of the King Code a listing requirement in 1995 on a "comply or explain" basis.[32]

King II

Following large-scale corporate governance failures in the United States, the United Kingdom, and at home, the second King Code of Corporate Governance (King II) was released in 2002. King II included sections on risk management, the role of the board, sustainability, and the suggestion that companies create an internal audit charter.[33] In a corporate context, "sustainability" was interpreted as a focus on "those non-financial aspects of corporate practice that . . . influence the enterprise's ability to survive and prosper in the communities within which it operates, and so ensure future value creation." Defined as the essence of corporate social responsibility, it means "the achievement of balanced and integrated *economic, social,* and *environmental* performance," or what is commonly called the "triple bottom line." The report clarified that these sustainability—or nonfinancial—issues should not and cannot be treated as secondary to established business mandates, noting, "It should also be pointed out that the reference to these issues as 'non-financial issues' is for ease of reference. There is no doubt . . . that these so-called non-financial issues have significant financial implications for a company."[34]

The concept of integrated reporting began to take shape in King II through the notion of an "integrated sustainability report." A chapter devoted to integrated sustainability reporting reviewed the stakeholder-inclusive model. The spirit of *Ubuntu,* an African values system, was suggested as a natural foundation for effective corporate governance. Reuel Khoza, Chairman of AKA Capital and The Nedbank Group and Chair of the Integrated Sustainability Reporting task team for King II, articulated the connection, saying, "The guiding principle of *Ubuntu* can be stated in one sentence:

'*Ubuntungubuntu.*' In English you can put it as, 'I am because you are, you are because we are.' We are interrelated beings, we operate best when we care about one another."[35]

As discussed above, King II linked a focus on sustainability to company survival over the long term. Thus, King II articulated relationships between good corporate governance and transparent reporting, transparent reporting and sustainability, and sustainability and corporate performance, especially over the long term. These elements remain at the center of the integrated reporting debate today.

In the years after King II was published, sustainability appeared with great frequency in the national dialogue. While still not enforced by legislation, key aspects of King II's code were further validated when the JSE developed a set of criteria to measure the "triple bottom line" performance of companies, making explicit reference to King II. The move to create a Sustainable Stock Index made South Africa both the first emerging market, and its stock exchange the first worldwide, to bring sustainability issues to the fore through a structured index. In 2008, the passage of the National Framework for Sustainable Development by the Cabinet of South Africa lent government support to the concept of sustainability.[36]

King III

Corporate governance visionaries, however, remained unsatisfied with the treatment of sustainability in King II, and King himself believed its placement of sustainability in an eponymous chapter had led companies to isolate it inappropriately from strategy and corporate governance. To underscore the importance of sustainability's integration into business strategy, the group revised the code to include the crucial recommendation that companies combine material financial and nonfinancial data in a single, integrated annual report. King I and II had already achieved the Committee's goal of placing South Africa at the vanguard of international corporate governance, and a third report would allow them to push the envelope again. Furthermore, changes in international governance trends, as well as the passing of the new Companies Act No. 71 of 2008, made a third report necessary.[37] In 2009, the third King Code of Governance (King III) was released, and it was applicable from March 2010 onward.

Departing from King I and King II, King III changed from a "comply or explain" to an "*apply* or explain" approach in the effort to be more flexible in the application of its now 76 principles. That is, King III was applicable to all public, private, and nonprofit entities, but those entities could opt out voluntarily by explaining why some of those principles were not applicable to their operations. The principles-based approach, rather than a rules-based one, was intended to allow companies to adapt those principles to their own situation to allow for a much wider scope of interpretation than a "comply" or explain approach. Still, many felt it would hinder King III's success unless companies had active shareholders to force them to account for their behavior. Because the United Nations (UN)-backed Principles for Responsible Investment (PRI)[38] believed there was not enough guidance in South Africa for institutional investors to behave as active asset owners, the King III Committee recommended the creation of a code according to which institutional investors should set their expectations in order to ensure companies apply the principles and suggested practices effectively.[39]

Structurally, the concept of integrated reporting developed in King III emphasized "a holistic and integrated representation of the company's performance in terms of both its finances and its sustainability" to be remarked upon annually in a single report.[40] How to represent these elements was subsequently defined in explicit, if aspirational, terms.[41] On a higher level, King III emphasized that integrated reporting was not just about year-end disclosure but integrating sustainable practices into company operations all the time—a phenomenon that has come to be referred to by many, including King, Roberts, and the IIRC, as "integrated thinking." This meant that the skill sets and responsibilities of audit committees would need to expand to account for nonfinancial considerations. Furthermore, emphasis was placed on "the principle of materiality, which links sustainability issues more closely to strategy, as well as the principle of considering a company's broader sustainability context."[42] Although King III acknowledged the helpfulness of international frameworks and guidelines like Global Reporting Initiative's (GRI's) G3 Guidelines, it suggested that companies should also develop criteria based on their unique circumstances. King III also advocated independent assurance of sustainability reporting and disclosure.[43] In recognition of the King Codes' pioneering nature, Kofi Anan, the Secretary-General of the UN, invited King to chair the UN Committee on Governance and Oversight.[44] Shortly thereafter, the King Reports were translated into Japanese.[45]

Meanwhile, the IRC of SA,[46] established in May of 2010, was created to develop integrated reporting guidelines for South African companies. In January 2011, its "Framework for Integrated Reporting and the Integrated Report Discussion Paper" (IRC of SA Discussion Paper)—the first attempt at integrated reporting codification—was released.

The Integrated Reporting Committee of South Africa's Discussion Paper

The IRC of SA Discussion Paper outlined three categories of principles for the integrated report. The first included principles to define the scope and boundary of the report.[47] The second pertained to the way in which the report's content was selected and the dependability of the information that comprised it: companies must ensure that the information they provide is appropriate (relevant), material, complete, neutral, and free from error. Thirdly, the information presented should be comparable and consistent, verifiable, timely, and understandable.[48] The IRC of SA Discussion Paper also suggested specific elements of the report. It was to include a profile outlining its scope and boundary and an organizational overview discussing business model and governance structure. The company operating context was to be explained by including information on material issues, impacts and relationships, and identifying risks and opportunities. Strategic objectives and targets were to be covered along with the Key Performance Indicators (KPIs), Key Risk Indicators (KRIs) that would track performance, and a demonstration of the competencies required to pursue the objectives. The IRC of SA Discussion Paper also emphasized that the account of organizational performance, financial and nonfinancial, should include a list of objectives and targets, along with a discussion of whether or not they were achieved. Companies were to state future performance objectives and internal activities along with the structures required to achieve them, remuneration policies should be brought to light, and an analytical commentary on the company's current state and anticipated performance in the context of strategic objectives was to be described.

The IRC of SA Discussion Paper also devoted a fair amount of attention to the topic of materiality, noting in its discussion of the second principle that it is defined differently for financial and nonfinancial information. For financial information, the IRC of SA Discussion Paper used the common definition: "For financial information, materiality is used in the sense of the magnitude of an omission or misstatement of accounting data that misleads users and is usually measured in monetary terms. Materiality is judged both by relative amount and by the nature of the item."[49] For nonfinancial information, the IRC of SA Discussion Paper observed, "In the context of sustainability, materiality is a more difficult measure to define and a great deal of judgment is required."[50]

Recommending assurance on sustainability disclosures by an independent third party under the oversight of the audit committee, the IRC of SA Discussion Paper noted that "the organisation's board should ensure the integrity of the integrated report."[51] Using a metaphor that has since gained considerable traction among members of the integrated reporting movement, it also observed that "Developing the ideal integrated report will be a journey for many organizations and so too will the extent and level of assurance."[52]

While companies were not required to follow the principles and elements in the IRC of SA Discussion Paper, and the JSE did not attempt to assess the extent to which they were doing so, it likely had credibility in the corporate community due to the impressive multistakeholder group that prepared it. The members of the Integrated Reporting Committee and the Integrated Reporting Committee Working Group included senior representatives from individual companies and investors, company and investor associations, accounting firms and the accounting association, the stock exchange, non-governmental organizations (NGOs), and academics.[53] After this groundbreaking publication was released, the International Federation of Accountants (IFAC) launched a revised edition of its sustainability framework, discussing the specifics of sustainable business operations—like stakeholder engagement, goal setting, carbon foot printing, KPIs, and the nature of integrated reporting.[54] The IRC is now promoting the international harmonization of integrated reporting by working with the IIRC[55] and, in March of 2014, the IRC of SA endorsed the International Integrated Reporting Framework (published in December 2013) as guidance for how to prepare an integrated report.

SOUTH AFRICAN ASSESSMENT OF THE SOUTH AFRICAN EXPERIENCE

As South African companies began practicing integrated reporting and issuing integrated reports, the Big Four accounting firms began to study them to identify trends and best practices. After the first mandatory integrated reporting season on an apply or explain basis concluded for 2011, Ernst & Young (E&Y) South Africa published a short report, "Integrated Reporting Survey Results," examining 25 companies listed on the JSE to interpret their understanding of integrated reporting and its perceived benefits and challenges.[56] The next year, the firm began to publish its annual "Excellence in Integrated Reporting" awards as a way to improve best practices by providing special scrutiny of the top 100 companies in terms of market capitalization. PricewaterhouseCoopers (PwC) followed suit, analyzing the top 100 companies listed on the JSE in the period after March 1, 2011, in the second full reporting season after the third King Report on Governance was released, and its analysis even contained screenshots of successful integrated report sections' layouts.[57] From 2011 to 2013, Deloitte and KPMG conducted similar surveys, publishing their results along with white papers reiterating the business case for integrated reporting, clarifying best practices, and addressing ongoing challenges. Local accounting firm Nkonki also began to produce an annual awards program covering the largest listed companies.[58]

Other organizations got involved in reflecting on the South African experience as well. For example, the University of Pretoria's Albert Luthuli Centre for Responsible Leadership collaborated with E&Y South Africa to interview 16 thought leaders, some of whom had been involved for over two decades in corporate governance and corporate reporting, lending nuance to the accounting firms' quantitative assessment of South Africa's integrated reporting experience.[59] Chartered Secretaries Southern Africa undertook an annual awards program for integrated reports. The IRC of SA began to release the results of a survey of the top 100 companies listed on the JSE covering general areas, such as the size of the reports. While one can assume that things have progressed in the past year since these reports were published, below we consider trends indicated by the most recent reports and surveys available at the time of this writing.

Report Quality

While Deloitte identified "pockets of excellence," the consensus among the Big Four remained that no one company could be indicated as exemplary in all aspects of integrated reporting.[60] Companies were increasingly engaging with sustainability issues, but there was no overall "Poster Child" Integrated Report due to, among other factors, the lack of definitive reporting guidance. Deloitte's 2012 report alone identified 15 potentially relevant frameworks, regulations, and standards[61] relevant to the process. It also addressed such issues as fear of disclosing competitive information related to strategy, board governance, how director remuneration was determined, and overall adjustment of internal controls, assurance, and data collection. Although the E&Y survey respondents demonstrated a solid understanding of the definition of an integrated report and the information it should represent, with all respondents agreeing that an integrated report was not simply a cross-reference between annual and sustainability reports, few disclosed these interdependencies in a useful manner.[62]

Overall, the following trends were indicated by most of the accounting firms: companies that had not embraced integrated reporting would become isolated; clear ways of telling the company narrative were improving, and companies relied more on visual storytelling and graphics than before; stakeholders were dealt with in greater detail in the reports; and companies were increasingly embedding sustainability issues into their business models. While KPMG estimated it would take up to three years for integrated reporting to become a fully established way of reporting business strategy and performance, the length of the journey depended entirely on a company's commitment to the spirit of King III in general and integrated reporting in particular. In some cases, companies were adopting a "tick-the-box" mentality to integrated reporting and simply outsourcing the production of the report to their audit firm or other consultants at a cost perceived to be high by the companies.

Materiality

Addressing the materiality of KPIs in a fulsome way remained one of the biggest hurdles for companies in their journey to integrated reporting, and it improved the least out of all other factors considered in the surveys from 2011 to 2013. South African shareholder activists like Theo Botha, Director of CA Governance,[63] viewed the uptake of integrated reporting as evolving on par with the development of appropriate KPIs that required a comprehensive definition of company-specific materiality. While companies had been culling nonfinancial information for sustainability reports for years, many surveyed described the difficulty of how to decide which material issues were the most relevant as a concern. Furthermore, too many companies failed to explain the methodologies behind the selection of material factors, simply saying things like "material issues are identified by the Board."[64] Deloitte found that only 11% of client companies disclosed the methodology used to assess materiality, and the link to stakeholder engagement was not clearly presented.[65] While deciding what is material enough to go into the report remains a challenge for companies to this day, the process has improved with the benefit of experience.

Disclosure of Nonfinancial KPIs

Integrated reporting was overwhelmingly credited with enabling management to redefine and focus its strategy to ensure sustainability's incorporation into its business model. This could be seen in the elevation of sustainability to the board level in some cases where it was not there before, the push for improved definitions of KPI data for measurement and management, inclusion into project decision-making, and an emphasis on an ongoing dialogue with stakeholders. Nevertheless, while companies had improved their integration of material environmental and social aspects into their overall business strategy, this improvement was not always reflected in their reporting practices. Many nonfinancial factors were still presented without context.[66] Companies showed a tendency to disclose nonfinancial KPIs in a separate section of the report without apparent thought for the relevance to their operations or context, resulting in a weak disclosure of the interdependencies between those indicators and company performance in a holistic way.[67] Indicators of how green a company is, for example, should only matter if measures like recycling or carbon emissions have a significant impact on business.

To make nonfinancial disclosure more useful for decision-making, E&Y suggested that mention of measures per unit produced or consumed, along with a comparison to industry norms, would give the KPIs greater meaning.[68] Noting that stated KPIs were not always relevant to business strategy, KPMG suggested that benchmarking was helpful in determining what the most relevant KPIs were and linking them to strategic imperatives.[69] As of 2013, PwC observed that while 55% of the 40 JSE-listed companies surveyed had identified one or more material capitals, only 6% effectively communicated their holistic performance.[70] Likewise, PwC found that 81% of the JSE's top 40 companies' reports could improve in their definition of KPIs and the provision of a rationale for their use. However, 71% of KPIs were quantified, indicating progress in the process of disclosing nonfinancial factors in a comparable, easily understandable way.[71] Although "silo reporting" was still evident, with KPIs sealed off in separate sections regardless of relevance to strategy, companies that considered the connections between KPIs and strategy found that their report content naturally addressed the most material issues affecting business value.[72]

Disclosure of Risks

While E&Y's 2013 "Excellence in Integrated Reporting" survey referred to risks that "will affect the businesses' ability to create value"[73] rather than dividing them into financial and nonfinancial risks, much like disclosure of nonfinancial KPIs, nonfinancial risk disclosure had often increased without being adequately linked to strategy or performance. While companies demonstrated an improved level of disclosure for items like the amount of money spent training staff or bursaries to build future capacity, the lack of links back to goals and strategies was disappointing to the accounting firms. Most companies surveyed had improved in presenting a balanced view of risks, but it was unclear how companies linked those risks to strategic objectives or how those risks translated into measurable KPIs. Many risks mentioned were generally applicable to any company in South Africa.[74] Few companies highlighted business opportunities arising from nonfinancial risks or linked risk disclosure of nonfinancial factors to International Financial Reporting Standards (IFRS) disclosures in statutory annual financial statements. While 97% of companies surveyed by PwC reported on principal nonfinancial risks,[75] only 52% integrated them into other areas of their reporting and only 10% of companies supported risk disclosure with quantitative information like KPIs. A mere 13% provided thorough insights into the dynamics of their risk profiles and how they could change over time.[76]

Director Remuneration and Board Transparency

Disclosure of director remuneration, introduced by King III, remained contentious. While PwC[77] observed that 51% of companies provided clear alignment between KPIs and remuneration policies, and Deloitte[78] conceded that disclosure had improved, it was clear that not many companies were assessing the effectiveness of the board as emphasized by King III. Moreover, detail regarding remuneration was scarce, and the way remuneration was aligned to facilitate the delivery of strategic objectives was not often addressed. E&Y found that little to no information was provided on how the variable portion of short-term bonuses was determined. When KPIs determining bonuses were discussed, there was seldom any sign of how those indicators translated to rand amounts or whether they were for previous or current accrual periods. Most of the information for director compensation was likewise convoluted.[79] Indeed, many companies were more comfortable reporting on board charters and terms of reference rather than actual activities undertaken by the board over the year. Only 16% of those surveyed by PwC described the activities of the board.[80] "Some companies have battled with what to include in their report about governance. The information that is most relevant is that which reflects how governance affects the value creation ability of the business," said Roberts.[81]

Disclosure of Forward-Looking Information

Although an area that had improved since the first reports, companies were loath to disclose too much forward-looking information. This was especially true when it came to environmental, social, and governance (ESG) factors.

While Deloitte found that companies disclosing KPIs generally included historical trends and future targets—an increase from 75% inclusion to 80% inclusion from Period 1 to Period 2 for fiscal 2011—future performance projections still suffered from a lack of completeness. Only one-third of those surveyed by Deloitte set measurable nonfinancial targets linked to strategy and stakeholder concerns.[82] Similarly, PwC found that only 13% of companies surveyed provided effective communication on future outlook. Only 10% provided future targets for KPIs. While 90% discussed future market trends, only 61% of companies linked them to strategic choices, and expected market rates and growth were, more often than not, not quantified. Nor was there much explanation of which factors would impact those trends in the future. However, 68% of companies did identify the time frame in which future viability had been considered.[83]

Reasons cited for the lack of disclosure were fear of regulatory reprisal and creating expectations that could be used against management in the future, as well as the simple fact that corporate reporting has traditionally been focused on past performance. In its 2011 assessment, KPMG suggested substantial cultural change was necessary to achieve a truly forward-looking perspective corroborated by a consideration of past performance against strategy and strategic perspectives, and that companies could guard against liability by wording their future performance goals and expectations carefully.[84] "This was a scary area for companies first stepping out on their integrated reporting journey," said Roberts. "But over the years disclosure has improved, with companies realizing that it was not about giving a profit projection; rather, the focus lay in transparency regarding the significant relationships and factors with the power to affect the future value creation ability. Companies have been quite inventive, using ratios, waterfall graphs, commodity reviews, and other clever ways to show true relationships."[85]

Characteristics of the Report

Company report preparers overwhelmingly felt that it was impossible to provide the amount of detail stakeholders would want in a single integrated report if that report were to remain clear and organized. Journalists like Ann Crotty feared that the reporting structure had succumbed to a gradual "densification" in which a checklist approach led to documents of 400 pages. However, analysis by the accounting firms showed that companies were slowly learning how to balance transparency with accessibility of reporting documents.[86]

Although all the accounting firms conceded that overall reports were still "too long," there was evidence that companies were trying to shorten their reports. While 35% of companies initially surveyed by E&Y in 2011 believed that an integrated report would be less than 50 pages and 44% were neutral, most respondents envisaged the next integrated report as being between 50 and 80 pages.[87]

In the following two years, the goal shifted to producing an integrated report between 80 and 120 pages. Graham Terry, Senior Executive at The South African Institute of Chartered Accountants (SAICA), noted that, in the application of integrated reporting, some principles would necessarily conflict with each other. Further, little guidance existed for what should or should not be included in the report.[88] Left to their own devices, some report preparers found that the most effective way to incorporate all of King III's requirements without producing information overload in the integrated report was to refer to other, more detailed documents with explicit links to the full IFRS financial statements and other detailed information like the sustainability report—a strategy Deloitte observed worked well when those links were clearly high-lighted.[89] E&Y noted that companies that appeared to have started from scratch in determining what and how to report often produced shorter and more effective reports.[90]

Although nearly all companies agreed that other reports were necessary, responses varied on exactly where and how information was being distributed. One hundred percent of the top 100 JSE-listed companies disagreed that integrated reporting was merely cross-referencing between annual reports and sustainability reports. This did not mean that other reports would disappear. During the first cycle of mandatory integrated reporting, 36% of companies reported a belief that a separate integrated report would be published alongside a sustainability report and the annual report on financial statements, 43% disagreed, and 21% expressed no strong belief that an integrated report should be published separately alongside the financial statements.[91] Mohamed Adam, a member of the King Committee, and Jo-Anne Yawitch, CEO of National Business Initiative,[92] noted that companies tended to get distracted by form (one report vs. multiple reports) when they should be focusing on the substance of the report itself.[93]

All accounting firms noted an increase in the use of graphics, charts, and images in conveying overviews of information. Heat maps for materiality were especially useful, and E&Y noted the increased use of waterfall charts[94] that explained the factors influencing movement in key measures such as profit over time.[95]

Internet Use

Although most companies initially made little use of the Internet in their integrated reporting efforts, all members of the Big Four firms and many South African thought leaders noted ways in which a more effective use of the Internet could ease the growing pains of integrated reporting. When it came to improving the treatment of materiality, Nigel Payne, a professional Non-Executive Director, suggested that those preparing an integrated report "need to be aware about the five or six things that are cooking at the moment" and put the details of these issues on the website. That is, thoughtful use of the company's integrated reporting site and the potential incorporation of Extensible Business Reporting Language (XBRL)[96] could assuage concerns about report length and content; by posting longer, more detailed documents on their website that need only be referenced in a concise integrated report, the company did not sacrifice completeness of information for clarity.

E&Y found in 2013 that many companies had improved in their use of navigation aids, icons, and other forms of cross-referencing to connect information across the report and that they had put detailed sustainability, corporate governance, and risk disclosure information on their website. While companies offered a few "quick reading"[97] options, some had begun to use XBRL[98] to tag information relevant to different stakeholders.

Auditing and Assurance on Nonfinancial Information

While companies surveyed had not sought uniform "reasonable"[99] assurance on nonfinancial information by an independent auditor, many agreed that it was desirable, and an increasing number of companies were seeking independent assurance on particular KPIs. E&Y noted that although more ESG indicators had received some form of external assurance, how those indicators were chosen did not always align with the material concerns of the business. E&Y suggested that the most material KPIs should receive the greatest consideration, as they were most relevant to the long-term sustainability of the business. Whether financial or nonfinancial, these KPIs selected for assurance based on materiality makes the business case for incurring the costs attached to the independent assurance of those indicators.[100] Achieving credibility of nonfinancial information was paramount and, from 2012, the topic of assurance of nonfinancial KPIs began to receive more attention from reporters.[101] That same year, an international group of accounting and legal experts led by the country's Independent Regulatory Board for Auditors was formed in South Africa to address the development of an appropriate assurance process over integrated reporting.[102]

OUR REFLECTIONS ON THE SOUTH AFRICAN EXPERIENCE

In tracing the origins of mandatory integrated reporting back to the period of 1990–1994, when the full consequences of the decision to end apartheid remained unknown, it becomes clear that South Africa's corporate governance journey developed from a unique set of circumstances. The emergence of mandated integrated reporting in South Africa was a small consequence of tumultuous political and social change as the country passed from apartheid to an era of social and economic inclusion. The architects of South Africa's new reality saw corporate governance as a way to rehabilitate the country's national image and attract the foreign capital that fled during the apartheid-era sanctions.[103] Sustainability reporting, and then integrated reporting, were simply one component of a much larger effort to make South African companies exemplars of corporate governance.

Still, the challenges facing South African companies plague companies all over the world. Shareholders and other stakeholders are demanding that companies be more responsive to ESG issues, and integrated reporting can help them identify, manage, and communicate how they are responding to these challenges in order to create value for shareholders over the long term. South African companies are on the vanguard of this social movement. While much can be learned from their experience, however, it is necessary to place it in the broader context of global efforts to shape the meaning of integrated reporting—the subject of the next chapter.

NOTES

1. A 2012 report compiled by Jess Schulschenk for Ernst & Young South Africa refers to the 2009 King Code as transitioning from a "comply or explain" to an "apply or explain" approach. Although integrated reporting is not "mandatory" in a strict legislative sense, for convenience we will use this term throughout the chapter with the understanding that it means "comply or explain," and following the 2009 King Code's appearance, "apply or explain." "Interview Summary Report." Compiled by Jess Schulschenk in

collaboration with the Albert Luthuli Centre for Responsible Leadership at the University of Pretoria. Published by Ernst & Young South Africa. August 2012. 1–40. In February 2010, the principles of the King Code of Governance of 2009 (King III), including those that recommend integrated reporting, were incorporated into the Johannesburg Stock Exchange's listing requirements and listed companies were obliged to apply the King III principles or explain their reasons for deviating from them (for financial years starting on and after 1 March 2010). SustainabilitySA. www.sustainabilitysa.org, accessed May 2014,

2. Not all listed companies produce integrated reports. There is no accurate number of the number of companies that do.

3. Nonfinancial information refers to environmental, social, and governance (ESG) information that reflects company performance in these areas.

4. On April 16, 2013, the European Commission issued a proposal to require large EU companies to report on social and environmental issues in annual financial reports. "Proposal for a Directive of the European Parliament and of the Council amending Council Directives 78/660/EEC and 83/349/EEC as regards disclosure of nonfinancial and diversity information by certain large companies and groups." European Commission. Strasbourg, France. April 16, 2013, http://eur-lex.europa.eu/LexUriServ/LexUriServ.do?uri=COM:2013:0207:FIN:EN:PDF, accessed April 2014. On April 15, 2014 the plenary of the European Parliament adopted this directive by a vote of 599 to 55 from its 28 member states. http://ec.europa.eu/internal_market/accounting/non-financial_reporting/index_en.htm, accessed April 16, 2014. In July of 2010, France took a step towards mandating integrated sustainability and financial reporting for large companies with a law called Grenelle II, Article 225 of which states that all listed companies on the French stock exchanges, including subsidiaries of foreign companies listed in France, and unlisted companies, must incorporate information on "the social and environmental consequences" of company activities or publish a justification for the exclusion of information if it is deemed irrelevant. Ernst & Young. "How France's new sustainability reporting law impacts US companies" 2012, http://www.ey.com/Publication/vwLUAssets/Frances_sustainability_law_to_impact_US_companies/$FILE/How_Frances_new_sustainability_reporting_law.pdf, accessed February 2014.

5. Brazil's BM&FBOVESPA and India's Bombay Stock Exchange have taken concrete steps to encourage listed companies to use sustainability reporting, and eight member exchanges of the World Federation of Exchanges (WFE) have joined the UN's Sustainable Stock Exchanges initiative to help research how stock exchanges can facilitate corporate transparency. In 2012, the WFE published the first "sustainability disclosure ranking" to benchmark the annual change in performance of global stock exchanges. Morrow, Doug.

"Measuring Sustainability Disclosure on the World's Stock Exchanges." World-Exchanges.org, http://www.world-exchanges.org/insight/views/measuring-sustainability-disclosure-world%E2%80%99s-stock-exchanges, accessed February 2014.

6. Also known as social accounting, nonfinancial reporting is the process of communicating the social and environmental effects of an organization's economic actions to society at large and particular stakeholders (interest groups). PwC. Audit and Assurance Services, "What is corporate reporting?" http://www.pwc.com/gx/en/corporate-reporting/frequently-asked-questions/publications/what-is-corporate-reporting.jhtml, accessed February 2014.

7. "Statistical Release for Census 2011 (embargoed until October 30, 2012)." Published by Statistics South Africa for the South African government, Private Bag X44, Pretoria 0001. Population was 51,770,560 people as of 2011. P0301.4. http://www.statssa.gov.za/publications/P03014/P030142011.pdf, accessed February 2014.

8. Empirical studies have shown that better corporate governance is highly correlated with better market valuation and operating performance, for example: Klapper, Leora F. and Inessa Love. "Corporate governance, investor protection, and performance in emerging markets." *Journal of Corporate Finance* 10, no. 5 (2004): 703–728.

9. King, Mervyn and Leigh Roberts. *Integrate: Doing Business in the 21st Century*, by Cape Town: Juta and Company, Ltd., 2013.

10. Ibid., pp. 40–44. The five forces are growing investor power supporting sustainability issues, requirements of large corporate customers for more sustainable business practices in their suppliers, increasing regulation on societal issues, pressures on companies from governments to deal with poverty and growing social inequality, and the need to reduce the waste of diminishing natural resources.

11. Ibid., pp. 5–9.

12. Ibid., pp. 16–22. The problems are: (1) too heavy for the postman, (2) yesterday's story, (3) not the whole story—the financial pictures only, (4) not the whole story—some intangibles are excluded, (5) not the whole story—some costs are excluded, (6) different reports for different users, (7) nonfinancial information is not considered mainstream by all, (8) reporting influences behavior, (9) short-termism, (10) reporting is behind the technology curve, and (11) no common system for preparing the annual report.

13. While 1994, the year of the first multiracial democratic elections, is commonly regarded as the end date of apartheid, making it a 46-year phenomenon, the process to dismantle apartheid legislation officially concluded in 1990, when the African National Congress ceased to be regarded as a terrorist organization by the South African state and was instead made a legal political party and all laws enforcing apartheid were abolished.

14. Knight, Richard. "Sanctions, Disinvestment, and U.S. Corporations in South Africa." *Sanctioning Apartheid*, edited by Robert Edgar, Trenton: Africa World Press, 1990.
15. Denmark, France, and Canada initiated bans on investment in and oil trade with South Africa, which Israel enacted in 1987 and Japan followed from 1986–88. To restrict loans and exports to South Africa, the United States passed its main anti-South Africa legislation, the Comprehensive Anti-Apartheid Act of 1986. Teoh, Siew Hong, Ivo Welch, and C. Paul Wazzan. "The Effect of Socially Activist Investment Policies on the Financial Markets: Evidence from the South African Boycott." *The Journal of Business*, Vol. 72, No. 1 (January 1999), pp. 35–89.
16. Ibid.
17. Knight, "Sanctions, Disinvestment, and U.S. Corporations in South Africa."
18. The 1973 Companies Act allowed for the establishment of private and public limited-liability companies, and most foreign firms that created South African subsidiaries capitalized on the private form. Other policies that indicated the government's keenness to attract foreign investors included the absence of a requirement for approval of foreign investors, who are subject to the same laws as domestic investors in most cases. The Close Corporation Act of 1984 (Act 69) also created a third legal form for corporations that is suited for small businesses, and no limit exists for the amount of foreign ownership or the rights of foreign owners outside of the banking sector. UNCTAD Investment Country Profiles: South Africa. pp 1–29. http://unctad.org/sections/dite_fdistat/docs/wid_cp_za_en.pdf, accessed January 2014.
19. Bjorvatn, Kjetil, Hans Jarle Kind, and Hildegunn Kyvik Nordas. "The role of FDI in economic development." The Research Council of Norway: Foundation for Research in Economic and Business Administration. Bergen, December 2001, http://brage.bibsys.no/nhh/bitstream/URN:NBN:no-bibsys_brage_24613/1/A62_01.pdf, accessed January 2014.
20. From 1956 to 1990, FDI as a percentage of GDP decreased from 34% to 9%. Fedderke, Johannes and A.T. Romm, 2004. "Growth Impact and Determinants of Foreign Direct Investment into South Africa, 1956–2003," Working Papers 12, Economic Research Southern Africa.
21. Schulschenk, "Interview Summary Report," p. 1.
22. Fedderke and Romm, "Growth Impacts and Determinants of Foreign Direct Investments into South Africa."
23. Nxasana, Sizwe (2012b). Ibid. At the corporate level, governance was, in the words of many interviewed, "absent." Sizwe Nxasana, CEO of FirstRand Limited & FirstRand Bank, remembered his experience as an articled clerk in the early 1980s as a time of unparalleled corporate licentiousness.

24. Bjorvatn, Kjetil, Hans Jarle Kind, and Hildegunn Kyvik Nordas. "The role of FDI in economic development." The Research Council of Norway: Foundation for Research in Economic and Business Administration. Bergen, December 2001, p. 17, http://brage.bibsys.no/nhh/bitstream/URN:NBN:no-bibsys_brage_24613/1/A62_01.pdf, accessed in January 2014.

25. IoDSA was founded to empower those charged with organizational governance duties with the right skills and ethics to execute on their duties based on the values of southern African society. "About the IoDSA" Institute of Directors in Southern Africa, http://www.iodsa.co.za/?page=About, accessed February 2014.

26. Schulschenk, "Interview Summary Report," p. 1.

27. Published in draft version in May 1992, the "Cadbury Report," formally titled *Financial Aspects of Corporate Governance*, was a report produced by The Committee on the Financial Aspects of Corporate Governance in Britain, chaired by Adrian Cadbury, that set recommendations on corporate boards and accounting systems to mitigate governance risks and failures. Hailed as an international vanguard, certain recommendations of the Cadbury report were used to establish other codes in the United States, the European Union, and the World Bank, among others. "Report of the Committee on the Financial Aspects of Corporate Governance." Gee (a division of Professional Publishing Ltd.) London. 1 December 1992, http://www.ecgi.org/codes/documents/cadbury.pdf, accessed February 2014.

28. "King Report on Corporate Governance for South Africa 1994, Chapter 20: The Code of Corporate Practices and Conduct," Institute of Directors South Africa, p. 2, http://www.ecgi.org/codes/documents/king_i_sa.pdf, accessed February 2014.

29. Schulschenk, "Interview Summary Report," p. 4.

30. Stout, Lynn A. "Bad and not-so-bad arguments for shareholder primacy." *S. Cal. L. Rev.* 75 (2001): 1189. "Milton Friedman is a Nobel Prize-winning economist, but he obviously is not a lawyer. A lawyer would know that the shareholders do not, in fact, own the corporation. Rather, they own a type of corporate security commonly called 'stock.' As owners of stock, shareholders' rights are quite limited . . . Thus, while it perhaps is excusable to loosely describe a closely held firm with a single controlling shareholder as 'owned' by that shareholder, it is misleading to use the language of ownership to describe the relationship between a public firm and its shareholders." (p. 1191)

31. Ibid. p. 14.

32. Schulschenk, "Interview Summary Report," p. 6.

33. A pro forma internal audit charter is contained in an appendix to King II, which describes the scope of an internal audit as "an independent objective assurance activity" that "brings a disciplined approach to evaluate risk

management, control and governance." King II Report on Corporate Governance: Summary of Code of Corporate Practices and Conduct. Appendix 4. 2009, 343, https://www.icsa.org.uk/assets/files/pdfs/BusinessPractice_and_IQS_docs/studytexts/corporategovernance2/w_CorpGov_6thEd_Study Text_Appendix4.pdf, accessed February 2014.

34. "King Report on Corporate Governance for South Africa 2002," King Committee on Corporate Governance. pp. 91–92. http://library.ufs.ac.za/dl/userfiles/documents/Information_Resources/KingII%20Final%20doc.pdf, accessed February 2014. As an idea, "sustainability" was gleaned from the way "Our Common Future" (commonly known as the Brundtland Report) defined the term "sustainable development" in 1987 to mean "development that meets the needs of the present without compromising the ability of future generations to meet their own needs." United Nations. "Report of the World Commission on Environment and Development: Our Common Future," no page numbers in online report, http://www.un-documents.net/wced-ocf.htm, accessed May 2014.

35. Schulschenk, "Interview Summary Report," p. 10.

36. "National Framework for Sustainable Development," Sustainability South Africa Website, http://www.sustainabilitysa.org/GlobalResponse/SAGovernmentsresponse/NationalFrameworksandPolicies.aspx, accessed February 2014.

37. "King Report on Corporate Governance for South Africa 2009," King Committee on Corporate Governance, Introduction and Background, The Need for King III, p. 2, http://www.library.up.ac.za/law/docs/king111report.pdf, accessed January 2014. When the Companies Act was revised in 2008, it fundamentally rewrote South African company law to give legal authority to some of the guidance in King II. In addition to introducing the concept of an Independent Review as a way to audit company financial statements, the Act touched upon issues like appointment of board members to the board of directors, which King III then sought to elaborate upon. For example, the Companies Act acknowledged the importance of appointing a board for company governance, but King III expanded extensively on the role and function of the board. The Companies Act clarified procedures for the appointment or election of directors, but King III went a step further to describe the qualities of people who might be appointed, also providing guidance for the appointment and duties of CEO and chairman, which were not discussed in the Companies Act. Further differences necessitating that a third King Code be published related to board committees in general, group boards, audit committees, social and ethics committees, risk committees, remuneration committees, and nomination committees. PricewaterhouseCoopers. "The board of directors and committees—a comparison between the new Companies Act and King III,"

October 2011, http://www.pwc.co.za/en_ZA/za/assets/pdf/companies-act-series-3.pdf, accessed February 2014.

38. The UN-supported Principles for Responsible Investment initiative is an international network of investors working together to understand the implications of sustainability for investors and to support signatories to incorporate such issues into their investment decision-making and ownership practices by putting the UN's six Principles for Responsible Investment into practice. UN Principles for Responsible Investment. About the PRI Initiative, http://www.unpri.org/, accessed February 2014.

39. "Institutional Investors." King III Introduction and Background, Section 7. http://www.library.up.ac.za/law/docs/king111report.pdf, accessed February 2014.

40. Institute of Directors in Southern Africa, "King Report on Governance for South Africa 2009," p. 109, http://african.ipapercms.dk/IOD/KINGIII/kingiiireport, accessed February 2014.

41. Ibid., p. 111. Clarity and a long-term outlook were emphasized: "Integrated reporting should be focused on substance over form and should disclose information that is complete, timely, relevant, accurate, honest, accessible, and comparable with past performance of the company. It should also contain forward-looking information." Sustainability was to be interwoven with financial reporting. In addition to reporting on the company's financial performance, the company should put its economic performance into context by discussing the environment in which it functioned and its impact on stakeholders, as well as strategies for mitigating any negative outcomes. In short, "the integrated report should describe how the company has made its money."

42. Ibid., p. 111.

43. Ibid., p. 111. Since King III was published, the interplay between the 2008 Companies Act and the King Code has begged a number of questions about the relationship between governance principles and legislation. King III was written to reflect the changes in company law, but the Companies Act did not go into effect until 2011, causing many to believe a process of refinement is necessary to bring the reports into alignment with legislation. This in itself has caused strong reactions among supporters of principles-based approach. While King III was more progressive than its predecessors by leaps and bounds, some felt it had gone too far. Amid these debates, integrated reporting gained cachet on the international and domestic stages.

44. The UN Committee on Governance and Oversight was formed to recommend improvements that affect management and the governing structures that serve the United Nations. For further information, see "Implementation of decisions contained in the 2005 World Summit Outcome for action by the Secretary-General: Comprehensive review of governance and oversight

within the United Nations and its funds, programmes and specialized agencies." Report of the Secretary-General. 10 July 2006. United Nations General Assembly, http://www.un.org/ga/president/62/issues/resolutions/a-60-883.pdf, accessed in February 2014.

45. Schulschenk, "Interview Summary Report," p. 9.
46. The IRC of SA was established by the joint efforts of the Association for Savings and Investment South Africa (ASISA), Business Unity South Africa (BUSA), Institute of Directors in South Africa (IoDSA), JSE Ltd, and the South African Institute of Chartered Accountants (SAIA).
47. The South African Institute of Chartered Accountants. The Integrated Reporting Committee (IRC) of South Africa "Framework for Integrated Reporting and the Integrated Report," https://www.saica.co.za/Technical/SustainabilityandIntegratedReporting/IRGuidance/tabid/2372/language/en-ZA/Default.aspx, accessed April 2014.
48. Ibid.
49. Ibid., p. 9.
50. The Paper further explains that materiality needs to be defined by answering three questions: (1) Are the "right things" being reported? (2) What level of error or omission in the data would influence the assessments and decisions of stakeholders in the organization?, and (3) Is the organization being response to the legitimate interests and expectations of its key stakeholders (sometimes referred to as stakeholder inclusiveness)? Ibid.
51. Ibid., p. 17.
52. Ibid., p. 17.
53. For a list of members see "Framework for Integrated Reporting and the Integrated Report Discussion Paper," by the Integrated Reporting Committee of South Africa, January 25, 2011, p. 25.
54. "IFAC Sustainability Framework 2.0," International Federation of Accountants. International Federation of Accountants Website, http://www.ifac.org/publications-resources/ifac-sustainability-framework-20, accessed February 2014.
55. SustainabilitySA. Integrated Reporting, The Integrated Reporting Committee of South Africa, http://www.sustainabilitysa.org/IntegratedReporting/TheIntegratedReportingCommitteeofSouthAfrica.aspx, accessed April 2014.
56. Ernst & Young South Africa. "Integrated Reporting Survey Results," 2011, pp. 1–15, http://hesabras.org/Portals/_Rainbow/images/default/download/Integrated%20Reporting.pdf, accessed February 2014.
57. PricewaterhouseCoopers. "Greater disclosure but little insight under new code," PwC, Corporate Reporting, http://www.pwc.com/gx/en/corporate-reporting/integrated-reporting/corporate-reporting-south-africa-king-iii.jhtml, accessed January 2014. Since this first evaluation, PricewaterhouseCoopers has produced an annual analysis of the Top 40 listed companies' integrated reports.

58. http://www.nkonki.com/IR/awards.php?a=integrated-reporting&page= Nkonki-Top-100-Integrated-Reporting-Awards-Winners. While Nkonki produced a special report in 2011 on the Top 40 IR Award Winners, the Nkonki Top 100 Integrated Reporting Awards began in 2012.

59. Schulschenk, "Interview Summary Report," p. 3.

60. Deloitte. "Integrated Reporting: Navigating Your Way to a Truly Integrated Report: Edition 2, February 2012," p. 20, http://www.deloitte.com/assets/ Dcom-SouthAfrica/Local%20Assets/Documents/Integrated%20Reporting% 20Publication%20II%20.pdf. The report, like Ernst & Young's "Excellence in Integrated Reporting" awards, analyzed 100 JSE-listed companies and identified top trends.

61. These included The Companies Act, No. 71 of 2008, King Code on Governance Principles, International Financial Reporting Standards, Global Reporting Initiative Third Generation, International Organization for Standardization, AccountAbility, Greenhouse Gas Protocol Corporate Accounting and Reporting Standard, United Nations Principles for Responsible Investment, Code for Responsible Investing in South Africa, International Council for Mining and Metals, United Nations Global Compact, Equator Principles, Carbon Disclosure Project, Water Disclosure Project, and eXtensible Business Reporting Language. Deloitte, "Integrated Reporting: Navigating Your Way to a Truly Integrated Report."

62. Ernst & Young South Africa. "Integrated Reporting Survey Results," 2011. http://hesabras.org/Portals/_Rainbow/images/default/download/Integrated %20Reporting.pdf, accessed February 2014.

63. CA Governance is a South Africa-based independent corporate governance entity that provides assurance of ESG information in reports to companies in addition to assurance and verification as called for in Global Reporting Initiative, CDP and Institute of Directors in Southern Africa GAI submissions. "An Introduction." http://www.ca-governance.co.za/, accessed February 2014.

64. Ernst & Young South Africa. "Excellence in Integrated Reporting Awards 2013," http://www.ey.com/Publication/vwLUAssets/EYs_Excellence_in_ Integrated_Reporting_Awards_2013/$FILE/EY%20Excellence%20in% 20Integrated%20Reporting.pdf, accessed February 2014.

65. Deloitte, "Integrated Reporting: Navigating Your Way to a Truly Integrated Report," p. 61.

66. Fifty-five percent of the companies analyzed by PwC described material capital inputs into their business models, but only 19% explained the resources and relationships relied upon to deliver the company strategy or the degree of dependence the company had on them. Fifty-five percent of companies assessed by PwC did not accomplish integration in governance because there was little linkage between company narrative and governance reporting. That is, leadership structure and the decision making process

were not explained. PricewaterhouseCoopers. "The Value Creation Journey: A Survey of JSE Top-40 Companies' Integrated Reports,"2013, PwC South Africa, The value creation journey, http://www.pwc.co.za/en/publications/integrated-reporting.jhtml, accessed May 2014.

67. Ernst & Young South Africa. "Excellence in Integrated Reporting Awards 2012," p. 7.
68. Ernst & Young South Africa, "Excellence in Integrated Reporting Awards 2013," p. 11.
69. "Integrated Reporting: Performance Insight Through Better Business Reporting, Issue 2: 2012." KPMG 2012. http://www.kpmg.com/Global/en/Issues AndInsights/ArticlesPublications/integrated-reporting/Documents/integrated-reporting-issue-2.pdf, accessed February 2014, p. 8.
70. PricewaterhouseCoopers. "The Value Creation Journey," p. 6 and p. 29.
71. PricewaterhouseCoopers. "The Value Creation Journey," p. 30.
72. Integrated Reporting: Performance Insight Through Better Business Reporting." Issue 2: 2011.
73. Ernst & Young South Africa, "Excellence in Integrated Reporting Awards 2011," p. 11.
74. Deloitte, "Integrated Reporting: Navigating Your Way to a Truly Integrated Report."
75. PricewaterhouseCoopers. "The Value Creation Journey," p. 9.
76. Ibid.
77. Ibid.
78. Deloitte, "Integrated Reporting: Navigating Your Way."
79. Ernst & Young South Africa, "Excellence in Integrated Reporting Awards 2013."
80. PricewaterhouseCoopers. "The Value Creation Journey."
81. Leigh Roberts email correspondence with Sydney Ribot, March 27, 2014.
82. Deloitte, "Integrated Reporting: Navigating Your Way to a Truly Integrated Report." In 2012, the numbers had not changed much.
83. PricewaterhouseCoopers. "The Value Creation Journey."
84. Ernst & Young South Africa, "Excellence in Integrated Reporting Awards 2012."
85. Leigh Roberts email correspondence with Sydney Ribot, March 27, 2014.
86. Schulschenk, "Interview Summary Report," p. 25.
87. Ernst & Young South Africa. "Integrated Reporting Survey Results," 2011. p. 5.
88. Schulschenk, "Interview Summary Report," p. 25.
89. Deloitte, "Integrated Reporting: Navigating Your Way to a Truly Integrated Report," p. 12.
90. Ernst & Young South Africa, "Excellence in Integrated Reporting Awards 2012."

91. Ibid.
92. Mohamed Adam is a longstanding member of the King Committee and, in 1991, he joined as legal adviser at South African state-owned utilities company Eskom. As of 2014, he serves as Eskom's Corporate Counsel and Senior General Manager of Regulatory Affairs. "Mohamed Adam." http://www.icsa.co.za/index.php?option=com_content&view=article&id=335&Itemid=479, accessed February 13, 2014. National Business Initiative is a South African organization that advocates for corporate citizenship and business leadership, facilitates collective business action and social dialogue, and implements strategic projects backed by rigorous policy analysis and research in order to foster public-private partnerships to build trust in and credibility of organizations via active engagement with members and the government. "Our Purpose." National Business Initiative. http://www.nbi.org.za/, accessed February 12, 2014.
93. Schulschenk, "Interview Summary Report," p. 24.
94. A waterfall chart or graph is a form of data visualization that shows the cumulative effect of sequentially introduced positive or negative values. Because its suspended columns are visually reminiscent of bricks or columns leaped over by the protagonist of the videogame Super Mario Brothers, it is also known as a "flying bricks chart" or "Mario chart." In finance, this chart is often known as a bridge chart.
95. Ernst & Young South Africa, "Excellence in Integrated Reporting Awards 2013," p. 12.
96. XBRL, or eXtensible Business Reporting Language, is a freely available global standard for exchanging business information, XBRL. XBRL Basics, http://www.xbrl.org/GettingStarted, accessed April 2014.
97. One of the criteria used by Deloitte in their research into the quality of integrated reports was the extent to which companies were effectively communicating the context in which they operate. A key measure of effective communication was the concept of a "quick reading" summary that included key performance indicators, historical trends, and future targets. Deloitte, "Integrated Reporting: Navigating Your Way to a Truly Integrated Report," p. 31.
98. Deloitte, "Integrated Reporting: Navigating Your Way to a Truly Integrated Report," p. 93.
99. In American parlance this is the same as "positive" assurance.
100. If management questioned the need for assurance, it is perhaps indicative that management should reconsider the motive for including that factor as a material KPI. Ernst & Young South Africa, "Excellence in Integrated Reporting Awards 2013."
101. Deloitte, "Integrated Reporting: Navigating Your Way to a Truly Integrated Report," p. 21.

102. "Integrated Reporting: Performance insight through Better Business Reporting." Issue 1. 2011. KPMG. http://www.kpmg.com/Global/en/IssuesAndInsights/ArticlesPublications/Documents/road-to-integrated-reporting.pdf, accessed February 2014.
103. From 1956 to 1994, FDI as a percentage of GDP decreased from 35% to 10%. Fedderke and Romm, "Growth Impacts and Determinants of Foreign Direct Investments into South Africa."

CHAPTER TWO

Meaning

W HAT EXACTLY AN INTEGRATED report signifies to its audience has been evolving through four continuous, overlapping phases of "meaning-making" (Figure 2.1). The first, *Company Experimentation*, began in the early 2000s with a handful of companies' efforts to produce their first integrated report. This phase is the *initiation in practice* of the idea of integrated reporting. Consultants, academics, and other experts instigated the second phase, which we call *Expert Commentary*, when they began to establish basic principles about integrated reporting based on observations of companies' practices. Including lessons about the costs, benefits, and challenges of integrated reporting and how to overcome them, this *theory-building* phase started in the mid-2000s. In the late 2000s, the third phase, *Codification*, began. It is centered on the development of *frameworks and standards* by nongovernmental organizations (NGOs) working with other actors in the movement, like companies, investors, and accounting firms. The fourth and most recent phase, *Institutionalization*, is based on influencing the regulatory and market environment to make it more conducive to the practice of integrated reporting. Starting in the early 2010s, this phase is built on *laws and codes of conduct.* In this chapter we will focus on the first two phases and introduce the third, which is further discussed along with the fourth phase in Chapter 3.

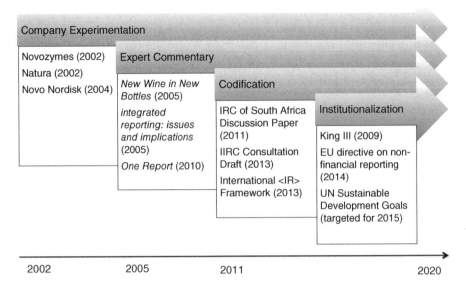

FIGURE 2.1 Four Phases in the Evolution of Meaning of Integrated Reporting

 COMPANY EXPERIMENTATION: EXAMPLES FROM THE FIRST INTEGRATED REPORTS

Eccles and Serafeim (2014) have argued that integrated reporting is superior to separate financial and sustainability reporting in its performance of both the "information" and "transformation" functions of corporate reporting.[1] "Corporate information that is more decision-useful is more likely to encourage all these counterparties to transact with the company and, all else equal, to transact with a company at better terms,"[2] they wrote. In other words, the information function affects resource allocation decisions of parties who do business with a company, but without allowing for feedback to the company from these counterparties. In contrast, "the transformation function relaxes this assumption, allowing for engagement and activism from the counterparties. The counterparties receive and evaluate the information. Where they see opportunities to influence corporate behavior to their benefit, and potentially to the benefit of the corporation, they actively try to bring change."[3] By affecting the resource allocation decisions of the company itself, "This engagement, activism, and change process enables a company to transform."[4]

Although supporters of integrated reporting vary in the relative importance they allocate to these two functions, they were implicit in the concept from its very earliest stages.

Like many new management ideas, integrated reporting began in practice.[5] When companies began to produce integrated reports in 2002, the notion of combining financial and nonfinancial data in a meaningful way arose in the same way as scientific ideas whose "time has come"—independently and simultaneously. The earliest integrated reporters were two Danish companies, Novozymes and Novo Nordisk, and a Brazilian company, Natura, all of whom gave essentially the same reason for the change: sustainability issues were now essential to the long-term success of the business, and integrated reporting was the best way to communicate about this. The integrated report's meaning lay in its capacity to help a company communicate that it was managing sustainability from a business perspective, and that it did not merely represent, to use a term from economics, a "transfer payment" from shareholders to stakeholders. Because integrated reporting was a nascent practice, general understanding of what it meant—or represented—was shallow. Consequently, further questions regarding report content and structure arose, focusing primarily on the information function. Although sustainability reporting guidance from the still-young Global Reporting Initiative (GRI) existed, at the time there was nothing to guide a company in what constituted an integrated report.

Despite the fact that the first companies to produce an integrated report differed in their report execution, many issues identified by these pioneers continue to be topical today. Materiality and stakeholder engagement (core to the transformation function) was challenging then, along with the questions of whether any kind of assurance should be provided on the report, the extent to which the Internet could be leveraged to supplement the paper report, the boundary of the report, the importance of intangible assets, understanding the relationship between financial and nonfinancial performance (often termed "ESG" performance because it refers to environmental, social, and governance factors), and the related struggle of going from a "combined report" to a truly "integrated report."

In 2008, a Dutch company (Philips) and an American company (United Technologies Corporation) raised further questions by issuing their first integrated reports.[6] The experience of Philips illustrates the evolutionary path of integrated reporting, and the intentions of United Technologies Corporation raise the issue of whether integrated reporting means less overall reporting by the company.

While the former is important for assessing the momentum of the movement today, the latter highlights a concern some advocates of sustainability reporting have voiced about integrated reporting: that in forcing concision, it will reduce the amount of information provided to stakeholders who represent civil society.

Novozymes

The first known company to produce an integrated report was the Danish industrial biotechnology company Novozymes. The second page of the company's compact 108-page 2002 annual report simply declares: "Integrated annual report, Environmental and Social Report."[7] In his CEO Statement,[8] President and CEO Steen Riisgaard declared:

Three bottom lines for future annual reports

This year and in future years Novozymes publishes a combined annual report with information on the areas that we believe to be most important for the majority of our stakeholders. This report is an integrated financial, environmental, and social report that also focuses on knowledge and the economic significance of our business. Our decision to bring everything together in one report is a natural consequence of business and sustainability moving ever closer together, and of various stakeholders asking for a wider overview of the business. We have chosen to keep the printed report relatively short and publish more detailed information on CD-ROM and on the Internet. We plan to expand this in-depth reporting for specific target groups in the coming years. Happy reading!

Riisgaard's use of the term "combined report," in contrast to the label, "integrated report," on the second page raised a debate that continues to this day. Although the degree to which interdependencies between financial and ESG performance must be disclosed to earn the title "integrated report" remains contentious, most parties would distinguish between a "combined report" that merely contains information on ESG performance and an "integrated report" insofar as the latter provides this information in a way that shows the relationships between them. Novozymes' integrated report was driven by the now-familiar themes of sustainability's increasing centrality to business success and the rising importance of stakeholders. Both issues point to the question, still being debated today, of exactly whom the audience for an integrated report should be.

Introducing the distinction between an *integrated report* and *integrated reporting*, Riisgaard pointedly noted the brevity of this 2002 integrated report, saying that supplementary information could be found on Novozymes' website. Integrated reporting both enables more detailed disclosure to specific stakeholders and more "real time" disclosures, albeit not necessarily in the format of a formal "report."

While it is clear that Novozymes' 2002 report was more combined than integrated, the progressive nature of its nonfinancial performance disclosures and consideration of noninvestor stakeholders demonstrate that the company had begun to build the foundation for a truly integrated report. In addition to revealing performance on a number of environmental and social indicators, the report presented a section titled "Knowledge as a strategic resource," which discussed process and technology, innovations, and the aggressive patenting of results. Also addressed were customer needs and organizational and employee development.[9] In considering these issues, Novozymes anticipated the intangible assets or "capitals" of intellectual, human, and social and relationship that feature prominently in "International <IR> Framework" (<IR> Framework) published by the International Integrated Reporting Council (IIRC) in December 2013.

In its commitment to better integration of social[10] and environmental[11] issues into the development of its overall strategic objectives, Novozymes arguably laid a foundation for exploring how environmental and social performance are linked to business success—and thus, integrated reporting. To do so, the company used GRI's G2 Guidelines as a basis for its Triple Bottom Line reporting,[12] indicating that GRI was involved with integrated reporting from the movement's inception and in the very early days of GRI itself. Although the term "materiality" was not mentioned in the report, the company established a 2003 goal to "Explore and implement new approaches to stakeholder engagement."[13]

Natura

The Brazilian cosmetics, fragrances, and personal hygiene company Natura also published its first integrated report in 2002.[14] Available in Portuguese and English, Natura's 2003[15] 143-page annual report stated, "For the second consecutive year, Natura presents in an integrated manner a report on its activities in the economic-financial, social and environmental fields. Therefore, it reaffirms the commitment made to the many sections of the general public with which it relates and that is stated in its Vision of the World, which is to seek sustainable development, as well as transparency when reporting its initiatives."[16] Like Novozymes, Natura emphasized a Triple Bottom Line approach without specifically using the term. The report stated that the challenge for the Natura Annual Report was to describe the impacts of Natura's economic, social, and environmental performance integration.[17] Despite a section titled "analysis of the economic-financial, environmental and social results," the report was, like Novozymes', more combined than integrated. Also like Novozymes, the company reported on a number of nonfinancial indicators like job creation and the company's relationship with the communities in which it operates.

Natura was ahead of its time in two critical areas: life cycle assessment (LCA) and supply chain management. The latter anticipated the "boundary" issue, or to what extent a company is responsible for the actions of its suppliers. This is discussed in the <IR> Framework. Not only did Natura address compliance by using a GRI indicator concerning the discussion of significant environmental impacts of principal products and services as an "integrated approach of concepts, techniques and procedures to access the environmental, economic, technological and social aspects of products and organizations with an aim to continuously improve the lifecycle prospect," it also set a 2004 target to carry out a packaging LCA study on 100% of products launched and to cover 100% of the packaging of the product portfolio.[18] Another 2004 target mentioned the Natura Environmental Management System and required the evaluation of environmental documentation of suppliers whose activities could impact the environment. No reference was made, however, to Accountability's AA1000 Assurance Standard[19] or to assurance, and the term "materiality" never appeared. While there was no mention of stakeholder engagement by name, three references to stakeholders surfaced in different contexts.[20]

Novo Nordisk

Along with Natura, Novo Nordisk is one of the most frequently cited examples today of a company producing a high-quality integrated report.[21] (Both companies have won numerous awards for their reports.[22]) Because Copenhagen-based Novo Nordisk and Novozymes formed a single company until a demerger in 2000, one can safely assume that Novo Nordisk was aware of Novozymes' first integrated report. Novo Nordisk followed suit in its 112-page 2004 annual report with what it referred to as its "Triple Bottom Line or TBL" reporting approach but did not call it an "integrated report."[23] It is highly unlikely that either of these Danish companies was aware of Natura in those early days, providing evidence that when "an idea's time has come," it occurs independently and simultaneously in different places. In the case of integrated reporting, the concept appeared in dramatically different industries separated by country and language.

Novo Nordisk gave an explanation similar to Novozymes' and Natura's for why it was producing an integrated report, but in its implementation this Danish company went further. Much like that of the previous two companies, its integrated report evolved out of a commitment to "sustainable development." Unlike the others, however, Novo Nordisk cited its management ethos, "The Novo Nordisk Way of Management," which "explicitly referred to the Triple Bottom Line (TBL) – social, environmental and financial responsibility – as the company's underlying business principle."[24] Furthermore, in March 2004 Novo Nordisk amended its Articles of Association to specify that the company will "strive to conduct its activities in a financially, environmentally and socially responsible way."[25] In doing so, the company made it clear that its approach was intended "to serve the long term interests of its shareholders."[26] Implicit in this statement was that shareholders' long-term interests are best served by taking account of other stakeholders' interests, an assertion that lies at the core of the movement's argument that it is in a company's long-term self-interest to adopt integrated reporting.

In its second integrated annual report, the company declared, "Novo Nordisk has chosen an integrated approach to reporting on its financial and non-financial performance. Hence, this report follows current international standards in terms of both mandatory and voluntary reporting."[27] In this 116-page report, Novo Nordisk showed leadership in addressing issues at the heart of the integrated movement today: materiality, stakeholder engagement, and assurance. The annual report had an explicit discussion about materiality, an issue absent in its 2004 report as well as the earlier reports of Novozymes and Natura. It also discussed how stakeholder engagement was used to help the company identify the material issues to be managed and reported on:

> Ongoing interactions with stakeholders, trendspotting, business monitoring and the integrated systematic risk management process are tools to identify the issues that are material to Novo Nordisk's business. The company's response to current and emerging business and societal challenges, in turn, is shaped in a closer dialogue with representatives of the stakeholders affected by the issue. As a result of this process, Novo Nordisk frames its strategic response and defines its targets. The company regularly reviews its key priorities to ensure

that they reflect current agendas, and reports on progress against performance targets.[28]

The company's Executive Management and Board of Directors affirmed that its nonfinancial reporting was prepared in accordance with Account-Ability's AA1000 AccountAbility Principles Standard 2003 and the 2002 GRI G2 Sustainability Reporting Guidelines,[29] and it included a Communication on Progress in support of the United Nations Global Compact.[30] Pricewater-houseCoopers reviewed the annual report to express a conclusion based on AccountAbility's AA1000 Assurance Standard 2003.

Philips and United Technologies

In 2008, Philips, a Dutch diversified technology multinational, and United Technologies Corporation (UTC), a U.S. manufacturing conglomerate, produced their first integrated reports. Since then, Philips has developed this practice to a much greater extent than UTC by, among other things, maintaining a sophisticated corporate reporting website. Although the term "integrated report" was only used once in its relatively bulky 276-page annual report, Philips was clear that producing an integrated report was its intention. It explained how this had evolved from previous nonfinancial reporting practices:

> In 1999 we published our first environmental annual report. We expanded our reporting in 2003 with the launch of our first sustainability annual report, which provided details on our social and economic performance in addition to our environmental results.
>   Now, for the first time, Philips is reporting on its annual financial, social and environmental performance in a single, integrated report. This approach reflects the progress we have made to embed sustainability in our way of doing business.[31]

Philips' evolution is fairly typical: companies begin with an environmental report, expand it to a broader sustainability (sometimes called a corporate social responsibility) report, and then make the leap to an integrated report. In fact, it follows general trends in "sustainability." Pressured heavily by climate change, companies tend to focus first on environmental issues, only later defining sustainability in broader "ESG" terms. When a company reaches the point of accepting that sustainability is no longer just a "program" but is core to strategy and operations, it has formulated the common argument for why integrated reporting makes sense.[32]

This is a necessary but not sufficient condition. While many companies today say they "really mean it" when it comes to sustainability, very few are publishing an integrated report. For us, this raises the question of how to separate sincerity from greenwashing. While we acknowledge that an integrated report can itself be used as a form of greenwashing, there are easier ways to do so if that is the company's intent. One discipline to prevent the practice and perception of greenwashing is to clarify which issues and audiences matter to the company and which do not. The basis of this distinction lies in what the company identifies as "material," something we explore in depth in Chapters 5 and 6.

Albeit in a more modest way than the companies discussed above, an American company can be considered a pioneer in integrated reporting as well: UTC.[33] Though UTC did not use the word "integrated" in a reporting context a single time in its svelte 98-page 2008 annual report,[34] it stated in a February 25, 2009, press release announcing the report that "United Technologies Corp. (NYSE: UTX) has become the first among the 30 members of the Dow Jones Industrial Average to publish a fully integrated annual and corporate responsibility report."[35] Echoing the argument of other companies that such integration makes business sense, albeit in the language of "corporate responsibility" rather than "corporate social responsibility" or "sustainability," the press release goes on to quote Andrea Doane, director of corporate citizenship and community investment: "UTC's 2008 Annual Report reflects the belief that corporate responsibility and profitability go hand in hand." Doane continued, "For UTC, the evolution to one report is natural, but we believe firmly in the years to come the practice of just one report will be not only widespread, but expected from those who believe corporate responsibility and profitability are inseparable."[36] As discussed in the next chapter, UTC's expectation that this practice would become "widespread" has not yet been met as of 2014.

In their "Dear Shareowner" letter, UTC Chairman George David and President and Chief Executive Officer Louis Chênevert stated, "For the first time, this Annual Report combines business and financial results with those on corporate responsibility." The report's subtitle, "More with less," speaks to UTC's efforts to be more efficient in its natural resource use. It is also suggestive of the consolidation of two reports into one, raising the more general question of whether an integrated report means "one report" or whether that additional information should be presented through other means. In 2010, Eccles and

Krzus made an argument that an integrated report does not strictly mean "one report"—an issue we will address in greater depth throughout this book.[37]

EXPERT COMMENTARY: THE FIRST REFLECTIONS ON INTEGRATED REPORTING

Not long after the first integrated reports were published, close observers of corporate reporting—a think tank, a consulting firm, and an academic and an accountant—began to reflect on the experiences of the early pioneers. Two publications appearing within a few months of each other in 2005 initiated the second phase of meaning: Expert Commentary.[38] Five years later, the first book on integrated reporting was published. These studies sought to give their own meaning to the concept of integrated reporting, to identify the benefits and challenges facing companies adopting it, and to make suggestions about what needed to be done to secure large-scale adoption of this practice. Though not treated in any depth, materiality was mentioned in all three studies. Stakeholder engagement received extensive attention in the book and the think tank article, although not in the article from the consulting firm.

New Wine in New Bottles

In a June 20, 2005, publication, Allen White, Vice President and Senior Fellow of Tellus Institute, a nonprofit research and policy organization, wrote, "A quiet renaissance in corporate reporting is gradually transforming its purpose, content and readership."[39] Although his piece primarily focused on nonfinancial reporting, he explicitly mentioned the term "integrated reporting." He did not specifically define the concept but described it as "embryonic" compared to the "pre-adolescence" stage of nonfinancial reporting.[40] Citing Novo Nordisk's 2004 Annual Report as providing a "glimpse of next-generation reporting," he went on to use the efforts of the pioneering cohort to explain the term. Examples he cited of companies combining financial and nonfinancial performance information in a single report included Swiss pharmaceutical company Novartis (2002), British automotive and aerospace engineering company GKN (2002), Canadian electric utility company BC Hydro (2003), Scandinavian airline SAS Group (2004), German chemical company BASF (2004), Dutch chemicals and life sciences company DSM (without giving a specific date), and Natura.[41]

White made the case for both the information ("It is integral to doing business and retaining the license to operate in the coming decades.") and transformation ("If wisely managed, it is also an opportunity to sharpen management's effectiveness while helping to position the firm in the vanguard of firms committed to corporate responsibility.") functions of integrated reporting.[42] Claiming that this "reporting renaissance is irreversible," White made five predictions which have largely emerged as true by 2014: (1) integration of financial and nonfinancial disclosure will accelerate, (2) metrics will continue to evolve "toward a set of generally accepted standards applicable to all companies," (3) sector-based initiatives will ensure that "disclosed information is in fact material information to stakeholders," (4) the use of technology "to communicate and access information will experience a quantum leap," and (5) indices and ratings will become as commonplace for nonfinancial performance as they are for financial performance today.[43]

The Solstice/Vancity Study

Two months later, the Canadian sustainability consulting boutique Solstice Sustainability Works published a study on integrated reporting sponsored by the Canadian cooperative bank Vancity.[44] In it, they defined integrated reporting as a fusion of financial and sustainability reporting into a single document: "The working definition of integrated reporting for this research was reporting that meets the needs of both statutory financial reporting and sustainability reporting. In practical terms, this will usually mean one annual report containing sustainability performance information and financial statements."[45]

As in White's paper, the views expressed in the report were based on company examples (12)[46] as well as interviews with experts in companies and other organizations. Without references or supporting data, a claim was made in the Introduction to the report that "For many years, integrated reporting has been something of a holy grail for advocates of accountability, something that has not been achieved through most efforts at triple bottom line reporting."[47] Solstice was more reserved in its assessment of integrated reporting as a practice, declaring, "Reporters should not count on significant tangible benefits of integrated reporting."[48] Instead, its authors saw the primary benefits to be largely intangible and internal: "challenge for staff, improved understanding of the links between sustainability and business strategy, consistent messaging, and improved decision making." This view was reinforced by their assertion that "there does not appear to be a significant external demand for integrated reporting, yet."[49]

While Solstice noted that the degree of integration in an integrated report varied and that some "combined reports sometimes look like different stories inexplicably bound in the same volume," it acknowledged that "the combined report could be seen as a useful first step in integrated reporting."[50] In identifying integrated reporting's benefits, Solstice listed reduced cost (not much), efficiencies in report preparation (mixed), recognition for leadership (maybe), interesting challenges for the reporting team (probably), improved internal understanding of business/sustainability linkages (yes), improved consistency of messages (yes), and forcing or reflecting integrated thinking (in theory, yes). In elaborating on integrated thinking, Solstice asked an important "chicken-and-egg" question which remains relevant: "Does integrated reporting encourage holistic management or does a holistic management approach naturally lead to integrated reporting?"[51] Major challenges cited for implementing integrated reporting included getting support from senior management, gathering information on nonfinancial information as quickly as information on financial performance, overly long reports or reports which lose important content on nonfinancial performance for the sake of brevity, the necessity for the team putting the integrated report together to build new skills, and that investors' information needs may dominate over those of other stakeholders.

Solstice addressed three other issues that remain central to the movement today. First, it concluded that regulation could not drive integrated reporting because it was focused on "only the most material social and environmental disclosures."[52] Second, they questioned whether an integrated report would lead to an integrated assurance opinion. Arguing that financial auditors do not have the skills to audit nonfinancial information, they remained noncommittal, expressing the concern "that bland or negative assurance will become the norm."[53] Third, they pointed out that technology was enabling a "shift in focus from the report to reporting," and that it could facilitate integration.[54]

One Report: The First Book on Integrated Reporting

In 2010, five years after the papers by White and Solstice were written, the first book on integrated reporting, written by us, was published.[55] In keeping with the assertions of pioneer companies and the arguments of White and Solstice, we argued that integrated reporting was an important mechanism for helping companies develop and implement a sustainable strategy, which we defined as "a commitment to corporate social responsibility that is contributing to a sustainable society that takes into account the needs of all stakeholders, of which shareholders are one type."[56]

We recognized the important transformation function of integrated reporting. Although the difficulty of trade-offs between financial and nonfinancial performance inherent in resource allocation decisions can be reduced or even reversed through innovation, a sustainable strategy requires a company to face them head-on.[57] Making these decisions assumes the company has a good understanding of the different relationships between the many dimensions of financial and nonfinancial performance. Answering the question asked by Solstice about the relationship between holistic management and integrated reporting, we saw integrated reporting as providing the discipline for developing this understanding and laying the groundwork for reporting on performance in an integrated way. Our view, then and now, is that the information and transformation functions of integrated reporting are mutually reinforcing.[58]

Since integrated reporting was still in its very early stages at the time, we framed our discussion of the information function in the institutional context of current financial and sustainability reporting practices. How integrated reporting builds on and/or conflicts with financial and sustainability reporting remains a core topic of debate today. While some companies, like UTC, have claimed integrated reporting saves money by turning two reports into one, we think this benefit is relatively trivial compared with its organizational change potential as a catalyst for integrated thinking. Furthermore, although we titled our book *One Report*, we made it clear that integrated reporting was not simply about producing a single document that contained both financial and nonfinancial information:

> One Report doesn't mean *Only* One Report. It simply means that there should be one report that integrates the company's key financial and nonfinancial information. It by no means precludes the company providing other information in many different ways that are targeted to specific users. Rather, One Report provides a conceptual platform that is supplemented by the technology platform of the company's Web site, from which much more detailed data can and should be provided to meet the information needs of a company's many stakeholders.

Based on the experiences of pioneering companies, we identified four major benefits of integrated reporting that form a self-reinforcing cycle. The first is greater clarity about the relationships between financial and nonfinancial performance and the commitments the company is making to specific performance targets. Second, it spawns better internal decision making for a sustainable strategy. Third is deeper engagement with stakeholders and reducing the distinction between shareholders and stakeholders by providing a common message to both. And fourth is lower reputational risk, which now ranks as the top risk, followed by regulatory risk and human capital risk (tied).[59] We also argued that the adoption of sustainable strategies by companies is necessary both for the long-term survival of those companies and for ensuring a sustainable society. Thus, we posited a societal level benefit from the broad scale adoption of integrated reporting.

Recognizing that the integrated reporting movement faces a collective action problem, in the last chapter we addressed the challenges to this form of reporting becoming a common practice. We identified the responsibilities of all key movement actors (companies, investors, standard setters, NGOs representing civil society, and regulators) to make this happen. Noting that success requires commitment from all groups, we argued that companies, as the reporting entities, must take the lead, with the support of their boards and auditors. Our view here has changed somewhat, and in Chapter 5 we will argue instead that the ultimate responsibility for integrated reporting lies with the board of directors, with support from executive management and the company's auditor. Finally, we also emphasized the importance of innovation and experimentation as the basis for principles-based "comply or explain" regulation, which we felt would ultimately be necessary but which would inevitably proceed at a different pace in different countries. This is still our position as discussed in Chapter 10.

 ## CODIFICATION: CREATING COMMON MEANING

The third phase in defining the meaning of integrated reporting is one of Codification. Differing from the first two phases in that it is not based on the efforts of individual companies or commentators, each expressing their own view, in Codification an authoritative body establishes a multistakeholder process to fashion an agreed-upon meaning of the concept of integrated reporting, supported by principles and guidelines to provide guidance on implementation. Others can decide whether to adopt this view or not. If the authoritative body establishing meaning is an organ of the State, its legitimacy is assured. Otherwise, broad credibility for the meaning codification depends upon the perceived legitimacy of the process for fashioning it, as well as the expertise, status, and influence of the individuals and organizations involved in it.

The Integrated Reporting Committee of South Africa

Introduced in the previous chapter, the first attempt at codification was the "Framework for Integrated Reporting and the Integrated Report Discussion Paper"[60] (IRC of SA Discussion Paper) by the Integrated Reporting Committee of South Africa (IRC of SA). Addressing both the information and transformation functions of integrated reporting, the IRC of SA Discussion Paper defined an integrated report as follows:

> An integrated report tells the overall story of the organisation. It is a report to stakeholders on the strategy, performance and activities of the organisation in a manner that allows stakeholders to assess the ability of the organisation to create and sustain value over the short-, medium- and long-term. An effective integrated report reflects an appreciation that the organisation's ability to create and sustain value is based on financial, social, economic and environmental systems and by the quality of its relationships with stakeholders.[61]

Although this definition does not include the word "sustainability" (but rather sustainable value creation—the source concept for the Sustainable Value Matrix as discussed in detail in Chapter 6), the word "sustainability" is used 52 times in the report.

Many themes developed in the first two phases of meaning appear in the IRC of SA Discussion Paper: the internal performance benefits of integrated reporting (e.g., how external issues can affect the company's strategy, better risk management, and developing a culture of innovation), the distinction between an integrated report and integrated reporting, the importance of stakeholder engagement for determining materiality, and the performance benefits of stakeholder engagement. As discussed in the previous chapter, the IRC of SA Discussion Paper identified three categories of "Reporting principles"—scope and boundary, selection of the report content, and the quality of the reported information. While it also suggested eight elements to be included in an integrated report, providing a detailed explanation of each and sometimes brief examples to make the point clear, it did not provide a detailed proscriptive format for what an integrated report should look like.[62]

The International Integrated Reporting Council

The second codification effort—and the most globally significant one to date—is "The International <IR> Framework" published in December 2013 by the IIRC following completion of the IIRC's due process procedures.[63] Based on seven "Guiding Principles" (Strategic focus and future orientation, Connectivity of information, Stakeholder relationships, Materiality, Conciseness, Reliability and completeness, and Consistency and comparability) and eight "Content Elements" (Organizational overview and external environment, Governance, Business model, Risks and opportunities, Strategy and resource allocation, Performance, Outlook, and Basis of preparation and presentation), the IIRC's definition of an integrated report is similar to that of South Africa's IRC. "An integrated report is a concise communication about how an organization's strategy, governance, performance and prospects, in the context of its external environment, lead to the creation of value over the short, medium and long term," it reads.[64] However, the 37-page Framework did not cast an integrated report as a fusion of a financial report and a sustainability report, as is the case in the South African publication. In stark contrast to the IRC of SA Discussion Paper, the term "sustainability" is only used three times[65] in the <IR> Framework. Table 2.1 shows the major similarities and differences in the two publications.

Echoing the conviction of *One Report*, the <IR> Framework stated that an integrated report "may be either a standalone report or be included as a distinguishable, prominent and accessible part of another report or communication."[66] Not to be confused with endorsing a "combined" report, this simply means the IIRC acknowledged that due to its intended concise nature, the integrated report could be viewed as an "entry point" to more detailed data, such as through hyperlinks on the company's website.[67] Furthermore, in a clear signal that the <IR> Framework was indeed intended to become a global standard for the meaning of an integrated report, it stated, "An integrated report should be prepared in accordance with this Framework."[68] This raises the obvious question of how an integrated report fits into the context of a company's regulatory reporting requirements.

The <IR> Framework further honed the distinction made in the IRC of SA Discussion Paper between an integrated report and integrated reporting by emphasizing the relationship between the information function of integrated reporting and the transformation function of integrated thinking. Each is defined as contributing to the other in a virtuous cycle. In fact, the very first

TABLE 2.1 Comparison of the IRC of SA's Discussion Paper and the IIRC's International <IR> Framework

Topic	IRC of South Africa Discussion Paper	IIRC International <IR> Framework
Concept		
Context	Corporate governance (in terms of integrity, transparency, and accountability)	Value creation over time
Integrated Thinking	Term not used	Core concept
Integrated Report vs. Integrated Reporting	The report—a work product—is different from reporting—a business process	The integrated report is a work product, which is different from integrated thinking. Integrated reporting supports integrated thinking
Principles-Based	Yes	Yes
Report audience	Multiple stakeholders	Providers of financial capital and other stakeholders interested in the organization's ability to create value over time
Framework users	Any organization	Private sector for-profit companies of any size, but adaptable to public sector and not-for-profits
Time Frame	Short, Medium, and Long Term	Short, Medium, and Long Term
Has a model for value creation	No	Yes
Sustainability	Core to the discussion	Core to the discussion to the extent that it has a material influence on value creation over time
Reporting		
Architecture of Framework	Three Reporting Principles, Eight Suggested Elements, and Nine Steps for preparing an integrated report (Annex 2)	Fundamental Concepts, Seven Guiding Principles, and Eight Content Elements

(continued)

TABLE 2.1　(*Continued*)

Topic	IRC of South Africa Discussion Paper	IIRC International <IR> Framework
Materiality	Defined by the company (in terms of issues affecting value over the short-, medium- and long-term) and distinguishes between financial and nonfinancial definitions	Defined by the company in terms of issues that substantively affect the organization's ability to create value over the short-, medium- and long-term
Stakeholder Engagement	Extensive discussion as Step 4 in the process of developing an integrated report in the context of determining materiality	"Stakeholder relationships" is one of the Guiding Principles; requires discussion of nature and quality and responsiveness to interests
Gives guidance on how to prepare an integrated report	Yes	Yes
General		
Discusses how to leverage the company's website on the Internet	Only that the integrated report should be posted on the company's website	Web-based content and hyperlinks are mentioned in the context of connectivity and conciseness
Has regulatory backing	The Johannesburg Stock Exchange; listed companies provide an integrated report on an apply or explain basis	No
Discusses Assurance	Yes in a dedicated section	Cursory reference to independent assurance enhancing reliability

sentence of the first section of the International <IR> Framework, "About Integrated Reporting," highlighted this relationship:

> The IIRC's long-term vision is a world in which integrated thinking is embedded within mainstream business practice in the public and private sectors, facilitated by Integrated Reporting (<IR>) as the corporate reporting norm. The cycle of integrated thinking and reporting, resulting in efficient and productive capital allocation, will act as a force for financial stability and sustainability.[69]

Emphasis on integrated thinking remains one of the IIRC's most important contributions to the meaning of integrated reporting. "Integrated thinking," the paper declared, "is the active consideration by an organization of the relationships between its various operating and functional units and the capitals that the organization uses or affects. Integrated thinking leads to integrated decision-making and actions that consider the creation of value over the short, medium and long term."[70]

If the IRC of SA Discussion Paper contextualized integrated reporting within corporate governance because of South Africa's particular circumstances, the <IR> Framework privileges value creation. Yet, governance remains important; it is cited as one of the eight Content Elements that should be included in the integrated report. "Those charged with governance are responsible for creating an appropriate oversight structure to support the ability of the organization to create value," the <IR> Framework stated.[71] The board has the ultimate responsibility for the company's strategy for sustainable value creation and for reporting on its results in an integrated report. Beyond governance, the integrated report should include the uses of and consequences to all of the "capitals" (financial, manufactured, intellectual, human, social and relationship, and natural) a company uses to create value. The importance of value creation in terms of the six capitals and the trade-offs that must be taken into account are reflected in the <IR> Framework's model of value creation (Figure 2.2).[72]

While both documents emphasized integrated reporting's role in helping companies create value over "the short, medium, and long term,"[73] the IRC of SA Discussion Paper and the <IR> Framework defined report audience somewhat differently. The IIRC focused on "providers of financial capital"; the IRC of SA had a multistakeholder approach, stating that an integrated report "allows stakeholders to assess the ability of the organization to create and sustain value over the short-, medium- and long-term."[74] That said, the <IR> Framework also noted, "An integrated report benefits all stakeholders interested in an organization's ability to create value over time."[75] Similarly, while the <IR> Framework contained materiality as one of its Guiding Principles, it did not distinguish between financial and nonfinancial information, simply defining materiality as "matters that substantively affect the organization's ability to create value over the short, medium and long term."[76]

Because the <IR> Framework is based on principles rather than rules, the IIRC was very clear that it "does not prescribe specific key performance indicators (KPIs), measurement methods or the disclosure of individual

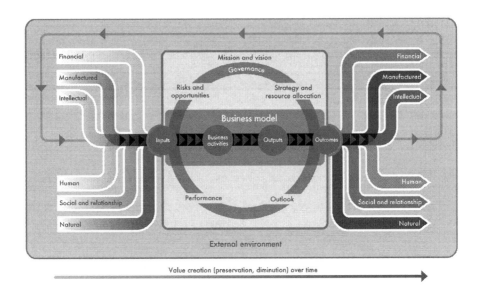

Value creation (preservation, diminution) over time

FIGURE 2.2 International <IR> Framework Value Creation Process

Source: International Integrated Reporting Council. International <IR> Framework, p. 13, http://www.theiirc.org/international-ir-framework/, accessed May 2014.

matters."[77] It simply states that the company should determine the material issues and how to disclose them, remaining agnostic about what these are and what standards to use, if any, assuming they exist, for reporting on them.

Such flexibility is less apparent in how the IIRC sees the relationship between its framework and the practice of integrated reporting. In the first section, "Using the Framework," the IIRC stated, "Any communication claiming to be an integrated report and referencing the Framework should apply all the requirements identified in bold italics."[78] In this sense, the IIRC is more ambitious than the IRC of SA, which never claimed that any use of the term "integrated reporting" referencing the IRC of SA Discussion Paper should follow its principles and guidelines. The fact that the IIRC is a nonprofit organization with no regulatory backing in any country raises the obvious question of how such a requirement would be enforced. As discussed in Chapter 10, this can happen through a combination of market and regulatory forces. Since the IIRC is a "global coalition of regulators, investors, companies, standard setters, the accounting profession and NGOs,"[79] it contains elements of both, making it one of the key actors accelerating the momentum of the integrated reporting movement.

NOTES

1. Eccles, Robert G. and George Serafeim. "Corporate and Integrated Reporting: A Functional Perspective." Harvard Business School Working Paper, No. 14-094, April 2014. (Revised May 2014.)
2. Ibid, p. 2.
3. Ibid, pp. 2–3.
4. Ibid.
5. Mol, Michael J. and Julian Birkinshaw. *Giant Steps in Management.* London: Financial Times Prentice Hall, 2007, pp. 2, 3, and 182–199. Bloomberg Business. "A History of Big Ideas," http://images.businessweek.com/ss/09/03/0312_game_changing_timeline/index.htm, accessed May 2014.
6. The convention used in corporate reporting is that the report year refers to the period of time covered by the annual report. For example, the United Technologies Corporation (UTC) Annual Report 2008 is for the year ended December 31, 2008, and was published in early 2009.
7. Novozymes. *Annual Report: The Novozymes Report 2002*, p. 2, http://www.zonebourse.com/NOVOZYMES-447531/pdf/8355/NOVOZYMES_Rapport-annuel.pdf, accessed January 2014.
8. Novozymes, *The Novozymes Report 2002*, p. 5.
9. Novozymes. *The Novozymes Report 2002*, http://www.novozymes.com/en/investor/financial-reports/Documents/The%20Novozymes%20report%202002.pdf, accessed March 2014.
10. Similar to the environmental commitment, the company asks whether social responsibility can be measured as it identifies goals and performance on social issues. Ibid.
11. The company positions itself for greater integration of environmental responsibility into the business model and strategy with a public commitment to "continuously improve our environmental performance by setting objectives and integrating environmental and bioethical considerations into our daily business." Ibid.
12. "The economic bottom line covers many different elements. The latest Global Reporting Initiative (GRI) guidelines for reporting on the Triple Bottom Line include a number of indicators that aim to paint a picture of companies' economic impact on the world around them. These indicators have served as our inspiration when reporting on the third bottom line." Ibid.
13. Ibid.
14. For a more detailed and recent discussion of integrated reporting at Natura, see Eccles, Robert G., George Serafeim, and James Heffernan. "Natura Cosméticos, S.A." Harvard Business School Case 412-052, November 2011. (Revised June 2013.)
15. The 2002 annual report is not available online.

16. Natura. *annualreport natura2003*, p. 19, http://natura.infoinvest.com.br/enu/1648/Eng_Annual_Report_2003.pdf, accessed January 2014.

17. Ibid.

18. Natura. *Annual Report 2003*, http://natura.infoinvest.com.br/enu/s-15-enu-2003.html, accessed March 2014.

19. In the 2003 edition of the AA1000AS the principles and the standard were published as a single document. This was changed in 2008 when separate versions of AA1000 Assurance Standard and the AA1000 AccountAbility Principles Standard 2008 were issued. AccountAbility. http://www.accountability.org/images/content/0/9/091/Introduction%20to%20the%20revised%20AA1000AS%20and%20AA1000APS.pdf, accessed April 2014.

20. The company mentions the Natura Environmental Management System as a channel for registering and replying to the notices of environmental impacts with stakeholders in its description of how the company manages impacts on communities affected by its activities. Natura, Annual Report 2003.

21. For a more detailed and recent discussion of integrated reporting at Novo Nordisk, see Eccles, Robert G. and Michael P. Krzus. "Novo Nordisk: A Commitment to Sustainability." Harvard Business School Case 412-053. Revised June 2013.

22. Novo Nordisk received the top ranking on Corporate Knight's list of Global 100 Most Sustainable Corporations in 2012. Reporting awards include Corporate Register's Best Integrated Report (three time winner), Corporate Register's Best Report for Openness & Honesty, top ranking by Lundquist CSR Online Awards Nordic, Globe Award for sustainability reporting, and Best Danish annual report. Novo Nordisk. http://www.novonordisk.com/sustainability/sustainability-approach/awards-and-recognition.asp, accessed March 2014. Natura was ranked second on Corporate Knight's list of Global 100 Most Sustainable Corporations in 2011 and 2012. Reporting awards include winner Aberje Award for Print Media (Annual Report), IR Magazine Brazil Awards for Best Social and Environmental Sustainability, and Transparency Trophy recognition as one of the five most transparent publicly traded companies. Natura. http://natura.infoinvest.com.br/enu/4381/RA_NATURA_2012_ENG.pdf, accessed March 2014.

23. John Elkington coined the phrase "triple bottom line." Elkington, J. "Towards the sustainable corporation: Win-win-win business strategies for sustainable development," *California Management Review* 36, no. 2. 1994. The "Triple Bottom Line" (TBL) reporting approach, which ultimately gave rise to the "ESG plus financials" approach favored today, appeared with the great frequency (11 times) in the 112-page 2004 report. Novo Nordisk. *Annual Report 2004: Financial, Social and Environmental Performance Report*, http://www.novonordisk.com/investors/download-centre/reports/annual/Annual%20Report%2004%20UK.pdf, accessed March 2014.

24. Ibid., p. 9.

25. Ibid.

26. Ibid.

27. Novo Nordisk. *novo nordisk annual report: financial, social & environmental performance 2005*, http://annualreport2005.novonordisk.com/annual-report/ images/2005/Annual%20Report%2005%20UK.pdf, accessed January 2014, p. 40.

28. Ibid., p. 6.

29. GRI G2 Guidelines were released at the August-September 2002 World Summit on Sustainable Development in Johannesburg. Global Reporting Initiative. https://www.globalreporting.org/information/about-gri/what-is-GRI/Pages/default.aspx, accessed April 2014.

30. The United Nations (UN) Global Compact is "a strategic policy initiative for businesses that are committed to aligning their operations and strategies with ten universally accepted principles in the areas of human rights, labour, environment and anti-corruption. By doing so, business, as a primary driver of globalization, can help ensure that markets, commerce, technology and finance advance in ways that benefit economies and societies everywhere." UN Global Compact. About Us, Overview, http://www.unglobalcompact.org/ AboutTheGC/index.html, accessed May 2014. "The UN Global Compact's ten principles in the areas of human rights, labour, the environment and anti-corruption enjoy universal consensus and are derived from: The Universal Declaration of Human Rights; The International Labour Organization's Declaration on Fundamental Principles and Rights at Work; The Rio Declaration on Environment and Development and The United Nations Convention Against Corruption. The UN Global Compact asks companies to embrace, support and enact, within their sphere of influence, a set of core values in the areas of human rights, labour standards, the environment and anti-corruption. Human Rights: Principle 1: Businesses should support and respect the protection of internationally proclaimed human rights; and Principle 2: make sure that they are not complicit in human rights abuses. Labour: Principle 3: Businesses should uphold the freedom of association and the effective recognition of the right to collective bargaining; Principle 4: the elimination of all forms of forced and compulsory labour; Principle 5: the effective abolition of child labour; and Principle 6: the elimination of discrimination in respect of employment and occupation. Environment: Principle 7: Businesses should support a precautionary approach to environmental challenges; Principle 8: undertake initiatives to promote greater environmental responsibility; and Principle 9: encourage the development and diffusion of environmentally friendly technologies. Anti-Corruption: Principle 10: Businesses should work against corruption in all its forms, including extortion and bribery." UN Global Compact. About Us, The Ten Principles, http://www.unglobalcompact.org/AboutTheGC/TheTenPrinciples/index.html,

accessed May 2014. "Business participants in the UN Global Compact commit to make the Global Compact ten principles part of their business strategies and day-to-day operations. Companies also commit to issue an annual Communication on Progress (COP), a public disclosure to stakeholders (e.g., investors, consumers, civil society, governments, etc.) on progress made in implementing the ten principles of the UN Global Compact, and in supporting broader UN development goals. "The Communication on Progress (COP) is frequently the most visible expression of a participant's commitment to the Global Compact and its principles. Violations of the COP policy (e.g., failure to issue a COP) will change a participant's status to non-communicating and can eventually lead to the expulsion of the participant." UN Global Compact. Reporting, What is a Cop? http://www.unglobal compact.org/COP/index.html, accessed May 2014.

31. Philips, *Annual Report 2008, Financial, social and environmental performance*, p. 180, http://www.philips.com/shared/assets/Downloadablefile/Investor/ Philips2008_AnnualReport.pdf, accessed January 2014.

32. Eccles, Robert G. and George Serafeim. "The Performance Frontier: Innovating for a sustainable strategy." *Harvard Business Review* 91, no. 5 (May 2013): 50–60.

33. For a detailed discussion of UTC's first integrated report and the evolution of its corporate reporting practices see, Eccles, Robert G. and Michael P. Krzus. *One Report: Integrated Reporting for a Sustainable Strategy*. New York: John Wiley & Sons, Inc., 2010. Chapter 2, pp. 29–50.

34. United Technologies. *United Technologies Corporation Annual Report: 2008 Financial and Corporate Responsibility Performance, More with less.* http:// www.cn.utc.com/utc_cn/Static%20files/About%20UTC/UTC%202008% 20Annual%20Report.pdf, accessed January 2014.

35. United Technologies. News, *United Technologies publishes combined Annual and Corporate Responsibility Report - determined to do "more with less,"* http://www .utc.com/News/United+Technologies+publishes+combined+Annual+and +Corporate+Responsibility+Report?Page=11&channel=/News/Archive/ 2009, accessed April 2014.

36. Ibid.

37. Eccles and Krzus, *One Report*, p. 10.

38. Given the timing of these papers, it is highly unlikely that either author knew about the other's work. This is yet another example of how separate events occur simultaneously when an idea's time has come.

39. White, Allen L. "New Wine, New Bottles: The Rise of Non-Financial Reporting." A Business Brief by Business for Social Responsibility, 2005, http://www .bsr.org/reports/200506_BSR_Allen-White_Essay.pdf, accessed May 2014.

40. Ibid., p. 2.

41. It is interesting that Novozymes is not mentioned and to this day Novo Nordisk has received a great deal more attention for its efforts in integrated reporting than its former sister company.
42. Ibid., p. 5.
43. Ibid.
44. Solstice Sustainability Works, Inc. *"integrated reporting: issues and implications for reporters,"* August 2005, https://www.vancity.com/lang/fr/SharedContent/documents/IntegratedReporting.pdf, accessed January 2014.
45. Ibid., p. 1.
46. Ibid., p. 4.
47. Ibid., p. 3.
48. Ibid., p. 1
49. Ibid., p. 2.
50. Ibid., p. 5.
51. Ibid., p. 7.
52. Ibid., p. 11.
53. Ibid., p. 13.
54. Ibid., p. 14.
55. Eccles and Krzus did not become aware of the White and Solstice papers until sometime after their book was published. These papers were buried deep in the Internet, suggesting that both were some years ahead of their time.
56. Ibid., p. 3.
57. Eccles and Serafeim. "The Performance Frontier."
58. Eccles and Krzus, *One Report*, Chapter 6, pp. 145–179.
59. The Economist Intelligence Unit. Reputation: Risks of Risks, white paper, December 2005, pp. 5, 22.
60. We have referred to the IRC Discussion Paper of South Africa so as to avoid confusion with the Discussion Paper of the IIRC.
61. Integrated Reporting Committee of South Africa. "Framework for Integrated Reporting and the Integrated Report," January 25, 2011. http://www.sustainabilitysa.org/Portals/0/IRC%20of%20SA%20Integrated%20Reporting%20Guide%20Jan%2011.pdf, accessed January 2014.
62. The eight elements are: 1. Report profile (What is the scope and boundary of the report?), 2. Organisational overview, business model, and governance structure (How do we create value and make decisions?), 3. Understanding of the operating context (What are the circumstances under which we operate?), 4. Strategic objectives, competencies, KPIs and KRIs (Where do we want to go and how do we intend to get there?), 5. Account of the organisation's performance (How have we fared over the reporting period?), 6. Future performance objectives (Informed by our recent performance, what are our future objectives?), 7. Remuneration policies (What is our approach towards remuneration?),

8. Analytical commentary (what are the views of the leadership about the organisation?), Ibid., Contents Page.

63. The Framework was developed in consultation with the Technical Task Force on the basis of feedback received from a range of sources including: the Working Group, responses to the 2011 Discussion Paper, consultation with Pilot Programme participants, discussions with Council members and round-tables conducted in various places around the world. The Consultation Draft was open for public comment for a period of 90 days. Prior to submitting the Framework to the IIRC Board for approval, all comments received on the Consultation Draft were considered, summarized, and the Board was advised of disposition. The process also required that at least two-thirds of the Working Group recommend the Framework to the Board and that two-thirds of the Council endorse the Framework. International Integrated Reporting Council. *IIRC Due Process*, http://www.theiirc.org/wp-content/uploads/2012/11/IIRC-Due-Process-25-09-12.pdf, accessed March 2014.

64. International Integrated Reporting Council. International <IR> Framework, p. 7, http://www.theiirc.org/international-ir-framework/, accessed May 2014.

65. The first mention seems to refer to the sustainability of the capital markets: "The cycle of integrated thinking and reporting, resulting in efficient and productive capital allocation, will act as a force for financial stability and sustainability." Ibid. p. 2. The second time is to emphasize that an integrated report is more than producing a single report that contains information on both financial and sustainability performance: "An integrated report is intended to be more than a summary of information in other communications (e.g., financial statements, a sustainability report, analyst calls, or on a website); rather, it makes explicit the connectivity of information to commu-nicate how value is created over time." Ibid. p. 8. The third time is in saying that information in the integrated report should be compatible with informa-tion in other reports: "For example, when a KPI covers a similar topic to, or is based on information published in the organization's financial statements or sustainability report, it is prepared on the same basis, and for the same period, as that other information." IRC of SA Discussion Paper, p. 30.

66. <IR> Framework, p. 8.

67. Ibid.

68. Ibid.

69. Ibid., p. 2.

70. Ibid.

71. Ibid., p. 13.

72. Ibid.

73. <IR> Framework, p. 2 and IRC of SA Discussion Paper, p. 6.

74. IRC of SA Discussion Paper, p. 13.

75. These stakeholders include employees, customers, suppliers, business partners, local communities, legislators, regulators, and policy-makers. <IR> Framework, p. 4.
76. International <IR> Framework, p. 19.
77. Ibid., p. 7.
78. Ibid., p. 8.
79. International Integrated Reporting Council. The IIRC, http://www.theiirc.org/the-iirc/, accessed April 2014.

CHAPTER THREE

Momentum

W HILE THE UNIVERSAL ADOPTION of integrated reporting is by no means inevitable, its current trajectory remains positive. Though less mature than sustainability reporting, integrated reporting is, at its core, a social movement.[1] When put into practice by companies and used by the audience of report consumers, it can transform the way resource allocation decisions are made inside companies and markets across the globe. Its social goal is to use corporate reporting as a means to influence companies and investors such that they incorporate the consequences of the positive and negative externalities of corporate decisions (most typically referred to as "sustainability"[2] regarding social and environmental issues) and the increasing importance of intangible assets. A key element of this is fostering longer-term thinking and taking more explicit account of all the "capitals" a company uses and transforms in creating value.

Defined as a loosely organized but sustained campaign in support of a social goal—often implementation of or resistance to a change in society's structure or values—social movements are by definition collective efforts.[3] Although they may differ in size, this type of group action results from the more or less spontaneous coalescence of individuals and organizations whose relationships are not defined by rules and procedures but by their common outlook on society.[4]

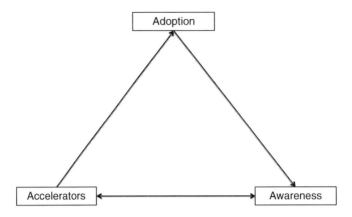

FIGURE 3.1　Adoption, Accelerators, and Awareness

The success of any social movement requires the participation, support, and collaboration of a wide range of actors. In the case of the integrated reporting movement, whose success ultimately depends on the global adoption of this practice by all listed companies, these actors include companies, analysts and investors, nongovernmental organizations (NGOs), regulators and standard setters, and accounting and technology firms. It is only through the global—or at least widespread—adoption of integrated reporting by most of the world's largest companies that the system-level benefits of integrated reporting will be achieved. In the meantime, individual companies stand to benefit for the reasons discussed in the next chapter, as can investors who learn how to incorporate the information in an integrated report into their investment decisions.

This chapter will catalogue evidence of the movement's momentum in terms of three interrelated dimensions: adoption, accelerators, and awareness (Figure 3.1).

As the company is the unit of analysis for integrated reporting, we use its *adoption* by companies outside of South Africa[5] as a litmus test of the movement's progress. If the number of companies using the practice is high and growing rapidly, momentum is increasing. *Accelerators* include regulation, multistakeholder initiatives and organizations, and endorsements that support integrated reporting.[6] Finally, *awareness* reflects the extent to which integrated reporting has received broad visibility in the business world and public sphere. *Accelerators* help speed the *adoption* of integrated reporting. Together, they raise the level of *awareness*. Although awareness can add energy to accelerators, it has little to no direct effect on adoption.

 **ADOPTION**

While it is difficult to assess the number of companies that have embraced integrated reporting or the rate at which this is happening, we can use the number of "self-declared" integrated reports, the rise of sustainability reporting, and data from annual reports that indicate that the "spirit" of integrated reporting is present as rough indicators of the level of adoption. At present, two limitations are to blame: (1) the lack of clear criteria for just what qualifies as an integrated report and (2) difficulty in determining how many annual or other types of reports fit these criteria.

Self-Declared Integrated Reports

Although integrated reporting principles were discussed as early as 2005, the first formal definition with reporting criteria did not appear until the Integrated Reporting Committee of South Africa published its 2011 Discussion Paper (IRC of SA Discussion Paper).[7] No database exists regarding how many reports fit these criteria. However, Global Reporting Initiative's (GRI's) Sustainability Disclosure Database for the period 2010–2013 provides a useful indicator of the rise in the number of integrated reporting companies, based on self-declared integrated reports.[8] The number of organizations declaring the publication of an integrated report grew from 287 in 2010 to 596 in 2012.[9] In 2013, for which we do not have a complete count at the time of this writing, 61% were listed companies; 31% unlisted, for-profit entities; and the remaining 8% were other organizations—like nonprofits and municipal governments.[10] Two-thirds were classified by GRI as "large" and another quarter as "multinationals."[11] While the main focus of the integrated reporting movement is listed companies, these statistics reveal that the idea has broader application—for instance, by cities.[12]

The fact that 51% of the reports came from European organizations, with only 3% from North America (just slightly below the 4% of the comparatively small Oceania region), suggests major differences in awareness of and receptivity to integrated reporting between these two regions. Compared to companies in the European Union (EU), U.S. companies perceive greater litigation risk surrounding voluntary disclosures. Latin America and the Caribbean accounted for 12% of the reports, Asia for 9%, and Africa—predominantly, South Africa—the remaining 21%. Even as many of these declared integrated reports might more aptly be labeled "combined," the volume of companies publicly declaring themselves to be advocates for integrated reporting is a positive sign of receptiveness.[13]

Trends in Sustainability Reporting

Companies that publish sustainability reports have taken a big step towards voluntary transparency and, in many cases, they have implemented systems to gather nonfinancial performance information. Thus, they represent a pool of candidates that might also be receptive to integrated reporting. At present, most companies that issue an integrated report did so after publishing a sustainability report for some number of years.[14]

Though only 1% of the world's 46,000 listed companies were self-declared integrated reporters in 2012,[15] companies producing sustainability reports are more numerous and the number is growing rapidly (Figure 3.2). In 1999, only 11 companies produced a sustainability report using GRI Guidelines. By 2012, the number of reports had grown to 3,704, for a compound annual growth rate of 56.5%. The growth rate in Asia (68.3%) was higher than in Europe (54.0%) and North America (43.5%), indicating a growing interest in sustainability reporting there. According to Peter DeSimone of the Sustainable Investments Institute, while only eight S&P 500 companies issued an integrated report in 2013, 89% (450) engaged in sustainability reporting, up from 76% in 2012,[16] and 43% of the S&P 500 made use of the guidelines, up from 36% in 2012.[17] Even in the United States, the strong growing trend of sustainability reporting could provide momentum for integrated reporting.[18]

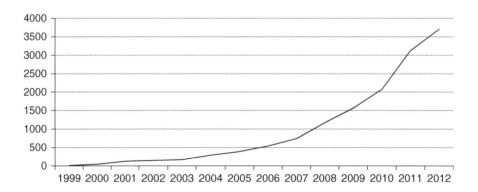

FIGURE 3.2 Number of GRI Reporters 1999–2012

Data Source: Global Reporting Initiative. Excel Spreadsheet of Sustainability Disclosure Database.

The Spirit of Integrated Reporting

In 2009, RobecoSAM, the organization that has prepared the Dow Jones Sustainability Indices (DJSI) since 1999, began to look for evidence of integrated reporting.[19] For the 2011 and 2012 annual reports, their Corporate Sustainability Assessment[20] of 2,000 of the world's largest companies looked for whether the company had provided data on how environmental and social initiatives have led to cost savings or increased revenues. While not the same thing as a fully integrated report, this is an indicator of companies putting some of the principles of integrated reporting into practice, particularly "connectivity of information" in the <IR> Framework.[21] Thus, we will take this as signifying the "spirit" of integrated reporting. Reasoning that only data from annual reports' main sections would signify true integration—as putting data in a sustainability section is indicative of a "combined" rather than integrated report—they found that only 12% of the companies provided an example of environmental or social cost savings or revenue generation in 2012. Still, this was up from 8% in 2011, a 50% increase.[22] Seventy-four percent of the 2012 examples concerned environmental initiatives split evenly between cost savings and revenue generation. For social initiatives, two-thirds concerned revenue generation and one-third cost savings.[23]

Supporting our use of these examples as indicators of the "spirit" of integrated reporting, a far greater proportion of these reporting examples concerned strategic, groupwide initiatives related to the company's core business (72%), as opposed to sustainability programs focused on noncore business activities or activities isolated in a single location (28%).[24] Reflecting the difficulty in quantifying these relationships between financial and nonfinancial performance, 60% of the total number of examples were expressed in qualitative terms.[25]

 ACCELERATORS

In any given market, the interactions of four market and regulatory forces increase the momentum of the integrated reporting movement or resist it. Explored below, these accelerators are regulation, multistakeholder initiatives, organizations, and endorsements.

Regulation

The only accelerating force to invoke the power of the State, regulation changes company behavior directly. It is a double-edged sword, however, whose successful implementation risks relegating integrated reporting to the status of a compliance exercise as companies, constrained in their ability to "tell their own story," might only adhere to the "letter" rather than the "spirit" of the law. Although only South Africa requires integrated reporting, regulations that support sustainability reporting are increasingly cropping up around the world. In the 2013 report "Carrots and Sticks," KPMG, the Centre for Corporate Governance in Africa, GRI, and the United Nations Environment Programme considered 180 policies in 45 countries to find that 72% were mandatory, compared with 62% in 32 countries studied in 2010, and 58% in 19 countries studied in 2006.[26] Major trends included framing regulation in terms of corporate governance and disclosure requirements, an increasing number of policies based on a "report or explain" basis, a focus on large and state-owned companies (with voluntary reporting by small and medium-sized enterprises), sustainability reporting as a listing requirement on some stock exchanges (discussed more below), and governments striving to harmonize the use of multiple frameworks.[27] Consistent with this trend toward mandated sustainability reporting, professors Ioannis Ioannou of London Business School and George Serafeim of Harvard Business School found that government adoption of mandatory corporate sustainability reporting led to positive organizational changes often linked to integrated reporting.[28] While integrated reporting and sustainability reporting are distinct practices, the spread of mandatory sustainability reporting and growing evidence of its benefits could encourage governments to consider regulations in favor of integrated reporting—most likely on a "comply or explain basis."

The latest piece of legislation covering a large geographical territory was initiated when, on April 16, 2013, the European Commission announced proposals[29] to amend the Fourth[30] and Seventh[31] Accounting Directives to improve business transparency and performance on social and environmental issues. On April 15, 2014, the plenary of the European Parliament adopted this Directive by a vote of 599 to 55 from its 28 member states: "Companies concerned will need to disclose information on policies, risks and outcomes as regards environmental matters, social and employee-related aspects, respect for human rights, anti-corruption and bribery issues, and diversity in their board of directors."[32] The Directive, expected to affect around 6,000 companies, applies to listed companies with 500 or more employees, as well as certain unlisted ones.[33] At the time of the legislation, only around 2,500 large EU companies were disclosing environmental and social information on a regular basis.[34] Companies could choose whether to include this information in their annual report (at least leading to a "combined report") or in a separate report.[35] They could also choose among various standards and guidelines for reporting this information, but they were not required to do so.

In a memorandum issued by the European Commission at the time the legislation was announced, the Commission explained its stance on integrated reporting:

> The Directive focuses on environmental and social disclosures. Integrated reporting is a step ahead, and is about the integration by companies of financial, environmental, social and other information in a comprehensive and coherent manner. To be clear, this Directive does not require companies to comply with integrated reporting.
>
> The Commission is monitoring with great interest the evolution of the integrated reporting concept, and, in particular, the work of the International Integrated Reporting Council.[36]

Thus, while the Commission made it clear that the Directive was not calling for integrated reporting, it explicitly acknowledged its existence and that of the International Integrated Reporting Council (IIRC) while positioning the current Directive as a possible step in the direction of integrated reporting. This simple statement conveys substantial institutional legitimacy for both the idea and the organization in the European Union.

Similar to what has been done in some jurisdictions with mandatory sustainability reporting,[37] the European Commission planned to develop implementation guidance. The proposal's implementation, however, would be determined by each Member State.[38] Steve Waygood, Chief Responsible Investment Officer at Aviva Investors and integrated reporting policy advocate,[39] expressed concern about the decision to leave implementation specifics and accountability to each individual country. He felt that if this were the case, "It is realistic to believe that fewer than these 6,000 large companies in the EU will be affected, taking realpolitik into account. Any number of countries may not do it effectively, and another category of countries will try to say the directives are already included in their legislation."[40]

Two central challenges exist: (1) each nation is responsible for creating its own accountability device for the legislation and (2) if the legislation is "comply or explain," there is no clear indication of who should be tasked with oversight, to which organizations companies should look to for guidance, and *how* to explain if they do not comply.[41] In contrast to countries, Waygood viewed the regulation's principles-based approach useful when it came to individual companies in preventing a "tick-the-box" compliance approach. "It would have been a mistake to attempt to create a one-size-fits-all approach that specified one set of key performance indicators for all individual sectors," he said, observing, "The proposals also recognize the individuality of each firm and give boards the discretion to report on what they believe to be relevant for their sector and explain why they have not included other measures."[42] As the proposed legislation does not include any discussion of materiality, companies will have to determine for themselves whether this idea is relevant to their determination of what is "concise, useful information" and, if so, how materiality should be determined. Despite its imperfections, Waygood was clear about the potential benefits of this legislation. "For us and other analysts, it makes more and more pertinent information available that can help us make more accurate valuation assessments for the benefit of end-investors. For the EC, it makes sense as part of the Single Market Act that envisaged creating a more sustainable capital market."[43]

Multistakeholder Initiatives

Multistakeholder initiatives change behavior by influencing those who can do so directly (the State) or indirectly, such as a club or industry association that can use moral suasion, membership criteria, and their recommended "best practices" to encourage companies to adopt a practice. Two initiatives particularly important to the integrated reporting movement are the Sustainable Stock Exchanges Initiative (SSE) and the Corporate Sustainability Reporting Coalition (CSRC).[44]

Sustainable Stock Exchanges Initiative

As noted by Ernst Ligteringen, chief executive officer (CEO) of GRI, "Stock market regulators are uniquely placed to drive change in [the sustainability arena] by smart regulation through listing requirements."[45] In most countries, the local stock exchange has regulatory powers given directly by legislation or deeded to it by the local securities commission. Because exchanges can change the behavior of every single company listed on them, they are good targets for multistakeholder initiatives. The SSE[46] is one of the most important ones.[47]

Pressure via a stock exchange listing requirement represents a moderate form of compulsion. Although companies can choose to delist if they do not want to comply, delisting or moving to another exchange is not always easy to do. Over the past 10 years, the number of environmental and social reporting requirements led by stock exchanges around the world has increased[48]—the most well known of these being the Johannesburg Stock Exchange's (JSE's) "apply or explain" requirement for integrated reporting.[49] To provide a platform for collaboration among investors, regulators, and companies, and to address corporate transparency-related environmental, social, and governance (ESG) issues, the UN launched the Sustainable Stock Exchanges Initiative in 2009.[50] Today, nine exchanges—BM&FBOVESPA, Bombay Stock Exchange Ltd., Borsa Istanbul Stock Exchange, Egyptian Exchange, JSE, NASDAQ OMX, Nigerian Stock Exchange, NYSE Euronext, and Warsaw Stock Exchange—comprise the SSE Partner Exchange.[51]

Waygood, a driving force behind the SSE, explains, "We think that the UN has responded very well to the concerns of many responsible investors in this area. The key focus for this initiative now needs to be ensuring that the stock exchanges take effective action, which is where the Corporate Knights' study that we commissioned comes in. Personally, we still regard the integration of Integrated Reporting into listing rules as the gold standard."[52] Members pledge to "voluntarily commit, through dialogue with investors, companies and regulators, to promoting long term sustainable investment and improved environmental, social and corporate governance disclosure and performance among companies listed on our exchange."[53] In order to push Partner Exchanges to comply with the spirit of their commitment, Aviva Investors and Standard & Poor's Rating Services commissioned CK Capital to conduct a benchmarking study of the sustainability disclosure practices of 3,972 companies listed on 45 large stock exchanges in 40 countries for the period 2007–2011.[54] Rankings are a time-honored way of influencing behavior. CK Capital's now-annual study ranked these 45 exchanges in 2013 based on the public disclosure scores of the large cap companies on each exchange.[55] SSE Partners ranked low have an incentive to improve, and non-SSE Partners have the opportunity to make a public statement about their commitment to sustainability.

Corporate Sustainability Reporting Coalition

Convened by Aviva Investors and announced in a September 20, 2011, press release, the CSRC[56] played an integral role in facilitating dialogue surrounding the 2014 EU Accounting Directive revision and the UN Conference on Sustainable Development in 2012 (Rio + 20) through a series of timely and informative publications.[57] With a membership that includes investors,[58] companies, NGOs representing a range of environmental and social interests (including GRI and the IIRC), accounting organizations, and UN-affiliated organizations the CSRC seeks to influence legislation that serves as the basis for regulation. While the SSE focuses on mobilizing existing regulators like stock exchanges, the heavy contingent of NGOs has made the CSRC more campaign-oriented.

In a 2011 press release, the CSRC called for companies to disclose and integrate material sustainability information into their annual report and accounts or explain why they are unable to do so, underlining a belief that an international policy framework should be developed to promote transparency and accountability.[59] To this end, extensive organizational and system-level benefits were also cited.[60] In anticipation of Rio+20, Aviva Investors published "Earth Summit 2012: Towards agreement on a declaration for corporate sustainability reporting at Rio+20." The document called upon delegates to commit to the development of a policy statement on sustainability reporting. Subsequently, "The Future We Want,"[61] Rio+20's outcome document, included "Paragraph 47," which called for companies "to consider integrating sustainability information into their reporting cycle."[62]

Though not as strong as the coalition had hoped it would be, Paragraph 47 demonstrated the support of countries attending the summit for a more integrated corporate accountability structure insofar as all countries that attended the summit endorsed it.[63] "Integrated reporting" was not mentioned, but the concept's essence was suggested in the phrase "integrating sustainability information into their reporting cycle" in which "reporting cycle" refers to the mandated financial reporting by all listed companies.

Following Rio+20, the CSRC turned its attention to Europe. In November 2012, Aviva Investors published, "European briefing: Towards an agreement on corporate sustainability reporting," to call on European policy makers to "consider a provision for a 'report or explain' standard for integrated corporate sustainability reporting."[64] It proposed that the European Union Accounting Directive discussed above be based on seven principles, such as a focus on business-relevant and material issues, the disclosure of corporate performance with quantified key performance indicators (KPIs), and the required integration of sustainability KPIs throughout the report and accounts—including strategy, risk, audit, and remuneration. Again, while the exact term "integrated reporting" was not used, "integrated corporate sustainability reporting" and the three principles cited evoked the idea. The nuances of the European briefing and the language in Paragraph 47 illustrate the challenges of building a social movement in which actors inevitably have overlapping but usually not identical interests, and perhaps not identical meanings, for the concept of integrated reporting.[65] This reflects the fact that a consensus has yet to emerge about the relationship between integrated reporting and sustainability reporting, a critical issue in establishing the meaning of the terms "integrated report" and "integrated reporting." Our position, explained in more detail in Chapter 6, is that sustainability reporting is an important complement to integrated reporting.

Organizations

Accelerating organizations include entities whose very mission is the adoption of integrated reporting (the IIRC), those whose mission is supportive of and broadly consistent with it (e.g., CDP, the Climate Disclosure Standards Board (CDSB), GRI, and the Sustainability Accounting Standards Board (SASB)), and those whose recommendations carry some weight of authority (e.g., the Financial Accounting Standards Board (FASB), the International Accounting Standards Board (IASB), the Big Four and other accounting firms, and the professional accounting associations). These organizations speed adoption by lending institutional legitimacy to the concept, encouraging companies to adopt it, and by providing them with frameworks, tools, education, and advice.

While a number of NGOs play key roles, we regard the IIRC as the principal accelerator because its explicit mission is global adoption of integrated reporting through its International <IR> Framework. GRI, SASB, CDSB, and CDP, in its role as Secretariat to the CDSB, support its efforts by pursuing missions that involve developing standards and frameworks for the measurement and reporting of nonfinancial information that can be used in integrated reporting. Complementary to the various reporting programs is the Global Initiative for Sustainability Ratings (GISR), whose mission is to accredit sustainability ratings that use as input data to their analytical models information reported according to the standards of the above organizations, as well as other sources. Unlike SASB, both the IIRC and GRI promote standards that are not country-specific. With an appropriate level of collaboration, the difference in jurisdiction and approach between these organizations should be complementary to each other.

The accounting firms Deloitte, Ernst & Young (E&Y), KPMG, and PricewaterhouseCoopers (PwC), and accompanying professional accounting organizations (of which each country has one or more), increase momentum through direct engagement with companies and working with them on materiality. Although the Big Four are primarily concerned with materiality in terms of auditing of financial statements, they and some major accounting associations have addressed it in sustainability and integrated reporting.[66] PwC has also produced its own "materiality matrix,"[67] which concept is the focus of Chapter 6.

IIRC [68]

On September 11, 2009, Paul Druckman, then Executive Board Chairman of The Prince's Accounting for Sustainability Project[69] (A4S), and Ernst Ligteringen, CEO of GRI,[70] invited us to a feedback meeting for a draft of our book *One Report*. At the session, 20 people representing accounting firms and accounting associations, civil society, companies, investors, standard setters, and United Nations' initiatives gathered in London to discuss steps to speed the adoption of integrated reporting. Toward the end of the meeting, a consensus was reached to petition the G20 to call for the creation of an international body to develop an integrated sustainability and financial reporting framework.[71]

On December 17, 2009, Professor Mervyn King, then Chairman of GRI, delivered remarks at The Prince's Accounting for Sustainability Forum[72] titled "The urgent need to establish a connected and integrated reporting framework and the required regulatory and governance response."[73] Later that afternoon, Paul Druckman called for the creation of the International Integrated Reporting Committee and of a globally accepted integrated reporting framework. On August 2, 2010, A4S[74] and GRI announced the formation of the International Integrated Reporting Committee.[75] Known today as the International Integrated Reporting Council (IIRC), the IIRC is a global coalition of regulators, investors, companies, standard setters, the accounting profession, and NGOs currently engaged in the promulgation and refinement of its <IR> Framework.[76]

Since its formation, the IIRC has worked to crystallize a common meaning for integrated reporting based on a notion of materiality that considers a matter's ability to substantively affect the organization's ability to create value and has published some important documents, such as the <IR> Framework discussed in the previous chapter.[77] Other activities encourage adoption through example and learning, such as its "Pilot Programme Business Network,"[78] or by generating investor interest, and thus "demand-pull," as through its "Pilot Programme Investor Network."[79] The IIRC has also engaged in efforts to educate regulators (such as the International Organization of Securities Commissions and the Federation of Euro-Asian Stock Exchanges), standard setters (such as FASB and the IASB), and other important organizations such as the UN Global Compact and the World Bank Group.[80] In an effort to ensure mutual understanding, cooperation, and collaboration between the major organizations relevant to integrated reporting, the IIRC has initiated a "Corporate Reporting Dialogue." In 2013, the IIRC signed Memorandums of Understanding (MoUs) to collaborate with other widely recognized organizations that share a mission to develop guidance and standards for corporate disclosure and reporting including CDP/CDSB,[81] GISR,[82] GRI,[83] SASB,[84] and a number of other organizations.[85]

GRI, SASB, CDP, and GISR

Although GRI, SASB, CDP, CDSB, and GISR are all nonprofit organizations with their own missions, those of GRI, CDSB, and SASB are most directly related to integrated reporting. CDP and GISR act as facilitators.

Global Reporting Initiative[86]

Based in Amsterdam, GRI was founded in 1997 as a joint project of the nonprofits Ceres[87] and the Tellus Institute.[88] GRI takes a multistakeholder audience approach in its definition of materiality with the goal of identifying issues important for companies to consider in support of sustainable development. Its success in spreading the practice of sustainability reporting provides a strong foundation on which the integrated reporting movement can build. With 5,980 organizations producing sustainability reports in its database, GRI, like sustainability reporting, today has a much broader reach than integrated reporting.[89] GRI and the IIRC differ in terms of their primary audience.[90] Although the latter distinction will likely affect their definitions of materiality, the attention it gives to integrated reporting and the relationship it sees between integrated and sustainability reporting will be, as discussed in Chapter 5, important in adding to the momentum of the movement.

While GRI predates the IIRC by some 13 years, it has smoothly assimilated integrated reporting into its mandate since the IIRC's formation. At its third global conference in Amsterdam on May 26–28, 2010, GRI introduced two strategic propositions that anticipated IIRC sentiments: (1) "By 2015, all large and medium-size companies in the Organisation for Economic Co-operation and Development (OECD) countries and large emerging economies should be required to report on their ESG performance and, if they do not do so, to explain why," and (2) "By 2020, there should be a generally accepted and applied international standard which will effectively integrate financial and ESG reporting by all organizations."[91] Importantly, GRI helped support the IIRC's mission by adding a section to its website to demystify the relationship between GRI Guidelines and the IIRC Framework. From GRI's perspective, sustainability reporting and integrated reporting are intrinsically related:

> . . . organizations must identify the material sustainability topics to monitor and manage to ensure the business survives and expands. This step is at the core of the sustainability reporting process provided by GRI's Sustainability Reporting Framework. GRI offers companies guidance on how to identify material sustainability topics to be monitored and managed, and to prepare for the integrated thinking process, which is the foundation for integrated reporting.[92]

In May 2013, GRI released its G4 Guidelines (G4).[93] Nelmara Arbex, former Deputy CEO of GRI, current Chief Advisor on Innovation and Reporting, and member of the IIRC Working Group, views GRI Sustainability Reporting Guidelines (G4) and the <IR> Framework as complementary. "Where sustainability information is material to a company's ability to generate value, it should be included in an integrated report as proposed by the IIRC," she explained. "G4 provides a basis for executives to understand the link between everyday activities and strategy, offering a globally accepted language to communicate a company's values, governance structure, and critical social and environmental impacts."[94]

Concurrent with the release of G4, GRI released a report, "The Sustainability Content of Integrated Reports—A Survey of Pioneers," whose key findings further underline the value of a dialogue between GRI and the IIRC about integrated reporting.[95]

- ▧ "Large companies are driving the year-on-year rise in the publication of self-declared integrated reports around the world.
- ▧ Leading countries in this sample are South Africa, the Netherlands, Brazil, Australia, and Finland.
- ▧ Globally, the financial sector self-declares more integrated reports than any other sector, followed by the utilities, energy, and mining sectors.
- ▧ About a third of all integrated reports clearly embed sustainability and financial information together and this proportion is growing year-on-year. In tandem, an increasing number of reports now have the title 'Integrated report' and clearly discuss the significance of integration as part of their content.

▓ About half of all self-declared integrated reports are two separate publications—an annual report and a sustainability report—published together under one cover, with minimal cross-connection."[96]

Unlike SASB, both the IIRC and GRI promote frameworks that are not country-specific. With an appropriate level of collaboration, the difference in jurisdiction and approach between these organizations should be collective strengths. As Christy Wood, the Chair of GRI, said, "The collective global thinking on sustainability is greater than the sum of its parts. These organizations [GRI, IIRC, and SASB] should be able to work together. If we have a united front, we can expedite and accelerate the uptake of integrated reporting."[97]

Sustainability Accounting Standards Board [98]

Based in San Francisco, the SASB was founded in July 2011 by its CEO Jean Rogers, John Katovich,[99] and Steve Lydenberg[100] as a not-for-profit organization to create industry-based sustainability standards for the recognition and disclosure of material environmental, social, and governance impacts by companies traded on U.S. stock exchanges.[101] At the time of this writing, SASB has issued standards for the healthcare, financial institutions, and technology and communications sectors and expects to have completed all 10 sectors by the beginning of 2016. These sectors are composed of more than 80 industries.[102] Because both SASB and the IIRC focus on investors, companies can use SASB's standards for the nonfinancial information they include in their integrated report.

Through evidence-based research; Industry Working Groups[103] comprised of corporations, investors, and other stakeholders; a 90-day public comment period; and review by an independent Standards Council,[104] SASB has established an exacting process[105] for standard setting. The rigor of its methodology earned SASB accreditation by the American National Standards Institute to establish sustainability accounting standards. Because SASB's process is based on a U.S. context, however, how its standards can be adapted to other countries remains undecided in spite of clear non-U.S. interest. As of May 1, 2014, of the 1,672 downloads of the healthcare sector standards, 991 (59%) were from the United States and 681 (41%) were from 55 other countries.[106] For the more recently released set of standards for financial institutions,[107] the 365 downloads were evenly split between the United States and 33 other countries on that same date. Because interest in SASB's standards outside the United States is high, whether and how SASB expands its industry-based expertise to the international market will have strategic repercussions for both the organization and the movement.

Using the Security and Exchange Commission's (SEC) definition of materiality,[108] SASB's goal is to set standards companies can use to provide information in their SEC filings, such as the Form 10-K (for U.S.-based companies) or Form 20-F (for foreign registrants). In light of this, Bob Herz, former Chairman of FASB, defined this benchmark for SASB's success as SEC incorporation: "The challenge for SASB is whether the SEC will enforce SASB standards based on the rigor of SASB's process and their use of the SEC's definition of materiality. Will the SEC refer to SASB standards when they review, for example, Forms 10-K and 10-Q? A related question is whether companies participating in the SASB process voluntarily begin making sustainability disclosures in their SEC filings."[109] While inclusion of sustainability performance information in the 10-K or 20-F would not turn these SEC-required documents into an "integrated report" as defined by the <IR> Framework, it would certainly accelerate the meaningful adoption of integrated reporting.

On May 1, 2014, SASB elected a new Chair, Michael Bloomberg (philanthropist, founder of Bloomberg LP, and the 108th mayor of New York City), and a new Vice Chair, Mary Schapiro (former SEC chairman).[110] According to GreenBiz, these appointments provide SASB with "two powerful allies who are well-poised to extend its influence within the business and investment communities."[111] We concur that these appointments will provide momentum to SASB's mission and, in our personal view, to the integrated reporting movement in general.

CDP[112]

CDP (previously the Carbon Disclosure Project) "is an international, not-for-profit organization providing the only global system for companies and cities to measure, disclose, manage and share vital environmental information."[113] With offices worldwide, its climate change, water, and forest programs are used by thousands of companies in more than 80 countries.

CDP was formed in 2001 after 35 signatories representing $4.5 trillion assets under management (AUM) signed a letter requesting that companies on the Financial Times 500 index disclose their carbon emissions data through CDP. As of the writing of this book, 767 investors who together represent $92 trillion in AUM have now signed this letter. CDP leverages this authority and, more recently, that of more than 60 major multinational purchasing organizations to survey companies on the disclosure and performance of their impacts on the environment and natural resources. According to Nigel Topping, CDP's Executive Director, "Approximately 4,500 companies disclosed climate change information through CDP's global platform in 2013. Of these, approximately 3,500 were listed (publicly traded) and represented about 54% of global market capitalization." Those remaining were in the supply chain.[114]

Climate Disclosure Standards Board[115]

CDP provides the secretariat for the Climate Disclosure Standards Board (CDSB), a consortium of business and environmental organizations formed at the World Economic Forum's annual Davos meeting in 2007. The CDSB was created to "overcome the patchwork of schemes designed to mitigate climate change that has resulted in an unclear disclosure landscape across different countries and aims to specifically harmonize reporting of environmental and sustainability performance and risk by having it included in, or linked to, an organization's financial report."[116]

CDSB released Edition 1.0 of the Climate Change Reporting Framework[117] in September 2010. The Framework is "a voluntary reporting framework designed to elicit climate change-related information of value to investors in mainstream financial reports. Created in line with the objectives of financial reporting and rules on non-financial reporting, the Climate Change Reporting Framework seeks to filter out what is required to understand how climate change affects a company's financial performance."[118] The CDSB updated the Framework in October 2012 and published "A guide to using CDSB's Reporting Framework in March 2013."[119] A further update is due in 2014 to expand the scope of its Framework to include fossil fuels and stranded assets, forest risk commodities (i.e., the drivers of deforestation), and water.[120]

CDSB views the disclosures contemplated by the Framework as being aligned with the efforts of the IIRC and has stated, "As a Framework that seeks to elicit information that connects the financial, governance and environmental impacts of climate change, CDSB's Climate Change Reporting Framework is on the frontier of how to apply the principles of integrated reporting with respect to reporting on climate change."[121]

Global Initiative for Sustainability Ratings[122]

While over 140 organizations provide sustainability ratings today, the quality and scope of these ratings varies widely. The degree of transparency about ratings methodologies is highly uneven, and ratings' organizations raise questions of conflict of interest by providing consulting services to the companies they rate. To strengthen the practice of ratings, the GISR was launched in June 2011—one month before SASB's foundation—as a joint project of Ceres and the Tellus Institute. As explained by its founder, Allen White, "The state of sustainability ratings today is comparable to sustainability reporting 20 years ago before the founding of both GRI (1997) and IIRC (2010)."[123] GISR's mission is "to design and steward a global sustainability (i.e., ESG) ratings standard to expand and accelerate the contribution of business and other organizations worldwide to sustainable development. GISR will not rate companies. Instead, it will accredit other sustainability ratings, rankings or indices to apply its standard for measuring excellence in sustainability performance."[124] In other words, GISR accredits rating methodologies to help drive excellence throughout the global community of rating organizations.

White sees a clear and complementary relationship between GISR and the work of organizations like GRI and SASB. "Raters have a vested interest in seeing high quality, comparable, and rigorous information flowing from various sources," he elaborated. "At the same time, high quality and credible ratings create incentives to improve companies' sustainability performance, making use of standards from groups like GRI and SASB in doing so."[125] Particularly if sustainability ratings evolve into "integrated ratings" of companies and credit, White also sees the potential for a similar self-reinforcing cycle between ratings and integrated reporting. A uniform framework for integrated reporting would enhance the quality of those ratings and those ratings, in turn, would create an incentive for companies to embrace this framework.

Ultimately, White speculated that the major credit rating agencies like Moody's and Standard & Poor's might incorporate sustainability issues more systematically into their ratings. Given the global bond market's size, which McKinsey estimated to have a value in 2010 of nearly three times that of the global equity market,[126] White sees the opportunity to encourage companies to view integrated reporting as essential to their communications with credit rating agencies. "If this were to evolve," he mused, "it would directly feed the information needs of integrated credit ratings which, in turn, would propel uptake of integrated reporting by companies."[127] At the time of this writing, GISR is establishing an accreditation program to give its "seal of approval" to ratings methodologies that align with the GISR framework. That framework is based on five process principles and seven content principles, which collectively comprise the first component of the three-part standard, with issues and indicators components to follow.[128]

Big Four Accounting Firms and Accounting Associations

Because they provide audits of financial and, increasingly, nonfinancial information, the Big Four accounting firms (Deloitte, E&Y, KPMG, and PwC) will be integral to the success of the integrated reporting movement.[129] Not only do clients look to them for a perspective on integrated reporting and what, if anything, they should be doing about it, each has published white papers explaining the concept, describing its benefits, addressing the challenges of its implementation, and providing a perspective on progress and prospects.[130] Further, they have all been supportive of the IIRC through actions like secondments and hosting Council meetings. However, since these organizations are networks of firms for legal and risk management reasons, the degree of support for integrated reporting within each firm varies by territory.

In addition to general support for the IIRC, professional accounting associations lend integrated reporting technical legitimacy through institutionalization. Every major country has a professional association of accountants whose members have passed their certification examination. Many of these, such as the AICPA (American Institute of Certified Public Accountants), CIMA (Chartered Institute of Management Accountants), ICAEW (Institute of Chartered Accountants of England and Wales), and IMA (Institute of Management Accountants), have endorsed integrated reporting through feedback on the IIRC's "Draft Framework," press releases supporting the publication of the <IR> Framework, white papers, videos, and research projects.[131]

The global accounting association ACCA (the Association of Chartered Certified Accountants) was the first to include integrated reporting in the training course for its certification examination: "Students will be examined on integrated reporting (<IR>) for the first time in the accountancy profession when ACCA (the Association of Chartered Certified Accountants) introduces it into its qualification from December 2014."[132] Making integrated reporting part of the body of knowledge one must have to earn ACCA certification is a tangible way of institutionalizing the idea in the context of more established accounting principles. After this, accounting professionals can educate and advocate for it with clients and employers.

Finally, the International Federation of Accountants (IFAC) has been an active supporter of integrated reporting. Its former CEO, Ian Ball, is Chairman of the IIRC's Technical Working Group at the time of the writing of this book.[133] An "association of associations" whose membership comprises "179 members and associates in 130 countries and jurisdictions, representing approximately 2.5 million accountants in public practice, education, government service, industry, and commerce,"[134] IFAC's role in the IIRC and the global scope of its membership imply buy-in from its members and signal to them the importance of the topic.

Endorsements

Endorsements are public demonstrations of support for integrated reporting that help contribute to its institutional legitimacy. The 100+ companies that form the IIRC's "Pilot Programme Business Network," which "provides the opportunity to discuss and challenge developing technical material, test its application and share learning and experiences," at least agree that the concept of integrated reporting is worth experimentation.[135] While they do not commit to publishing an integrated report, they invest resources to help develop an asset, the <IR> Framework, that other companies can freely use. Similarly, the 36 investors in the IIRC's "Pilot Programme Investor Network," which "provides an investor's perspective on the shortfalls of current corporate reporting; providing constructive feedback on emerging reporting from the Pilot Programme Business Network," also form a complementary endorsement.[136]

Several individual high-profile investment funds have also provided public endorsements for integrated reporting. APG (a big Dutch pension fund), California Public Employees' Retirement System (CalPERS, the big California state pension fund), and Norges Bank Investment Management (the Norwegian sovereign wealth fund) jointly submitted a letter on December 15, 2011, to the IIRC providing commentary on its "Discussion Paper on Integrated Reporting," saying, "we are supportive of the concept of Integrated Reporting as set out in the high-level Discussion Paper."[137] CalPERS took this one step further in 2012 when it listed integrated reporting as one of its "key initiatives" for its Global Governance Program in 2013.[138] Generation Investment Management listed mandated integrated reporting as its second recommended action to create "a paradigm shift to Sustainable Capitalism."[139]

 AWARENESS

An outcome of both adoption and accelerators, general awareness of integrated reporting as a concept and a movement can provide further, although modest,

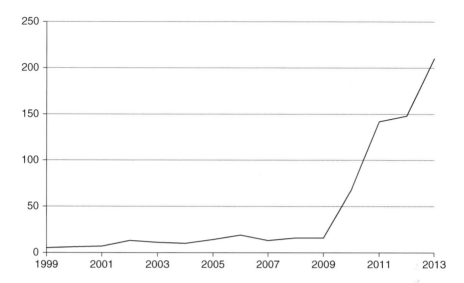

FIGURE 3.3 Citations on Integrated Reporting

additional momentum. Compared to adoption, where actual counts (whatever their limitations) can be taken, and accelerators, where the existence of regulations, multistakeholder initiatives, organizations, and public statements can be definitively established, awareness is difficult to measure. However, we can assess it in two simple ways.

First, we looked at academic and practitioner citations in the literature (Figure 3.3). Between 1999 and 2009, citations were minimal and flat. The year 2010 saw a substantial increase. This number doubled for the years 2011 and 2012, and 2013 again saw a steep increase to an amount triple that of 2010. While it is impossible to directly link the accelerators discussed above to this increase, integrated reporting citations have grown dramatically over the last four years—the time since *One Report* was published.[140]

The second way we assessed awareness was through word counts of the terms "integrated report" and "integrated reporting" (Figure 3.4). During the period 1995–2001, there was little awareness and only a very modest growth rate. This increased slightly for the period 2002–2008. Between 2008 and 2010, word count spiked, slowing somewhat and even flattening out in 2012 and 2013. Time will tell if the publication of the <IR> Framework and other contributors to momentum will reinvigorate this index of awareness.

We did the same word count on the term "International Integrated Reporting Council." Reflecting the creation and growing awareness of the

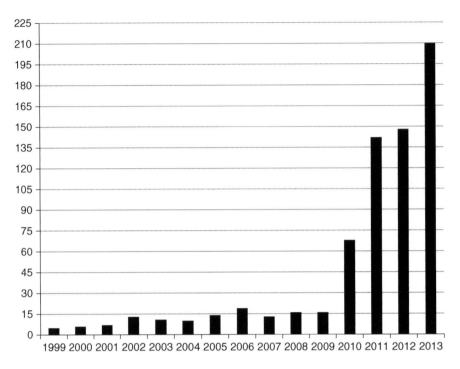

FIGURE 3.4 Growth in Awareness of Integrated Report and Integrated Reporting

IIRC, this count increased from virtually 0 in 2010 to 4 in 2011, 119 in 2012, and 268 in 2013. Given the motive of the IIRC to spread the adoption of high-quality integrated reporting, this increasing awareness is encouraging. The extent to which the awareness of the IIRC and integrated reporting itself continues to grow will be influenced by the motives of all the other actors involved in the movement.[141]

 NOTES

1. Encyclopedia Britannica. Social Movement, http://www.britannica.com/EBchecked/topic/551335/social-movement, accessed January 2014.
2. Sustainability has many definitions. For us, we focus on defining it from the perspective of a company. A sustainable strategy is one that enables a company to create value for its shareholders over the long term while

contributing to a sustainable society. It is one that can meet the needs of the present generation without sacrificing those of future ones.

3. Tilly, Charles and Lesley J. Wood. *Social Movements, 1768–2012.* Boulder: Paradigm Publishers, 2009. Adapting to communication trends is a theme among successful social movements.

4. In Charles Tilly's study of historical social movements, he provides a framework by which we can recognize them, defining social movements as a series of contentious performances, displays, and campaigns by which ordinary people make collective claims on others through sustained activity. Campaigns are defined as "sustained, organized public efforts making collective claims of target authorities." "Repertoires of contention" are the use of different combinations of political action (creating special-purpose coalitions and associations, public meetings statements to and in public media, and so on). Finally, in Tilly's scheme, "WUNC displays" are those in which the participants' public representation of "worthiness, unity, numbers, and commitments" on the part of their constituencies or themselves is demonstrated. Ibid.

5. As discussed in great detail in Chapter 1, South Africa remains the only country in which integrated reporting is required on an "apply or explain" basis as of this book's publication.

6. These accelerators can act both directly and indirectly from a company-push (i.e., encouraging or demanding companies to practice integrated reporting) or demand-pull (e.g., encouraging shareholders, stakeholders, and regulators to call for integrated reporting by companies) perspective.

7. We have no way of knowing how many South African companies used the "IRC of South Africa Discussion Paper" to prepare their integrated report. Similarly, since the Johannesburg Stock Exchange does not formally review these reports to see if they truly are an integrated report through some kind of assessment, there is no database regarding the quality of these reports.

8. "The GRI Sustainability Disclosure Database includes reports that GRI is currently aware of. Some reports may be omitted, in particular those in non-Latin scripts or that are not published online; reports based on GRI Guidelines without a GRI Content Index are included as 'GRI-Referenced' reports in the database and are not considered to be GRI reports; not all GRI reporters publish reports annually. Therefore, the total number of GRI reports per publication year does not correspond with the total number of GRI reporters." Global Reporting Initiative. Excel Spreadsheet of Sustainability Disclosure Database, Discover the Database, What's Included, https://www.globalreporting.org/reporting/report-services/sustainability-disclosure-database/Pages/Discover-the-Database.aspx, accessed April 2014.

9. GRI collects data about "self-declared integrated reports" (1) directly from reporting organizations, (2) through an international network of GRI Data Partners and (3) ad-hoc searches or data entry by GRI staff. Companies submit report data to GRI through an online form. One of the questions asks, "Does the reporting organization consider this to be an integrated report, meaning it includes financial as well as nonfinancial disclosures beyond basic economic data? Note: a sustainability report that covers economic, environmental and social disclosures (e.g. the requirements of the GRI Guidelines) is not considered an integrated report by itself." The company must make a Yes/No choice and GRI staff does not make any judgment on this selection. GRI Data Partners and GRI staff entering report data are trained by the GRI Database Coordinator on application of the Data Classification scheme used by GRI. To ensure objectivity in the process to capture data about integrated reports, Data Partners and GRI staff only a "Yes" in the field if there is explicit reference to "integrated reporting" in the report itself. Ian van der Vlugt, email correspondence with Robert Eccles and Andrew Knauer, February 18, 2014. As of April 15, 2014 the database contained 337 integrated reporting companies for 2013. This total is incomplete as GRI continually collects data. We believe the 2013 numbers, however, to be accurate depictions of the differences in type of company, size, and geography. Duplicate company observations from GRI database were removed before making calculations. Ibid.

10. These numbers were calculated using the listed/nonlisted variable from GRI database, supplemented with the sector variable to identify nonprofits, public agencies, and universities. Ibid.

11. The rest were small and medium-sized enterprises. Ibid.

12. Eccles, Robert G., Annissa Alusi, Amy C. Edmondson, and Tiona Zuzul. "Sustainable Cities: Oxymoron or the Shape of the Future?" *Infrastructure Sustainability and Design*, edited by Spiro Pollalis, Andreas Georgoulias, Stephen Ramos, and Daniel Schodek, 247–265. New York: Routledge, 2012.

13. While some companies may see more brand benefits than substantive benefits in doing so, one should not be too cynical about their intentions given the concerns many companies raise about integrated reporting. For a company to declare that it is publishing an integrated report is no trivial statement. In doing so, the company commits itself, if only implicitly, to improving the annual report's quality as frameworks and standards are developed and "best practices" are learned from the experiences of other companies.

14. As the relationship between integrated reporting and sustainability is better understood, however, this could change. Using the GRI database, the average number of years a company produces a sustainability report before publishing an integrated report is 2.1. Global Reporting Initiative. Excel Spreadsheet of Sustainability Disclosure Database, https://www.globalreporting.org/

reporting/report-services/sustainability-disclosure-database/Pages/Discover-the-Database.aspx, accessed April 2014.

15. Based on the World Federation of Exchanges, the number of listed companies in 2012 was 46,332. World Federation of Exchanges, 2012 WFE Market Highlights, http://www.world-exchanges.org/files/statistics/pdf/2012%20WFE%20Market%20Highlights.pdf accessed April 2014. Definition: "Number of companies which have shares listed on an exchange at the end of the period, split into domestic and foreign, excluding investment funds and unit trusts. A company with several classes of shares is counted just once. Only companies admitted to listing are included." World Federation of Exchanges, Number of Listed Companies definition, http://www.world-exchanges.org/statistics/statistics-definitions/number-listed-companies, accessed April 2014. Based on GRI data, 596 companies in 2012 produced integrated reports—approximately 1.29% of all listed companies.

16. "This includes all companies who voluntarily report sustainability information on their websites, from a policy or two or summaries of practices to full-blown reports with five-plus years of data on key metrics." Peter DeSimone, email correspondence with Robert Eccles, January 26, 2014.

17. The criterion used was that the company declared its annual report to shareholders to also be their sustainability report. The eight companies were AEP, Clorox, Dow Chemical, Eaton, Ingersoll Rand, Pfizer, Southwest Airlines, and United Technologies Corporation (UTC). Only UTC was not a GRI reporter. Data for 2012 are from IRRC Institute and Sustainability Investments Institute. "Integrated Financial and Sustainability Reporting in the United States," http://irrcinstitute.org/projects.php?project=63, accessed May 2014. Data for 2012 are from IRRC Institute and Sustainability Investments Institute, "Integrated Financial and Sustainability Reporting in the United States" and data for 2013 are from Peter DeSimone, email correspondence with Robert Eccles.

18. Global Reporting Initiative. Excel Spreadsheet of Sustainability Disclosure Database.

19. We are grateful to Cecile Churet and her colleagues at RobecoSAM for providing us the data to do this analysis. "Founded as the first asset manager focused exclusively on Sustainability Investing, SAM was acquired by Robeco Group in 2007 in-line with Robeco's strategic ambition to further develop into the thought leader in the field. With Robeco's global presence, SAM has grown into one of the world's most prominent Sustainability Investment groups. In 2013, SAM was renamed RobecoSAM as part of Robeco's strategy to further align its group-wide Sustainability Investing activities. With approximately 130 specialist staff located in Zurich and Rotterdam, RobecoSAM offers clients a comprehensive range of differentiated and complementary Sustainability Investing solutions including indices,

actively managed diversified and thematic equities, private equity, active ownership and corporate sustainability benchmarking services. RobecoSAM's long-standing experience in assessing companies and developing and managing successful sustainable investment strategies and Robeco's more than 80-year history of serving institutional investors and private investors with investment solutions across a broad range of asset classes are ideally complementary to each other. Leveraging Robeco's global network of sales, service and investment professionals, our Sustainability Investing products and services are represented in over 20 countries." RobecoSAM, http://www.robecosam.com/en/about-us/about-robecosam.jsp, accessed April 2014.

20. For detail on the CSA methodology see Eccles, Robert G. and Cecile Churet. "Integrated Reporting, Quality of Management, and Financial Performance" *Journal of Applied Corporate Finance*, Winter 2014, Volume 26 Number 1, p. 2 and http://www.robecosam.com/en/sustainability-insights/about-sustainability/robecosam-corporate-sustainability-assessment.jsp, accessed February 2014.

21. The Guiding Principle of Connectivity of information states, "An integrated report should show a holistic picture of the combination, interrelatedness and dependencies between the factors that affect the organization's ability to create value over time." "International Integrated Reporting Framework," http://www.theiirc.org/international-ir-framework/, accessed April 2014.

22. International <IR> Framework, p. 10.

23. Ibid., p. 11.

24. Ibid., p. 9.

25. Ibid., p. 11. Roughly two-thirds of the program examples were qualitative for both program and strategic examples.

26. KPMG, Centre for Corporate Governance in Africa, Global Reporting Initiative, and UNEP (United Nations Environment Programme). "Carrots and Sticks: Sustainability reporting policies worldwide—today's best practice, tomorrow's trends," 2013 edition, https://www.globalreporting.org/resourcelibrary/Carrots-and-Sticks.pdf, accessed February 2014, p. 9.

27. Ibid.

28. Ioannou, Ioannis, and George Serafeim. "The Consequences of Mandatory Corporate Sustainability Reporting." Harvard Business School Working Paper, No. 11-100, March 2011. (Revised May 2012, October 2012.) Ioannou and Serafeim found that government adoption of mandatory corporate sustainability reporting (CSR) led to positive organizational changes often linked to integrated reporting. The social responsibility of business leaders increases, while sustainable development and employee training become a higher priority. The authors also found that mandatory CSR led to improved corporate governance, company implementation of more ethical practices, a decrease in bribery and corruption, and an

increase in managerial credibility. In countries with stronger law enforcement and more widespread assurance of sustainability reports, these effects of CSR are larger.

29. European Union. "DIRECTIVE OF THE EUROPEAN PARLIAMENT AND OF THE COUNCIL, amending Council Directives 78/660/EEC and 83/349/EEC as regards disclosure of non-financial and diversity information by certain large companies and groups," http://ec.europa.eu/internal_market/accounting/non-financial_reporting/, accessed January 2014.

30. The Fourth Directive provides the requirements for content and presentation of annual accounts and reports. European Union. Fourth Directive: annual accounts of companies with limited liability, http://europa.eu/legislation_summaries/internal_market/businesses/company_law/l26009_en.htm, accessed January 2014.

31. The Seventh Directive provides the requirements for the consolidation of company accounts. European Union. Seventh Directive, Seventh Directive: consolidated accounts of companies with limited liability, http://europa.eu/legislation_summaries/internal_market/businesses/company_law/l26010_en.htm, accessed January 2014.

32. European Commission. The EU Single Market, Accounting, Non-Financial Reporting, http://ec.europa.eu/internal_market/accounting/non-financial_reporting/index_en.htm, accessed April 2014.

33. Unlisted companies include banks, insurance companies, and other companies that are so designated by Member States because of their activities, size, or number of employees. European Union. Europa, Press releases database, http://europa.eu/rapid/press-release_MEMO-14-301_en.htm, accessed April 2014.

34. Ibid.

35. Examples cited were the UN Global Compact, ISO 26000, and the German Sustainability Code.://ec.europa.eu/internal_market/accounting/non-financial_reporting/index_en.htm, accessed April 16, 2014.

36. European Union. Europa, Press releases database.

37. Sustainability reporting in the EU is often "principles-based" rather than prescriptive about what frameworks and standards should be used.

38. "A directive has to be then implemented into national legislation by each member state." Steve Waygood, telephone interview with Robert Eccles and Sydney Ribot, March 20, 2014.

39. Waygood, Steve for Aviva Investors. "A Roadmap for Integrated Capital Markets: Aviva's proposals for how the UN Sustainable Development Goals and the UN Framework Convention on Climate Change can harness the capital markets." May 2014. 1-54.

40. Steve Waygood, telephone interview.

41. Ibid.

42. Waygood, Steve. "Finally, regulation that investors can support." *Financial News* online. March 17, 2014. http://www.efinancialnews.com/story/2014-03-17/non-financial-reporting-directive-steve-waygood?ea9c8a2de0ee111045601ab04d673622, accessed May 7, 2014.

43. Steve Waygood, telephone interview, March 20, 2014.

44. Though materiality was not defined by either one of these initiatives, it was highlighted in the CSRC. While not directly about integrated reporting, the CSRC is focused on changing corporate reporting in a way that helps shape the context to make it easier for companies to adopt integrated reporting.

45. CK Capital. "2013 Trends in Sustainability Disclosure: Benchmarking the World's Stock Exchanges," October 2013, "Foreword" by Ernst Ligteringen (no page number).

46. Sustainable Stock Exchanges Initiatives. http://www.sseinitiative.org, accessed May 2014.

47. A similar initiative was announced not long before this book was sent to the publisher. The Ceres-sponsored Investor Initiative for Sustainable Exchanges is seeking to engage global stock exchanges via the World Federation of Exchanges (WFE) to establish possible uniform reporting standards for sustainability reporting by all exchange members. http://www.ceres.org/press/press-releases/world2019s-largest-investors-launch-effort-to-engage-global-stock-exchanges-on-sustainability-reporting-standard-for-companies, accessed April 2014. The recommendations are contained in the report "Investor Listing Standards Proposal: Recommendations for Stock Exchange Requirements on Corporate Sustainability Reporting," https://www.ceres.org/resources/reports/investor-listing-standards-proposal-recommendations-for-stock-exchange-requirements-on-corporate-sustainability-reporting/view, accessed April 2014.

48. Initiative for Responsible Investment at Harvard University. Our Work, Global CSR Disclosure Requirements, http://hausercenter.org/iri/about/global-csr-disclosure-requirements, accessed January 2014.

49. The South African Institute of Chartered Accountants (SAICA). "An integrated report is a new requirement for listed companies." SAICA, News, News Articles and Press & media releases, https://www.saica.co.za/tabid/695/itemid/2344/An-integrated-report-is-a-new-requirement-for-list.aspx, accessed January 2014.

50. Specifically, it was launched under the auspices of the United Nations Global Compact Office, the United Nations Conference on Trade and Development, the United Nations Principles for Responsible Investment, and the United Nations Environment Programme Finance Initiative. United Nations Environment Programme Finance Initiative. http://www.unepfi.org, accessed January 2014.

51. Sustainable Stock Exchanges Initiative. Partner Exchanges, http://www.sseinitiative.org/partners/stock-exchanges/, accessed January 2014.

52. Steve Waygood, email correspondence with Robert Eccles, Louise Haigh, Mike Krzus and Sydney Ribot, April 29, 2014.

53. Steve Waygood, telephone interview with Robert Eccles and Sydney Ribot, January 29, 2014.

54. CK Capital is the investment research arm of Corporate Knights, based in Toronto, Canada. CK Capital offers investment products and services to asset owners and managers. Corporate Knights is a publishing company which calls itself "The Company for Clean Capitalism." http://www.corporateknights.com/about/corporate-knights-policy, accessed February 2014. CK Capital. "2013 Trends in Sustainability Disclosure: Benchmarking the World's Stock Exchanges," October 2013. In the other Foreword to this report, Paul Druckman, the CEO of the IIRC, points out that "Integrated Reporting will help hardwire sustainability issues, amongst other 'capitals,' into mainstream decision-making and reporting," and that "stock exchanges have a major role to play in setting the agenda, as well as responding to cultural and behavioural shifts in market practice."

55. An exchange's disclosure score is the sum of three sub-scores: disclosure, disclosure growth, and disclosure timeliness. These scores are based on indicators regarding energy, water, waster, greenhouse gas emissions, employee turnover, and lost-time injury rate. For more details on the methodology used see CK Capital. "2013 Trends in Sustainability Disclosure: Benchmarking the World's Stock Exchanges," October 2013, pp. 15 and 38. Reflecting the fact that integrated reporting is not the same as sustainability reporting, the top five stock exchanges, ranked from one to five, respectively, were BME Spanish Exchanges, Helsinki Stock Exchange, Tokyo Stock Exchange, Oslo Stock Exchange, and Johannesburg Stock Exchange. The bottom five exchanges, ranked from 45th to 40th, respectively, were Tel Aviv Stock Exchange, Qatar Stock Exchange, Lima Stock Exchange, Saudi Arabia Stock Exchange, and Kuwait Stock Exchange. The highest rated SSE Partner was the Johannesburg Stock Exchange. The lowest rated was NASDAQ OMX at 36, with NYSE Euronext at 33.

56. Corporate Sustainability Reporting Coalition. http://www.aviva.com/media/news/item/aviva-convenes-corporate-sustainability-reporting-coalition-13023/, accessed May 2014.

57. Aviva Investors. News Releases, Aviva convenes Corporate Sustainability Reporting Coalition, http://www.aviva.com/media/news/item/aviva-convenes-corporate-sustainability-reporting-coalition-13023/, accessed January 2014.

58. These investors represented $1.6 trillion in assets under management at the time of announcement. Aviva Investors. News Releases, Investor led

coalition calls for UN declaration requiring companies to integrate material sustainability issues into reporting, http://www.aviva.com/media/news/item/investor-led-coalition-calls-for-un-declaration-requiring-companies-to-integrate-material-sustainability-issues-into-reporting-13203/, accessed April 2014.

59. Ibid.

60. Organizational benefits cited for these actions included enhanced long-term profitability for companies and better long-term returns for investors. Additionally, the systems-level benefits of higher quality stock markets, increased macro financial stability, and improving the lives of people everywhere who are impacted by corporate activity were also cited. Paul Abberley, then CEO of Aviva Investors, commented "We believe that all corporate boards should be required to consider the future sustainability of the firm they govern. This should not only enhance long-term profitability and returns to investors, but also improve the quality of stock markets, increase macro financial stability and make a material contribution to the lives of those impacted by corporate activity. This is why we are calling on the United Nations member states to commit to develop policy on Corporate Sustainability Reporting. Markets are driven by information. If the information they receive is short term and thin then these characteristics will define our markets." Ibid.

61. United Nations Conference on Sustainable Development. "The Future We Want," http://www.uncsd2012.org/thefuturewewant.html, accessed January 2014.

62. "47. We acknowledge the importance of corporate sustainability reporting, and encourage companies, where appropriate, especially publicly listed and large companies, to consider integrating sustainability information into their reporting cycle. We encourage industry, interested governments and relevant stakeholders, with the support of the United Nations system, as appropriate, to develop models for best practice and facilitate action for the integration of sustainability reporting, taking into account experiences from already existing frameworks and paying particular attention to the needs of developing countries, including for capacity-building." Ibid., p. 9.

63. Representatives from 191 UN member states and observers, including 79 Heads of State or Government, attended Rio+20, IISD Reporting Services. Earth Negotiations Bulletin. http://www.iisd.ca/vol27/enb 2751e.html, accessed April 2014. Paragraph 1 of the "The Future We Want," renewed their "commitment to sustainable development, and to ensure the promotion of economically, socially and environmentally sustainable future for our planet and for present and future generations." Ibid., p. 1.

64. Long Finance. "European briefing: Towards an agreement on corporate sustainability reporting," http://www.longfinance.net/images/PDF/csrc_eusustrep_2013.pdf, accessed January 2014.

65. The linguistic relativity principle, commonly referred to as the Sapir-Whorf hypothesis, holds that differences in the way language symbolizes certain cultural and cognitive categories impacts the way people think about those categories such that speakers of different languages tend to behave and think differently depending on the language they use. It is usually considered in a "strong" or "weak" form. The strong version of the hypothesis holds that language determines thought and linguistic categories delimit cognitive categories. The weak version holds that linguistic categories influence thought and some forms of nonlinguistic behavior. In light of either version, the way that meaning is articulated in the integrated reporting movement, the way that the evolution of companies' reporting practices is referred to as a "journey," has consequences for the way that actors in the movement view integrated reporting. Koerner, E.F.K. "Towards a full pedigree of the Sapir-Whorf Hypothesis: from Locke to Lucy." *Explorations in Linguistic Relativity*, edited by Martin Pütz and Marjolijn Verspoor, 1-25. Amsterdam: John Benjamins Publishing Company, 2000.

66. Deloitte. "Disclose of long-term business value: What matters?" http://www.deloitte.com/assets/Dcom-UnitedStates/Local%20Assets/Documents/us_scc_materialitypov_032812.pdf, accessed March 2014; Deloitte. "Does materiality matter? Should the principle of materiality be applied more consistently to non-financial reporting?," https://www.deloitte.com/assets/Dcom-UnitedStates/Local%20Assets/Documents/us_scc_materialitydebate_032712.pdf, accessed March 2014; Ernst & Young. "The concept of 'materiality' in Integrated Reporting," http://www.ey.com/Publication/vwLUAssets/The_concept_of_materiality_in_Integrated_Reporting/$FILE/EY_'Materiality'%20in%20Integrated%20Reporting%20April%202013.pdf, accessed March 2014;

67. PricewaterhouseCoopers. "Materiality - choosing our sustainability priorities," http://www.pwc.co.uk/corporate-sustainability/materiality.jhtml, accessed March 2014.

68. International Integrated Reporting Council. http://www.theiirc.org, accessed May 2104.

69. The Prince's Accounting for Sustainability Project. http://www.accountingforsustainability.org, accessed December 2013.

70. Global Reporting Initiative. https://www.globalreporting.org/Pages/default.aspx, accessed December 2013.

71. Krzus, Mike. Personal notes on "Roundtable meeting to discuss 'One Report,' a book being written by Bob Eccles and Mike Krzus." September 11, 2009, Clarence House, London, U.K.

72. International Integrated Reporting Council. Key Milestones for the IIRC, http://www.theiirc.org/about/the-work-plan/, accessed December 2013.

73. Agenda. The Prince's Accounting for Sustainability Forum. December 17, 2009, St. James's Palace, London, U.K.

74. Accounting for Sustainability (A4S) was instrumental in building a foundation for the IIRC through its work on "connected reporting" by publishing a "Connected Reporting Framework" in 2007, followed by a "how to guide" in 2009. Since then, this idea has been absorbed into integrated reporting. For more information on how A4S sees the relationship between connected reporting and integrated reporting see http://www.accountingforsustainability.org/connected-reporting/connected-reporting-a-how-to-guide, accessed May 2014.

75. International Integrated Reporting Council. Press Releases, Formation of the IIRC, http://www.theiirc.org/category/press/iirc-key-press-releases/page/4/, accessed December 2013.

76. On October 11, 2011, Sir Michael Peat, the founding Chairman of the IIRC retired and Mervyn King was appointed the Chairman. http://www.theiirc.org/2011/10/11/iirc-appoint-mervyn-king-as-chairman-to-lead-next-steps-of-integrated-reporting-framework-2/, accessed December 2014. Paul Druckman is its Chief Executive Officer.

77. The "Draft Framework" was published in April 2013, and "The International <IR> Framework," in December 2013. See "International <IR> Framework Consultation Draft," April 2013 and "The International <IR> Framework" December 2013. Documents related to the International <IR> Framework include, "Basis for Conclusions: International <IR> Framework," December 2013; and "Summary of Significant Issues: International <IR> Framework," December 2013. International Integrated Reporting Council. International <IR> Framework, http://www.theiirc.org/international-ir-framework/, accessed May 2014. Previously, the only other guidance was the "Framework for Integrated Reporting and the Integrated Report Discussion Paper," by the Integrated Reporting Committee of South Africa, January 25, 2011.

78. International Integrated Reporting Council. IIRC Pilot Program, Pilot Program Business Network, http://www.theiirc.org/companies-and-investors/pilot-programme-business-network/, accessed February 2014.

79. International Integrated Reporting Council. IIRC Pilot Program, Pilot Program Investor Network, http://www.theiirc.org/companies-and-investors/pilot-programme-investor-network/, accessed February 2014.

80. Examples cited are members of the IIRC's Council or Working Group. http://www.theiirc.org, accessed May 2014

81. International Integrated Reporting Council. The IIRC, About, Memorandums of Understanding, CDP and Climate Disclosure Standards Board, http://www

.theiirc.org/wp-content/uploads/2014/01/MoU-IIRC-CDP+CDSB-FINAL-20130415.pdf, accessed April 2014.

82. International Integrated Reporting Council. The IIRC, About, Memorandums of Understanding, Global Initiative for Sustainability Ratings, http://www.theiirc.org/wp-content/uploads/2014/03/MoU-IIRC-GISR.pdf, accessed April 2014.

83. International Integrated Reporting Council. The IIRC, About, Memorandums of Understanding, Global Reporting Initiative, http://www.theiirc.org/wp-content/uploads/2013/02/MoU-IIRC-GRI-20130201-1.pdf, accessed April 2014.

84. International Integrated Reporting Council. The IIRC, About, Memorandums of Understanding, The Sustainability Accounting Standards Board, http://www.theiirc.org/wp-content/uploads/2014/01/MoU-IIRC-SASB-Final.pdf, accessed May 2014.

85. International Federation of Accountants, IFRS Foundation for International Accounting Standards Board, United Nations conference on Trade and Development, World Intellectual Capital Initiative, and World Business Council for Sustainable Development. http://www.theiirc.org/the-iirc/, accessed April 2014.

86. Global Reporting Initiative. https://www.globalreporting.org/Pages/default.aspx, accessed May 2014.

87. "Ceres is a non-profit organization advocating for sustainability leadership. We mobilize a powerful network of investors, companies and public interest groups to accelerate and expand the adoption of sustainable business practices and solutions to build a healthy global economy." Bob Massie was president at the time of GRI's founding. http://www.ceres.org/about-us, accessed February 2014. He is now President of the New Economy Coalition whose mission "is to build a New Economy that prioritizes the well-being of people and the planet," http://neweconomy.net/about_us, accessed February 2014.

88. At that time Allen White was a Vice President and Senior Fellow of the Tellus Institute and he still is today. "At this perilous juncture in human affairs, Tellus Institute works to advance a global civilization of sustainability, equity, and well-being through research, education, and action." http://www.tellus.org/about/, accessed February 2014.

89. Global Reporting Initiative. Excel Spreadsheet of Sustainability Disclosure Database.

90. GRI has a multistakeholder focus whereas the IIRC's primary audience is "providers of financial capital."

91. Global Reporting Initiative. Conference 2010, https://www.globalreporting.org/information/events/gri-global-conference/conference-2010/Pages/default.aspx, accessed January 2014.

92. Ibid.

93. GRI released their G4 Guidelines on May 22, 2013, at the 2013 Global Conference. Global Reporting Initiative. Information, News and Press Center, "G4 is future of sustainability reporting, say business leaders," https://www.globalreporting.org/information/news-and-press-center/Pages/G4-is-future-of-sustainability-reporting-say-business-leaders.aspx, accessed May 2014.

94. Nelmara Arbex, email correspondence with Robert Eccles, March 19, 2014.

95. Global Reporting Initiatives. Current Priorities, Resources, "The Sustainability Content of Integrated Reports—A Survey of Pioneers," https://www.globalreporting.org/resourcelibrary/GRI-IR.pdf, accessed January 2014.

96. Ibid., p. 5.

97. Christy Wood, telephone interview with Robert Eccles, Mike Krzus, and Sydney Ribot, October 28, 2013.

98. Sustainability Accounting Standards Board. http://www.sasb.org, accessed January 2014.

99. John Katovich is a capital markets lawyer who also teaches in the Presidio Graduate School MBA Program in San Francisco, which focuses on sustainability, http://k2-legal.com/aboutus/ourteam/john/, accessed February 2014.

100. Steve Lydenberg is the Partner, Strategic Vision for Domini Social Investments, http://www.domini.com/about-domini/Management/index.htm, accessed February 2014 and an Adjunct Lecturer in Public Policy at the Harvard Kennedy School, http://www.hks.harvard.edu/about/faculty-staff-directory/steve-lydenberg, accessed February 2014 where he helped establish the Initiative for Responsible Investment, http://www.hks.harvard.edu/news-events/news/press-releases/pr-hauser-iri-mar10, accessed February 2014.

101. The Sustainability Accounting Standards Board is a 501(c)3 non-profit engaged in the creation and dissemination of sustainability accounting standards for use by publicly-listed corporations in disclosing material sustainability issues for the benefit of investors and the public. Sustainability Accounting Standards Board. About, Vision and Mission, http://www.sasb.org/sasb/vision-mission/, accessed March 2014.

102. Sustainability Accounting Standards Board. Standards, Key Dates & Status, http://www.sasb.org/standards/status-standards/, accessed March 2014.

103. Sustainability Accounting Standards Board. Engage, Join an Industry Working Group, http://www.sasb.org/engage/join-an-iwg/, accessed February 2014.

104. Sustainability Accounting Standards Board. About SASB, Standards Council, http://www.sasb.org/sasb/standards-council/, accessed May 2014.

105. Sustainability Accounting Standards Board. Approach, Our Process, http://www.sasb.org/our-process/, accessed February 2014.

106. Amanda Medress, email correspondence with Robert Eccles, Jean Rogers, Mike Krzus, and Sydney Ribot, April 30, 2014. SASB released its Healthcare standards on July 31, 2014. SASB. Standards, Key Dates & Status, http://www.sasb.org/standards/status-standards/, accessed May 2014.

107. SASB released its Financials standards on February 25, 2014. Ibid., SASB, Standards.

108. SASB uses the Securities and Exchanges Commission definition of materiality as interpreted by the U.S. Supreme Court. See Securities and Exchange Commission Staff Accounting Bulletin: No. 99—Materiality, http://www.sec.gov/interps/account/sab99.htm, accessed January 2014 and 22 TSC Industries v. Northway, Inc., 426 U.S. 438, 449 (1976). See also Basic, Inc. v. Levinson, 485 U.S. 224 (1988).

109. Bob Herz, telephone interview with Robert Eccles, Mike Krzus, and Sydney Ribot, October 4, 2013.

110. PR Newswire. "Michael R. Bloomberg and Mary Schapiro Appointed to SASB's Board Leadership," http://www.prnewswire.com/news-releases/michael-r-bloomberg-and-mary-schapiro-appointed-to-sasbs-board-leadership-257486101.html, accessed May 2014.

111. GreenBiz.com. "Finance powerhouses Michael Bloomberg and Mary Schapiro to lead SASB," http://www.greenbiz.com/blog/2014/05/01/sasb-taps-star-power-mike-bloomberg-and-former-sec-chair, accessed May 2014.

112. CDP. https://www.cdp.net/en-US/Pages/HomePage.aspx, accessed May 2014.

113. CDP. About CDP, https://www.cdp.net/, accessed January 2014.

114. Nigel Topping, telephone interview with Bob Eccles, Mike Krzus, and Sydney Ribot, October 15, 2013.

115. Climate Disclosure Standards Board. http://www.cdsb.net, accessed May 2014.

116. Climate Disclosure Standards Board. Climate Change Reporting Framework, http://www.cdsb.net/climate-change-reporting-framework/why-we-need-framework, accessed January 2014. It was established at the annual meeting of the World Economic Forum.

117. Climate Disclosure Standards Board. "Climate Change Reporting Framework," http://www.cdsb.net/sites/cdsbnet/files/cdsbframework_v1-1.pdf, accessed January 2014.

118. Ibid.

119. Ibid.

120. Climate Disclosure Standards Board. CDSB Framework Consultation, http://www.cdsb.net/climate-change-reporting-framework/framework-consultation, accessed March 2014.

121. Climate Disclosure Standards Board. CDSB's Framework for integrated reporting, http://www.cdsb.net/climate-change-reporting-framework/cdsbs-framework-integrated-reporting, accessed January 2014.

122. Global Initiative for Sustainability Ratings. http://ratesustainability.org, accessed May 2014.

123. Allen White, telephone interview with Robert Eccles, Mike Krzus, and Sydney Ribot, February 17, 2014.

124. Global Initiative for Sustainability Ratings. About GISR, Vision and Mission, http://ratesustainability.org/about/, accessed February 2014.

125. Allen White, telephone interview.

126. McKinsey estimated the global bond market in 2010 at $158 trillion. The global equity market was $54 trillion. Roxburgh, Charles, Susan Lund, and John Piotrowski, "Mapping global capital markets 2011," McKinsey Global Institute, p. 2, c., 2011.

127. Allen White, telephone interview.

128. The 12 Principles comprise two categories: Process and Content. Process principles pertain to the design, application, and maintenance of a rating to ensure excellence, credibility, and integrity. The five process principles are Transparency, Impartiality, Continuous Improvement, Inclusiveness Development, and Assurability. Content principles relate to the scope, quality, and measurement aspects of a rating. The seven content principles are Materiality, Comprehensiveness, Sustainability Context, Long-Term Horizon, Value Chain, Balance, and Comparability. Global Initiative for Sustainability Ratings. Standard, Principles, GISR Standard Component 1: Principles, http://ratesustainability.org/standards/principles/, accessed February 2014.

129. "Based on 2012 year-end data, the four largest registered public accounting firms and their global affiliates audited more than 98 percent of the global market capitalization of U.S. issuers. The next three firms and their global affiliates audited another 1.1 percent of this market capitalization." Franzel, Jeannette M. "Accountability: Protecting Investors, the Public Interest and Prosperity," Public Accounting Oversight Board, July 17, 2013.

130. Deloitte. "Integrated Reporting: The New Big Picture," *Deloitte Review*, Issue 10, 2012, pp. 124–137. Ernst & Young. "Driving value by combining financial and non-financial information into a single, investor-grade document." 2013. KPMG. "Integrated Reporting: Performance insight through Better Business Reporting," 2013. PricewaterhouseCoopers. "Integrated Reporting: Going beyond the financial results," August 2013.

131. American Institute of Certified Public Accountants, http://www.aicpa.org/PRESS/PRESSRELEASES/2013/Pages/AICPA-Commends-IIRC-for-Release-of-International-Integrated-Reporting-Framework.aspx, accessed February 2014; Chartered Institute of Management Accountants, http://www.cimaglobal.com/Thought-leadership/Integrated-reporting/, accessed February 2014; Institute of Chartered Accountants in England and Wales, http://www.icaew.com/en/

about-icaew / newsroom / press-releases / 2013-press-releases / integrated-reporting-is-a-catalyst-to-improve-business-reporting-says-icaew, accessed February 2014; Institute of Management Accountants, http://www.imanet.org/about_ima / advocacy_activity / advocacy_activity_all / details_all / 13-06-17/Integrated_Reporting_Draft_Framework.aspx, accessed February 2014.

132. Association of Chartered and Certified Accountants, http://www.accaglobal.com / gb / en / discover/news/2014 / integrated-qualification.html, accessed February 2014.

133. International Federation of Accountants, https://www.ifac.org/news-events/2013-12/ifac-welcomes-release-international-integrated-reporting-frame-work, accessed February 2014.

134. Ibid.

135. International Integrated Reporting Council. IIRC Pilot Program, http://www.theiirc.org/companies-and-investors/pilot-programme-business-network/, accessed January 2014.

136. International Integrated Reporting Council. Pilot Program Investor Network, http://www.theiirc.org/companies-and-investors/pilot-programme-investor-network/, accessed April 2014.

137. California Public Employees' Retirement System. http://www.calpers-governance.org/docs-sof/marketinitiatives/initiatives/joint-submission-to-iirc.pdf, accessed February 2014.

138. California Public Employees' Retirement System. http://www.calpers.ca.gov/eip-docs/about/board-cal-agenda/agendas/invest/201211/item09a-00.pdf, accessed February 2014.

139. Generation Investment Management. "Sustainable Capitalism," p. 1, http://www.generationim.com/media/pdf-generation-sustainable-capitalism-v1.pdf, accessed April 2014.

140. These counts are based on a database comprised of academic and practitioner journals.

141. These counts are based on the Factiva database of general press articles. There is no overlap between this database and the one used for counting article citations.

4

Motives

S IX GROUPS OF ACTORS, each with their own motives, comprise the integrated reporting movement: (1) companies, (2) the audience or users of integrated reports and integrated reporting, (3) supporting organizations, (4) supporting initiatives, (5) regulators, and (6) service providers. Each group's motives are a function of whether they are mission-driven, profit-driven, or some combination of the two. Companies are largely profit-driven, although some have a strong mission element as well. Audience includes a diverse set of report users: investors and other providers of financial capital (e.g., debt and project finance), sell-side analysts, rating agencies, employees, customers, suppliers, and nongovernmental organizations (NGOs). With the exception of NGOs, which are by definition mission-driven, these are largely profit-driven and interested in financial information. The mission-driven members are interested in nonfinancial information. One of the challenges a company practicing integrated reporting faces is to educate these different members on the value of taking a more holistic view of the company's performance. Regulators and supporting organizations and initiatives are mission-driven. Regulators can also be considered members of the audience. Finally, service providers are profit-driven.

These actors' relationships with each other make positive action possible. When two actors are both profit-driven, their relationship is one of shared economic self-interest based on resource exchange. From a company perspective, this is true of their relationship with profit-driven audience members and service providers. In profit-driven/mission-driven relationships, the relationship is based on gaining or resisting influence, such as those between companies and supporting organizations and initiatives and companies and regulators. Relationships between different mission-driven organizations are also based on influence, such as those between supporting organizations and initiatives and regulators.

The integrated reporting movement's momentum is a function of the extent to which these actors succeed in providing resources and exercising influence in ways that accelerate adoption and increase awareness. Accelerating adoption can be accomplished both directly by companies and indirectly by shaping the context through laws and codes of conduct in the institutionalization phase of meaning. Examples of the former from a resource perspective are providers of capital creating incentives for a company to produce an integrated report and service providers that furnish advice and technology to help them do so. From an influence perspective, examples would include supporting organizations that seek to encourage companies to adopt integrated reporting as a "best practice" or to "show leadership" or get "brand value" from doing so. Examples of entities that indirectly accelerate adoption include supporting organizations and initiatives that influence regulators, such as securities commissions, and those with some regulatory authority, such as stock exchanges, to require or create incentives for companies to adopt integrated reporting. Finally, there are many ways in which supporting organizations and initiatives attempt to influence each other and regulators in order to codify and institutionalize the meaning of integrated reporting as a way to accelerate its adoption.

 ## COMPANIES

Absent regulation mandating that companies publish integrated reports, the decision of whether or not to produce one lies with each company. Company motivation to produce an integrated report generally stems from the belief that its tangible (e.g., better financial performance) and intangible (e.g., enhanced reputation) benefits will exceed the tangible (e.g., resources) and intangible (e.g., litigation risk) costs of doing so. In making this assessment, executives must be aware of the concept and important related concepts like integrated thinking and materiality. Although this varies by country, most executives we have encountered today have a modest understanding of integrated reporting at best due to the relative youth of the movement. If these executives are sufficiently senior and occupy the right roles—such as chief executive officer (CEO), chief financial officer (CFO), or board member—they can, however, take the next step and make it an item for consideration, debating its costs and benefits.

The litmus test for both advocates and skeptics is whether integrated reporting leads to better corporate performance through integrated thinking, all of which should be ultimately reflected in a company's stock price. Today, it would be very difficult to analyze this contention due to the limited number of companies practicing integrated reporting for any length of time. However, it is possible to gain insights from company experiences to date, as reflected in their perceptions of the costs and benefits of integrated reporting, even though no algorithm exists to net these out into a "bottom line." Moreover, even experienced companies find it difficult to quantify the costs and benefits of integrated reporting.

Thus far, surveys have shown integrated reporting's benefits as perceived by companies to be modest and largely intangible. An Ernst & Young (E&Y) survey[1] conducted with GreenBiz[2] asked company representatives to provide their reasons for why it makes sense to voluntarily adopt integrated reporting (Table 4.1). A total of 282 companies in 17 sectors, all with revenues of $1 billion or more, 85% of which were in the United States, responded to the survey. The top three benefits by a wide margin were all intangible: increased external sustainability awareness, improved transparency and data accuracy, and enhanced brand and reputation. These are cited by over 50% of the respondents. By comparison, tangible benefits such as improved reporting efficiency and cost reductions are ranked relatively low, cited by one-third and one-quarter of respondents, respectively.

Table 4.1 also provides insights into the meaning companies ascribe to integrated reporting. The fact that nearly 40% cited "creating competitive advantage" and "driving collaboration between different parts of the business" suggests that some companies see a relationship between integrated reporting and integrated thinking. However, only one-third or less thought that integrated reporting will improve their communications with investors and enable them to better understand the company, leading to a higher valuation. Except for increased sustainability awareness—and, as noted in Chapter 2, the International <IR> Framework (<IR> Framework) is not couched in

TABLE 4.1 Reasons for Voluntary Adoption of Integrated Reporting

Reasons	Percent Making This Statement
Increase sustainability awareness with investors and customers	63
Improve transparency and data accuracy	56
Enhance brand and reputation	54
Create competitive advantage	37
Drive increased collaboration between different parts of the business	37
Improve communication with media and general public	36
Improve reporting efficiency	35
Improve analysis and valuation	32
Preempt questions from investors and others stakeholders	28
Drive cost savings/reductions	28
Enhance employee recruiting	25
Improve innovation	24

Data Source: Ernst & Young and GreenBiz Group, "2013 six growing trends in sustainability reporting," p. 30.

"sustainability" terms—more companies cite the internal benefits of integrated reporting than the external benefits. These modest percentages suggest that most companies have yet to be convinced about the full range of integrated reporting's benefits. Until they are, adoption will be slow and momentum will be minimal.[3]

Similarly, a 2012 survey of 43 organizations in the International Integrated Reporting Council's (IIRC) Pilot Programme Business Network conducted by Black Sun Plc[4] confirmed the importance of internal benefits, all of which are primarily intangible but most of which are consistent with integrated thinking:

1. "One of the most mentioned benefits of Integrated Reporting is the opportunity it provides to connect teams from across an organisation, breaking down silos and leading to more integrated thinking.
2. Changes to systems driven by Integrated Reporting requirements are providing greater visibility across business activities and helping to improve understanding of how organisations create value in the broadest sense.
3. A shift to Integrated Reporting is increasing the interest and engagement of senior management in issues around the long-term

sustainability of the business, which is helping them to gain a more holistic understanding of their organisations.

4. Better understanding of organisational activities is enabling companies to establish a holistic business model and helping to streamline communications.

5. Organisations are starting to identify ways to measure the value to stakeholders of managing and reporting on sustainability issues."[5]

Unlike the benefits of creating an integrated report, the costs are very tangible, thereby making the decision to adopt integrated reporting a difficult one. Financial and human resource costs include organizing and executing on a process to produce an integrated report[6] (which includes determining the material issues to be included and necessarily higher levels of stakeholder engagement), investments in technology and control systems to produce sufficiently reliable nonfinancial information on a timely basis[7] (which can also be thought of as a benefit), the costs of producing an additional report (if it is one), making changes in the company's website to support the integrated report, and educating users about how to get the most benefit out of it. Difficult-to-quantify costs include increasing expectations by the audience and subsequent reputational risk, and legal risk from increased disclosure.

While little empirical evidence exists to confirm the existence or magnitude of these costs and benefits, one could argue that this is beside the point. What is important is that inside the company, management and the board make an informed decision about whether to produce an integrated report or not. Equally important is the fact that some barriers commonly cited to practicing integrated reporting are not seen as significant by most companies. For example, in the E&Y/GreenBiz survey, respondents ranked challenges to preparing an integrated report (Table 4.2). While legal risk is often cited as a reason against integrated reporting, only 18% of respondents considered it the most difficult challenge. Further evidence that legal risk is more of an excuse than a legitimate reason to refrain from producing an integrated report is that there is very little evidence of lawsuits or regulatory enforcement actions against companies for voluntary disclosures. Rather, the problem is one of inaccurate or fraudulent disclosures—or the failure to disclose material items.[8] All other challenges on the list are cited by 15% or fewer of respondents. With the exception of lack of guidance from standard setters and regulators, cited by only 12% (showing that this is not a significant barrier), all other challenges are internal.[9]

TABLE 4.2 Challenges to Integrated Reporting

Challenges	Percent of Respondents Ranking the Challenge as Most Difficult
Balancing the demands for transparency against legal risk and other considerations of releasing such information	18
Aligning sustainability reporting processes with financial processes	15
Lack of C-suite and board buy-in	15
Lack of CFO buy-in	14
Budget and staff to prepare the report	13
Time constraints	13
Adequate guidance from standard setters and regulatory bodies (e.g., U.S. SEC)	12

Data Source: Ernst & Young and GreenBiz Group, "2013 six growing trends in sustainability reporting," p. 31.

AUDIENCE

Perhaps the broadest category of actor, the integrated reporting audience includes shareholders and other providers of financial capital (e.g., bond holders and bank lenders), sell-side analysts, rating agencies, stakeholders of various kinds (including employees, customers, suppliers, and NGOs), potential acquirers, and joint venture partners. In the next chapter, we will simplify the treatment of this group by distinguishing between the "direct audience" of providers of financial capital and the "indirect audience" that includes everyone else. However, this chapter requires more nuanced audience segmentation. For the audience, the significance of an integrated report lies in its potential to help them make better resource allocation decisions or better provide advice that influences the resource allocation decisions of others. For a profit-driven audience, these decisions will be made based on an economic calculus. For the mission-driven audience of NGOs and concerned citizens, these decisions will be in terms of whether to support or confront the company on their issues of concern.

Since integrated reporting is still in its early stages of adoption, it is difficult to assess its impact on audience resource allocation decisions, just as it is difficult to assess its impact on company resource allocation decisions through the integrated thinking that it engenders. The Black Sun survey described above provides some data on companies' perceptions of audience benefits. Here too the results were modest: 21% of respondents believed integrated reporting benefits analysts and investors and 23% for employees, but only 8% of respondents said private shareholders.[10] Respondents were more bullish about the future benefits of integrated reporting as it develops, with 64% citing benefits to analysts, 49% to institutional investors, and an impressive 95% to employees. The present and future data on employees are consistent with the conversations we have had with executives who said that of all their different stakeholders, employees are among the first to benefit when a company starts practicing integrated reporting because it gives them a better understanding of the company. Executives also believed that this benefits the company since better understanding leads to greater employee engagement and, in turn, more efficient and effective employees.

Two surveys queried investors on whether and how they use non-financial information, including data likely to be in an integrated report. E&Y released "Tomorrow's investment rules: Global survey of institutional investors on non-financial performance" in 2014.[11] Investors rated the sources for nonfinancial information used in investment decision-making and concluded that annual reports (77%), corporate websites (62%), and integrated reports (61%) are "essential" or "important." Specific issues that emerged as essential or important to investors are business impact of regulation (86%), minimizing risk (83%), and evidence of improved future valuation with business forecast (71%).[12] Investors were also asked to rate disclosures considered to be "beneficial" to investment decisions. The three highest-scoring disclosures were sector or industry-specific reporting criteria and key performance indicators (65%), statements and metrics on expected future performance and links to nonfinancial risks (64%), and company disclosures based on what they feel is most material to their value creation story (60%).[13] The importance of focusing on issues that are material to a given audience is underscored by the revelation that 50% of investors who do consider ESG issues when making decisions cite lack of clarity in corporate disclosures about whether information is material.

A November 2012 survey by SustainAbility,[14] *Rate the Raters Phase 5, The Investor View*,[15] looked into how often investors considered environmental, governance, and social (ESG) data and ranked the importance of ESG issues. Sixty percent of investors considered governance issues "always" or "often," followed by social (40%) and environmental (35%) issues. The highest rated ("important/very important") governance issue was ethics

(79%). About 75% of the respondents chose customer relationship management as the highest rated social issue, and energy efficiency (59%) was the top rated environmental issue.[16]

Despite the limitations on rigorous research into the benefits of integrated reporting to companies and their audience, we can suggest hypotheses, largely taken from the arguments of those who support integrated reporting, about the benefits for different audiences and how this leads to company benefits. An integrated report can provide information to investors interested in a company's ability to create value over the long term based on all relevant capitals, resulting in the company having a greater proportion of stable, long-term investors.[17] Sell-side analysts seeking to provide useful research to such investors will be able to provide better insights based on the information in an integrated report, potentially making them more bullish on the company.[18] Similarly, rating agencies may find an integrated report useful in doing credit analysis for the providers of financial capital who use these ratings to make resource allocation decisions. More accurate credit ratings can result in either a higher or lower cost of capital to the company. Largely based on an economic calculus, employees, customers, and suppliers can use an integrated report to make their own resource allocation decisions, potentially in favor of the company.

A company issuing an integrated report may attract higher quality employees or even equally skilled employees for a lower wage. This can be attributed to both the symbolic value of issuing an integrated report and the information it contains if it provides evidence of the company's ability to create value over the long term, thereby reducing the risk of accepting a job at the company. Integrated reporting, especially when it includes high levels of stakeholder engagement, can increase the overall level of engagement of employees. Research has shown a strong relationship between engagement and productivity.[19]

Similarly, customers are unlikely to accept a higher price, and suppliers, a lower price simply due to integrated reporting. However, it can "break the tie" for the same reason as employees, especially if the company significantly engages with them in putting its integrated report together. Customers may give an integrated reporting company a greater "share of wallet," and suppliers may give the company priority in times of demand shortages. We admit that these arguments make a heroic assumption about corporate reporting as an input into decision-making by employees, customers, and suppliers. That is, they assume that these audience members will take the time and effort to access and understand the information provided in an integrated report.

In contrast, it is *not* a heroic assumption to posit that potential acquirers and joint venture partners would be influenced by the information contained in an integrated report. These decisions involve substantial, long-term resource commitments. Today, acquirers, including private equity firms, have already made ESG issues an important part of their due diligence process.[20] An integrated report would not only place these issues in a financial performance context, but it would also address other issues based on all six capitals that affect a company's ability to create value over the short-, medium-, and long-term. Since the success of the partnership will depend upon how well the partner will be able to perform over these periods of time, such information is equally useful to potential joint venture partners.[21] In turn, a strong integrated report can make a company attractive to an acquirer or joint venture partner. It can also make it attractive as a buyer of another company.

While providers of financial capital comprise the primary audience of an integrated report, NGOs focused on environmental and social issues can also find it valuable. The report will enable them to see the company's view on whether their issue is part of its value creation strategy and how it is managing the capitals of interest to the NGO. Based upon the report, an NGO can decide if and how it wants to engage with the company, including shaping the content of the integrated report itself and the process by which it is constructed. Since NGOs' focus tends to be fairly narrow, they have a tendency to ignore the fact that companies are subject to multiple, often-conflicting, pressures from providers of financial capital and their many stakeholders. By having a more holistic understanding of the company's strategy and performance, the NGO can engage more effectively with the company, whether in private or through a public campaign.[22] Given the severe resource limitations typical of most NGOs, this is important. While an integrated report can provide these NGOs with useful information, NGOs must develop the skills to read and understand it in order to reap this benefit. From the company's perspective, it will be able to engage more effectively with NGOs to understand and address their agenda if the NGO has a holistic view of the company and is practicing some degree of integrated thinking itself.

More generally, we hypothesize that any member of the audience can achieve the same benefits of integrated thinking gained by a company during its report production process by learning how to understand an integrated report. Whatever its motives or the nature of its relationship with the company, the report audience will have a deeper understanding of how to meet its own long-term objectives. In fact, integrated reporting can be the basis of greater engagement to the benefit of both the company and its audience. Trade-offs will always remain, but at least they will be mutually understood. For this reason, companies practicing integrated reporting are well-served by making an effort to help their audience understand how to use and benefit from their integrated report. They should not assume this will automatically happen—an assumption being made by companies when they complain, "we aren't getting any credit from our investors for our integrated report."

 ## SUPPORTING ORGANIZATIONS AND INITIATIVES

Two types of mission-driven actors are influencing the momentum of the integrated reporting movement: supporting organizations and supporting initiatives. Both believe that integrated reporting will benefit society through better resource allocation decisions by companies and markets in order to create a more sustainable society—and more sustainable companies. In the previous chapter, we discussed the most important supporting organizations and initiatives. Here, we simply want to raise the issue of how these organizations and initiatives work together—or not—as each attempts to create system-level change.

The basic question is whether supporting organizations should collaborate with or compete against each other. An important argument in favor of collaboration is that it will eliminate, or at least reduce, confusion in the marketplace. Companies already complain about the "alphabet soup of acronyms" created by the various supporting organizations, asking if they somehow fit together or if the company has to choose one or two of them. While less affected, investors raise this question as well. To the extent that regulators are the targets of influence attempts by these organizations, they too will want to know if choices need to be made and if doing so will put them in the crosshairs of competing organizations and initiatives. A further argument for collaboration is that by reducing this confusion, each actor will actually enhance its ability to achieve its own separate mission, as well as to support integrated reporting, which all claim to believe in.

The argument in favor of competition holds that by "letting many flowers bloom," the most effective organization or initiative will "win" in the market and regulatory spheres. This framing is similar to that of those who support and do not support, respectively, convergence in accounting standards[23]—a framing based on two premises. The first is that there actually is competition, just as in product markets, and that the better product will get the biggest market share or at least, that each "product" will find its appropriate market niche. The second premise is that the resources spent on collaboration by these severely resource-constrained organizations and initiatives are better spent focusing on their main mission.

In reality, collaboration and competition will coexist. The real issue will be striking the right balance between the two. This is already the case today—with a tilt, in our view, toward "competition." We believe that the movement and its specific organizations and initiatives would benefit from more collaboration. It is our view that, on balance, the gains to each will exceed the costs. Of course, each supporting organization must make its own decisions about the nature and degree of collaboration with others. Some degree of competition will always exist—such as for funding, for companies to serve as pilots, and for investor and regulatory support. However, if "co-opetition," a game theory–based theory of strategy, can exist in the profit-driven product markets, it can also exist in the mission-driven sector, even though competition here sometimes makes the product markets look tame.[24]

 ## REGULATORS

In a corporate reporting context, regulators' role is to ensure that investors are getting the high-quality information they need in order to make informed decisions. At a system level, regulators are responsible for ensuring orderly markets. Exactly what these regulations are, the form in which they are issued (such as rules vs. principles-based), and which organization is responsible for making and enforcing them varies by country. In the United States, for example, this is the role of the Securities and Exchange Commission (SEC).[25] All countries with a capital market have an SEC-equivalent and are members of the International Organization of Securities Commissions (IOSCO).[26] In some countries, such as South Africa, the stock exchange has substantial regulatory powers. In others, such as in the United States, it has less.[27] Any regulator that chooses to mandate integrated reporting, whether in a "hard" (you must do this) or "soft" (comply or explain) way, would do so out of a determination that integrated reporting would enable it to more effectively fulfill its legislated mandate. A regulator choosing to do so would have some degree of freedom, perhaps a great deal, to define what integrated reporting means in its jurisdiction.

Getting regulatory support will be difficult in the short term, especially in countries like the United States Consider the remarks made by U.S. SEC Chairman Mary Jo White in October 2013 where she expressed skepticism about whether the benefits of additional disclosure about environmental or social matters (both likely to be discussed as risks or opportunities in an integrated report) outweigh the costs associated with mandating such disclosure.[28] White specifically mentioned rulemaking petitions seeking additional disclosures about environmental matters and companies' equal employment practices, noting that the SEC concluded, "disclosure of such non-material information regarding each of the identified matters would render disclosure documents wholly unmanageable and increase costs without corresponding benefits to investors generally."[29] White also asked whether more disclosure makes it difficult for investors to focus on information that is material and most relevant to their decision-making. White's remarks indicate that the SEC is not convinced about the materiality of environmental and social issues that might be addressed in an integrated report and is likely to view integrated reporting with skepticism if it is seen as just arguing for more disclosure. The real crux of the matter here is "materiality," the subject of the next chapter.

While unlikely, a regulator could mandate integrated reporting and use the <IR> Framework as the basis of its regulation, including whatever monitoring and enforcement it deems necessary. Since every regulator exists in a web of previously established reporting requirements and guidelines, it would be hesitant to replace them, or even part of them, with integrated reporting because of the sheer cost burden this would place on the corporate community. Simply making integrated reporting an additional requirement would also add costs and potentially create confusion about how it exists with current required reports—contextual pitfalls of which the IIRC is well aware. Because listed companies have regulatory filing requirements, it recognizes that companies may face legal prohibitions to disclosing certain information.[30]

Any regulator supportive of integrated reporting would most likely incorporate its broad principles, even if not the term itself, into existing reporting regulations. Whether or not it drew from aspects of the <IR> Framework, if the regulator used the term, it would then be putting its own "meaning stamp" on integrated reporting. Such is the power of the State. Views will differ on the consequences of the State exercising it. For example, in the admittedly far-fetched scenario that the SEC were to issue a new regulation for an amended "Integrated Form 10-K" by stating that companies should use Sustainability Accounting Standards Board's (SASB) standards for guidance on materiality for nonfinancial information, some would see it as a major accelerator of the movement because the SEC does not lightly decide lightly to issue new reporting regulations. Others would consider it as a step backward for the movement—a misappropriation of the term that muddles its meaning in perhaps damaging ways. Another likely concern is that integrated reporting in the United States would become a compliance exercise and achieve none of the benefits of integrated thinking.

Whatever one's view, this scenario raises an interesting dilemma for the movement in terms of the costs and benefits of regulatory support. Those seeking regulatory backing must accept the fact that, in doing so, the regulator will impose its own meaning on "integrated reporting." Should this happen in many countries, it is likely that there would be many meanings, just as there were many country Generally Accepted Accounting Principles (GAAP) not so long ago.[31] How similar or different these meanings turn out to be would be a function of when these regulations took effect and how widespread adoption already was by companies. If many companies in many countries were already practicing integrated reporting, more or less according to the <IR> Framework, these country-based meanings would be more similar than if regulation occurred before substantial adoption had already taken place.

This is a moot point today. Outside of South Africa, no legislation or regulation in any country mandates integrated reporting—even on a "comply or explain" basis. While the supporting organizations discussed above are, to varying degrees, seeking government support for what they are doing (some of this in the public domain and some not), acquiring overt support from the State is difficult and takes time and resources. It also inevitably involves lobbying, as the mere existence of an initiative guarantees the existence of those who oppose it. Because the impact of regulation is pervasive in that all companies must comply, the State is typically cautious in its decisions as it attempts to balance conflicting demands when issuing new regulations. The effectiveness with which companies comply is a function of the quality of the regulation, along with how effectively it is monitored and enforced.[32]

 ## SERVICE PROVIDERS

Helping companies prepare and publish their integrated report, profit-driven service providers include accounting firms and others who provide assurance on sustainability reports, consulting firms who help companies prepare and publish integrated reports (including the advisory practices of accounting firms, boutique sustainability consulting firms, and public relations firms), and information technology vendors who provide software and services that are useful in producing an integrated report. Service providers vary in terms of whether they are "meaning makers" or "meaning takers." "Meaning makers" seek to influence the definition of integrated reporting and an integrated report, and how each should be accomplished. "Meaning takers" seek to understand the existing consensus on meaning so that they can design and deliver products and services

The Big Four accounting firms, along with boutique consulting firms deeply involved in the movement, tend to be "meaning makers." As experts on the topic of corporate reporting, they feel compelled to offer their own point of view on integrated reporting through white papers, webinars, and conferences. In doing so, they consciously or unconsciously shape the meaning of the concept. In contrast, IT firms tend to be "meaning takers." Their business models are based on designing software and services to help companies accomplish a task. In the reporting world, these tasks are typically defined by regulation and these firms provide products and services to ensure that their customers are in compliance with them, a mentality most IT firms apply to integrated reporting. As its meaning becomes clearer—and the more detailed and prescriptive the better—the better able they are to design the requisite software and services.

All of these service providers see an economic opportunity in integrated reporting. Whether larger assurance fees for an integrated audit, consulting fees, or sales of software and services, we do not denigrate this motive. It remains an incentive that can help create a market for integrated reporting. In order to create and grow this market opportunity, service providers must develop a deep understanding of integrated reporting, first selling the merits of the concept to their clients before they can "make the pitch" on how they can be helpful. In their product development and marketing efforts, these organizations can learn things that are useful to supporting organizations and initiatives, and even regulators, such as through benchmarking and identifying "best practices." That said, most service providers are "market followers" rather than "market leaders" in that they wait for other forces (typically a combination of client demand and regulation) to develop the market for them to serve.

It is unlikely that service providers will see integrated reporting as simply a revenue-generating opportunity without any real degree of conviction in its merits. These service providers must make their own resource allocation decisions about which new markets to create and pursue. Because there is hardly a market for integrated reporting today beyond South Africa, investments here must be considered risky ones with a long-term payoff. Unless a service provider "believes" in integrated reporting—although not to the extent of economic irrationality—it is not going to make these investments. These investments can be substantial, ranging from cash and soft dollar support to supporting organizations and initiatives (e.g., secondments, office space, and hosting meetings and conferences) to cash and soft dollar investments made for product and service development. In taking on this risk, the service provider also incurs the opportunity cost from not investing these resources in other opportunities. More intangible investments include putting the service provider's brand behind the concept.

Service providers may also see the costs in producing their own integrated report as an investment. By showcasing their integrated report, they signal that it can be done, demonstrate their belief in the concept, and establish a "moral high ground" for recommending it to their clients along with how they can help them implement it. Suggestive of this, the large software firm SAP published its first integrated report in 2012. In its second integrated report, one of its prominent features revised its approach to materiality.[33] We now turn our attention to this fundamental but elusive concept.

 ## NOTES

1. Ernst & Young and GreenBiz Group. "2013 six growing trends in sustainability reporting," http://www.ey.com/Publication/vwLUAssets/Six_growing_trends_in_corporate_sustainability_2013/$FILE/Six_growing_trends_in_corporate_sustainability_2013.pdf, accessed February 2014. The report is also available from GreenBiz Group, http://www.greenbiz.com/research/report/2013/05/26/six-growing-trends-corporate-sustainability, accessed February 2014.
2. The GreenBiz Group "provides clear, concise, accurate, and balanced information, resources, and learning opportunities to help companies of all sizes and sectors integrate environmental responsibility into their operations in a manner that supports profitable business practices." GreenBiz Group. About Us, http://www.greenbizgroup.com, accessed March 2014.
3. Ernst & Young and GreenBiz Group, "2013 six growing trends in sustainability reporting," p. 30.
4. Black Sun Plc is a London-based consultancy focused on helping clients integrate their corporate reporting, sustainability, and digital communications. http://www.blacksunplc.com/corporate/, accessed March 2014.
5. Black Sun conducted the research in association with the International Integrated Reporting Council (IIRC). They emailed all Pilot Programme

participants a detailed baseline survey that was administered online. In total, 44 individuals from 43 companies completed the questionnaire, which comprised 44 questions. The research took place between June and August 2012. Black Sun interviewed 19 of these organizations by telephone. These 19 organizations provided detailed examples of what they were doing. Survey participants included 21 listed companies, 11 private companies, 6 public sector organizations, and 7 other organizations, including a development bank and a member-owned credit union. Black Sun Plc. "Understanding Transformation: Building the Business Case for Integrated Reporting," http://www .blacksunplc.com/corporate/iirc_understanding_transformation/projet/ BUILDING-THE-BUSINESS-CASE-FOR-INTEGRATED-REPORTING.pdf, accessed February 2014.

6. Over 50% of public company respondents to a 2013 survey conducted by the Boston College Center for Corporate Citizenship and Ernst & Young LLP cited lack of resources as a reason why they had not yet prepared an integrated report. The survey covered ESG reporting, including costs and benefits and making connections to financial performance, a core concept of integrated reporting. "Value of sustainability reporting," http://www.ey.com/US/en/ Services/Specialty-Services/Climate-Change-and-Sustainability-Services/Value-of-sustainability-reporting, accessed March 2014.

7. Over 60% of respondents to the 2013 Boston College and Ernst & Young survey cited both availability of data and accuracy and completeness of data as obstacles to reporting. Ibid., p. 15.

8. A word search of "2012 YEAR-END SECURITIES LITIGATION UPDATE" by Gibson Dunn, January 2013, shows not a single mention of the words or phrases corporate social responsibility, sustainability, voluntary disclosure, nonfinancial, or risk factors. However, there is substantial mention of "material" and "materiality," the focus of Chapter 5. Lending support to the fact that there is very little legal risk in voluntary disclosures for sustainability or integrated reporting, "SEC Enforcement Data Analyses" of SEC cases filed in 2013, Morvillo Abramowitz notes that in 2014 the SEC's "Enforcement's Financial Reporting and Audit Task Force will focus on violations relating to the preparation of financial statements, issuer reporting and disclosure, and audit failures." Morvillo Abramowitz Grand Iason & Anello PC, "SEC Enforcement Data Analyses," Analyses of cases filed by the SEC in calendar year 2013, Q1 2014, 5. This too suggests that the focus is reporting done by companies under existing regulations.

9. Ernst & Young and GreenBiz Group, "2013 six growing trends in sustainability reporting," p. 31.

10. Black Sun Plc, Understanding Transformation, p. 20.

11. Ernst & Young. "Tomorrow's investment rules: Global survey of institutional investors on non-financial performance," http://www.ey.com/Publication/

vwLUAssets/EY-Institutional-Investor-Survey/$FILE/EY-Institutional-Investor-Survey.pdf, accessed April 2014. The Custom Research Group of *Institutional Investor* magazine (http://www.institutionalinvestor.com/Institutional-Investor-Magazine.html?StubID=10334) retained E&Y to examine investors' views on using nonfinancial information in investment decision-making. Using a jointly designed questionnaire, E&Y gathered 163 responses from senior investment decision makers around the world through an online survey in September 2013. Follow-up interviews were conducted with investors who completed the survey. Survey respondents represent large financial institutions such as third-party investment managers, banks, pension funds, foundations, endowments, sovereign wealth funds, insurance companies, and family offices. Fifty-nine percent of respondents work for institutions with more than $10 billion in assets under management. Approximately 72% of the investors were domiciled in the United States, Canada, and Latin America. Eleven percent were based in Europe or the United Kingdom and the remainder were in the Middle East, Africa, or Asia-Pacific.

12. Ibid., p. 11
13. Ibid., p. 17.
14. SustainAbility was founded by John Elkington and Julia Hailes in 1987, the same year that the Brundtland Commission published *Our Common Future.* SustainAbility describes itself as a "think tank and strategy consultancy working to inspire transformative business leadership on the sustainability agenda." http://production.sustainabilitylt.netdna-cdn.com/content/ftpfiles/safactsheet/1/sustainability_factsheet.pdf, accessed April 2014.
15. SustainAbility. *Rate the Raters Phase 5, The Investor View,* http://www.sustainability.com/projects/rate-the-raters#projtab-9, accessed April 2014. SustainAbility partnered with Bloomberg to survey over 1000 investment professionals, of which almost 50% were research analysts or portfolio managers. About half of these professionals had over 11 years' experience and 74% covered equities. The survey had global coverage, including 33% from the U.S., 8% U.K., 6% India, 4% Brazil, 3% China, and 3% Germany.
16. Some investors track selected environmental data for use as a proxy for production efficiency and cost control. See Eccles, Robert G. and Michael P. Krzus. "Novo Nordisk: A Commitment to Sustainability." Harvard Business School Case 412-053, p. 10.
17. "Long-term investors, who are interested in relevant, credible, and timely information for assessing the long-term prospects of the firm, could be more likely to hold shares of firms that practice IR. These firms presumably provide information that is value relevant in the long-term, decreasing information asymmetry between interested investors and corporate managers thereby decreasing financing frictions and monitoring costs. Thereby, all else equal, I expect long-term investors will be attracted to firms that practice IR."

Serafeim, George. "Integrated Reporting and Investor Clientele." Harvard Business School Working Paper, No. 14-069, February 2014. p. 13.

18. We should qualify this statement by noting that most sell-side analysts are notoriously short-term oriented, focusing heavily on quarterly earnings estimates largely within a one-year time frame.

19. Eccles, Robert G., Kathleen Miller Perkins, and George Serafeim. "How to Become a Sustainable Company," *MIT Sloan Management Review* 54 No. 4 (2012): 48.

20. George Roberts, a private equity financier and co-founder of KKR in 1976 with Henry Kravis and Jerome Kohlberg, has declared that integrating environmental, social, and governance (ESG) factors into private equity is both "good business and the right thing to do" and suggested that in doing so private equity houses should swallow short-term costs in favor of long-term value. Speaking at a conference in New York organized jointly by the United Nations-backed Principles for Responsible Investment and Private Equity International, Roberts said KKR wanted to be: "Skating towards where the puck is going, not where it has been." He said this meant "shared value" between investors and stakeholders, alluding to an article published in the *Harvard Business Review* at the beginning of 2011 by professors Michael Porter and Mark Kramer, which argues for creating economic value in a way that also creates value for society. At the end of 2010, KKR published its first ESG report titled: "Creating Sustainable Value." The report said that its Green Portfolio Program, established in partnership with the Environmental Defense Fund, covers 16 of its portfolio companies and had identified $160m in cost savings and 345,000 metric tons of CO_2 avoided at eight of those. Roberts said that before embarking on the program he was worried: "I said that if we are going to do this then it has to work and that we needed metrics and proper auditing." He said that since its introduction the program had become a "bottom-line business issue." Wheelan, Hugh. "Long-term value should outweigh short-term cost says KKR founder." Responsible Investor, June 6, 2011. The next phase of the Green Portfolio initiative resulted in a KKR collaboration with Business for Social Responsibility (BSR). KKR and BSR developed a framework for analyzing supply chain risk. The framework outlined six risk categories, including: executive commitment, quality of program in-place (e.g., codes and standards), quality of implementation, geography, types of products, and industry. Eccles, Robert G., George Serafeim, and Tiffany A. Clay. "KKR: Leveraging Sustainability." Harvard Business School Case 112-032, September 2011. (Revised March 2012.)

21. Principles for Responsible Investment and PricewaterhouseCoopers. "The Integration of Environmental, Social and Governance Issues in Mergers and Acquisitions Transactions," January 2013, http://www.pwc.com/gx/en/sustainability/publications/esg-impacts-private-equity.jhtml, accessed March 2014. Universities Superannuation Scheme. "Responsible Investment Private

Equity toolkit," May 2010, http://www.uss.co.uk/Documents/USS%20PE%20internal%20guidance%202010.pdf, accessed March 2014. KKR. "Creating Sustainable Value, Progress Through Partnership," 2012 ESG and Citizenship Report, http://www.kkr.com/_files/pdf/KKR_ESG-Report_2012.pdf, accessed March 2014.

22. "NGO strategies have become much more sophisticated. Recent years have seen NGOs use a broad range of interventions, including: the production of investment analysis in support of campaign issues; direct attempts to move capital into certain investment projects and out of others; ongoing programmes of communication with investors in relation to specific issues of corporate social responsibility (CSR); public policy advocacy on rules that govern the capital markets; and, in some cases, formal programmes of collaboration between investors and NGOs." Waygood, Steve. *Capital Market Campaigning*. London: Haymarket House, 2006, p. 3.

23. Because the capital markets play a central role in today's global economies, legislators and regulators must address the question of how to assure effective functioning of these markets and how to develop a sound financial reporting infrastructure. Experience suggests that these reporting infrastructures should be built on consistent and comprehensive accounting standards that enable financial reports to reflect underlying economic reality. Rezaee, Zabihollah, Murphy L. Smith and Joseph Z. Szendi "Convergence in Accounting Standards: Insights from Academicians and Practitioners." *Advances in Accounting*, Vol. 26, No. 1, pp. 142–154, 2010, http://papers.ssrn.com/sol3/papers.cfm?abstract_id=1703584, accessed April 2014. Herz, Robert H and Kimberly R. Petrone "International Convergence of Accounting Standards-Perspectives from the FASB on Challenges and Opportunities." *Northwestern Journal of International Law & Business*, Volume 25 Issue 3 Spring, 2005, http://scholarlycommons.law.northwestern.edu/njilb/vol25/iss3/27/, accessed April 2014. PricewaterhouseCoopers. "Convergence of IFRS and US GAAP." *ViewPoint*, April 07, http://www.pwc.com/gx/en/ifrs-reporting-services/pdf/viewpoint_convergence.pdf, accessed April 2014. Tweedie, David and Thomas R, Seidenstein "Setting a Global Standard: The Case for Accounting Convergence." *Northwestern Journal of International Law & Business*, Volume 25, Issue 3, Spring 2005, http://scholarlycommons.law.northwestern.edu/njilb/vol25/iss3/25/, accessed April 2014.

24. Adam M. Brandenburger, a professor at New York University's Stern School of Business, and Barry J. Nalebuff, a professor the Yale School of Management, are credited with developing the principles and practices co-opetition. See Brandenburger, Adam M. and Barry J. Nalebuff. *Co-opetition*. New York: Doubleday, 1996. "Co-opetition is a business strategy that uses insights gained from game theory to understand when it is better for competitors to work together.

Co-opetition games are mathematical models that are used to examine in what ways cooperation among competitors can increase the benefits to all players and grow the market. The models also examine when it's best to allow competition to divide the existing benefits among players in order to provide the leading competitors with more market share. The co-opetition model starts out with a diagramming process called the value net, which is represented as a diamond with four defined player designations at the corners. The players are customers, suppliers, competitors and complementors (competitors whose products add value). The goal of co-opetition is to move the players from a zero-sum game, in which the winner takes all and the loser is left empty-handed, to a plus-sum game, a scenario in which the end result is more profitable when the competitors work together. An important part of the game is to learn which variables will influence the players to either compete or cooperate and when it is to a player's advantage not to cooperate." Search CIO. http://searchcio.techtarget.com/definition/co-opetition, accessed April 2014.

25. The U.S. Securities and Exchange Commission (SEC) views itself as an advocate for investors. This is reflected in its simple yet powerful mission statement. "The mission of the U.S. Securities and Exchange Commission is to protect investors, maintain fair, orderly, and efficient markets, and facilitate capital formation." The SEC's description of what it does goes on to say, "The laws and rules that govern the securities industry in the United States derive from a simple and straightforward concept: all investors, whether large institutions or private individuals, should have access to certain basic facts about an investment prior to buying it, and so long as they hold it. To achieve this, the SEC requires public companies to disclose meaningful financial and other information to the public. This provides a common pool of knowledge for all investors to use to judge for themselves whether to buy, sell, or hold a particular security. Only through the steady flow of timely, comprehensive, and accurate information can people make sound investment decisions." U.S. Securities and Exchange Commission, About the SEC, http://www.sec.gov/about/whatwedo.shtml#.U1E5Y16kJfM, accessed April 2014.

26. "The International Organization of Securities Commissions (IOSCO), established in 1983, is the acknowledged international body that brings together the world's securities regulators and is recognized as the global standard setter for the securities sector. IOSCO develops, implements, and promotes adherence to internationally recognized standards for securities regulation, and is working intensively with the G20 and the Financial Stability Board (FSB) on the global regulatory reform agenda. IOSCO's membership regulates more than 95% of the world's securities markets. Its members include over 120 securities regulators and 80 other securities markets participants (i.e. stock exchanges, financial regional and international organizations etc.). IOSCO is the only international financial regulatory organization which includes all the major

emerging markets jurisdictions within its membership." The objectives of IOSCO are similar to the mission of the U.S. SEC; ". . . to cooperate in developing, implementing and promoting adherence to internationally recognised and consistent standards of regulation, oversight and enforcement in order to protect investors, maintain fair, efficient and transparent markets, and seek to address systemic risks; to enhance investor protection and promote investor confidence in the integrity of securities markets, through strengthened information exchange and cooperation in enforcement against misconduct and in supervision of markets and market intermediaries; and to exchange information at both global and regional levels on their respective experiences in order to assist the development of markets, strengthen market infrastructure and implement appropriate regulation." IOSCO. About IOSCO, http://www.iosco.org/about/, accessed April 2014.

27. Lütz, Susanne. "The revival of the nation-state? Stock exchange regulation in an era of globalized financial markets." *Journal of European Public Policy* 5.1 (1998): 153–168. While this article focuses primarily on German stock exchanges, it provides a comparative perspective for other stock exchanges on pages 10–13.

28. White, Mary Jo. "The Importance of Independence." 14th Annual A.A. Sommer, Jr. Corporate Securities and Financial Law Lecture, Fordham Law School, October 3, 2013. U.S. Securities and Exchange Commission. Speeches, Chairman, http://www.sec.gov/News/Speech/Detail/Speech/1370539864016# .U1FAFl6kJfM, accessed April 2014.

29. Ibid., p. 7.

30. Other valid reasons for not disclosing a piece of information are that it is not sufficiently reliable or that it may cause competitive harm. In these cases, the IIRC recommends that the company indicate the nature of the information that has been omitted and why. When the reason is unavailability of data, the company should explain what it is doing to correct this situation and how long it will take. "The International <IR> Framework" p. 8, http://www.theiirc .org/international-ir-framework/, accessed March 2014.

31. The Deloitte IAS*Plus* website summarizes on a country basis the use of International Financial Reporting Standards as the primary GAAP by domestic listed and unlisted companies in their consolidated financial statements for external financial reporting. http://www.iasplus.com/en/resources/ifrs-topics/ use-of-ifrs, accessed March 2014.

32. "Regulation is extremely important for an effective information function in the same way that regulation is necessary to establish accounting standards. Regulation could be less important for the transformation function and, some would argue, can actually inhibit it. The high-level, principles-based framework of the IIRC enables companies to determine the most material issues through stakeholder engagement and then to continue the engagement

process. If regulation is more prescriptive and 'rules-based,' the risk is that integrated reporting becomes more of a compliance exercise." Eccles, Robert G. and George Serafeim. "Corporate and Integrated Reporting: A Functional Perspective," Social Science Research Network, 2014, http://papers.ssrn.com/sol3/papers.cfm?abstract_id=2388716, accessed March 2014.

33. SAP. Integrated Report 2013, About This Integrate Report, Materiality, http://www.sapintegratedreport.com/2013/en/nc/about-this-integrated-report/materiality.html?sword_list%5B0%5D=materiality, accessed May 2013.

CHAPTER FIVE

Materiality

ATERIALITY FORMS THE CONCEPTUAL bedrock of corporate reporting, yet no authoritative definition of it exists. In "Securities Regulation,"[1] Louis Loss points out that the legal field offers no specific definition of the word. Court opinions on materiality have merely sketched its conceptual contours. Every time materiality has been relevant to a legal case in the United States, the court has opined that it must be decided on a case-by-case basis.[2] The U.S. Supreme Court has also asserted that this determination must be based on both qualitative and quantitative factors based on the "total mix" of information made available.[3] Further complicating the "total mix" standard set by the Supreme Court for evaluating potentially material omissions or misstatements, the Court left open the issue of "circularity" in its definition of materiality.[4] Finally, the courts have also made clear that materiality must be determined with complete clarity. These opinions do not discuss "degrees" of materiality; materiality is binary. A fact is either material, in which case it should be reported, or is not material, in which case it does not need to be reported.

These "delicate assessments" are to be made by the corporation itself. Since investors have no voice in a company's materiality determination process other than through lawsuits (which lead to further guidance instead of specific answers), it is management's, and ultimately the board's, responsibility to ascertain what information its "reasonable investors" would want to know. In the end, materiality is determined by the corporation itself and it is entity-specific.[5] While there may be no easy *rule* to follow in determining materiality, how companies go about making the ultimate decision of which externalities and issues are included in an integrated report should be a clearly defined *process* with solid lines of responsibility. The company's board of directors has the ultimate responsibility for putting in place a process that will enable it to make the final determination of what the company deems is material. In doing so, it establishes the legitimacy of the corporation's role in society.

In this chapter, we will not attempt to offer a precise definition of materiality. As accountant and historian Carla Edgley[6] has shown, such crystallization of meaning is neither historically probable nor necessary for the term to accomplish what it should.[7] There is also evidence that cultural context influences the meaning of materiality.[8] Rather than pin the idea down, this chapter seeks to widen our understanding of *what* materiality is by reviewing how it has been treated in the worlds of financial and nonfinancial reporting. In scrutinizing the assumptions and historical precedents upon which the notion of materiality is based, we will show *how* integrated reporting materiality should be determined by focusing on *who* should define materiality and for *whom* it is determined.

THE SOCIAL CONSTRUCTION OF MATERIALITY

Although materiality forms the conceptual bedrock of corporate reporting, it is ultimately a social construct. In *The Construction of Social Reality*, philosopher John Searle observes that society's institutional structures share a special feature of social construction: symbolism.[9] The United Nations, Harvard University, the New York Stock Exchange, Rolex, the Red Cross, and Apple, for example, signify something beyond the sum of their parts. Their symbolic value is similar to brand power in that the mere mention of these institutions conjures expectations beyond what can be explained by their present "assets" and activities. As Apple is not the only company that makes innovative, imaginative products with attractive design, its products alone cannot explain the company's public monopoly on that combination of attributes or the fact that *Forbes* ranked it the world's most valuable brand in 2013.[10] The fragmented body that is society projects meaning onto these institutions. Because societal agents like judges, commissioners, legislators, trustees, and board members consciously and intentionally foster this symbolism by reinforc-ing the reputation of these institutions, it can be said that these institutions are *socially constructed*: they exist only to the degree that meaning is shared between a given institution and its audience. Thus, meaning can exist without definition and, conversely, definition does not confer meaning.

Consider fraud. Fraud is analogous to materiality in its treatment by the courts. Like fraud, materiality does not lack for meaning in that people generally have a sense of what qualifies, but it has notoriously evaded definition for practical reasons. Loss wrote, "The courts have traditionally refused, whether at common-law deceit, or under securities laws, to define fraud with specificity."[11] Similarly, materiality is grounded in law that speci-fies that its meaning must be defined in practice by the particular circum-stances of the company. In this spirit, the accountant William Holmes encouraged us to "continue to discuss, dispute, dissect, deplore, and generally 'look before and after and pine for what is not' in this matter of materiality," concluding that the solution is to "widen our understanding and narrow our judgments—short of official standards."[12] We take this to mean that rather than looking for an ultimate definition, we should instead focus on how to exercise judgment to determine what is material on a case-by-case basis.

Because materiality is a firm-specific social construct, it poses certain challenges for the integrated reporting movement. Since every board and management team protects a unique brand, what the corporation symbolizes for society is unique to each firm. The judgment of which limited matters are, in the language of the International Integrated Reporting Council (IIRC), "relevant and important,"[13] is also firm-specific. As each firm can define its own materiality threshold within the boundaries of accepted and evolving standards, our understanding of materiality must encompass all integrated reporting firms. In "Westphalian"[14] terms, materiality for the firm becomes materiality for its audience.

Regardless of whether or not its wishes are heeded, the involvement of an "audience" begs the question of *to whom* the firm is reporting. Recalling Searle, a social construct like materiality is a form of human agreement that involves the capacity of an institution, or more specifically its agents, to symbolize it. In the context of materiality for integrated reporting, one must ask, "*Whom* do the institution's agents address when they determine *which* issues are material, and which issues are *not?*"

Although providers of financial capital form the "direct audience"[15]—that is, the "users"—of an integrated report, the "indirect audience" of stakeholders also exerts pressure on the firm's selection of material issues. Firms are driven to engage with stakeholders because stakeholders wield varying degrees of influence on the providers of capital, and the implications of that influence are often too great to ignore. Consequently, when the firm decides what information is material, it must, for its own good, take into account the perspectives of stakeholders beyond those who provide financial capital.[16] Furthermore, as Berle and Means[17] have argued, society has granted corporations special privileges not given to individual persons, which suggests these same corporations have a moral, if not a civic, duty to think beyond profits to consider the good of society. Logically, corporations would then be morally obliged to not only "perform" in such a way, but to report back to society "material actions" beyond the profit-driven.

This does not mean, however, that issues that are "material" to stakeholders will be material to the firm. In the end, the corporation as represented by its board of directors will determine what is material for reporting purposes. In doing so, it chooses which stakeholders to address, how to obtain their input, and the relative weightings to assign to issues and audience members. The next chapter explores this in more detail in terms of the concept of a "Materiality Matrix" or, for reasons we will explain, what we prefer to call the "Sustainable Value Matrix." Here we will briefly use the case of environmental reporting to introduce a more general discussion about how materiality has been treated in the worlds of financial and nonfinancial reporting, compare the two, and then give our view of this concept's relevance for integrated reporting.

 ## MATERIALITY IN ENVIRONMENTAL REPORTING

Even in the context of financial reporting, information is not required to be a financial metric or even quantitative to qualify as material. To a limited extent, regulators have attempted to provide some guidance for reporting on "non-financial" environmental, social, and governance (ESG) issues, most recently on climate change or environmental issues more generally. In doing so, they illustrate the perils of regulatory intervention. Time will tell how regulators in European Union countries implement the legislation discussed in Chapter 3 and how central the concept of materiality will be in their efforts to do so.[18]

In January 2010, the Securities and Exchange Commision approved *Commission Guidance Regarding Disclosure Related to Climate Change* [19] regarding climate disclosures that might impact a company's operations. In its release, the Commission did not issue any new regulations. It simply stated, "This interpretive release is intended to remind companies of their obligations under existing federal securities laws and regulations to consider climate change and its consequences as they prepare disclosure documents to be filed with us and provided to investors."[20] While noting that companies could voluntarily disclose climate-related issues in a sustainability report, the Commission also remarked, "Securities Act Rule 408 and Exchange Act Rule 12b-20 require a registrant to disclose, in addition to the information expressly required by Commission regulation, 'such further material information, if any, as may be necessary to make the required statements, in light of the circumstances under which they are made, not misleading.'"[21] According to Ceres,[22] this guidance has not been aggressively implemented by corporations or enforced by the SEC.[23]

In its release, the Commission is clearly using the same "rational investor"[24] definition of materiality for climate change issues as for financial information when it reviews "the most pertinent non-financial statement disclosure rules": description of business (Item 101 of Regulation S-K), legal proceedings (Item 103 of Regulation S-K), risk factors (Item 503 (c) of Regulation S-K), and management's discussion and analysis (Item 303 of Regulation S-K). The release then interpreted these general rules for disclosures related to climate change by discussing "some of the ways climate change may trigger disclosure by these rules and regulations." Furthermore, the impact of legislation and regulation, international accords, indirect consequences of regulation or business trends, and physical impacts of climate change are given as examples.[25]

The mostly negative reaction from the corporate community was very strong. A *Forbes* op-ed piece scathingly denigrated the SEC move as "an effort to remain relevant after Madoff," forecasting that "while there are no completely new disclosure requirements here, the 'interpretation' could impose a world of hurt and uncertainty on firms without benefiting (and likely even hurting) investors."[26] As of 2013, an estimated 73% of publicly traded companies were still not providing disclosures on climate change.[27] Given that materiality is an entity-specific concept, it is impossible to know what percent regarded climate change as a material issue but chose to ignore the SEC's guidance and what percent simply did not see this as material to their business.

COMPARING DIFFERENT DEFINITIONS OF MATERIALITY

Materiality's centrality in disclosure means that any organization whose mission concerns disclosures by companies *must address how it defines the term*. Five organizations—AccountAbility, CDP, Global Reporting Initiative (GRI), the

IIRC, and the Sustainability Accounting Standards Board (SASB)—are particularly important in framing the concept for integrated reporting. In contrast to regulators and accounting standard setters, these organizations are heavily, if not exclusively, focused on nonfinancial reporting. None has official support from the State in any country. Their definitions of materiality vary in terms of: (1) the audience targeted by the organization (shareholders vs. other stakeholders), (2) whether the determination of materiality depends on some degree of engagement with the audience, (3) whether other information is considered as relevant context, and (4) the organizational boundary of the disclosed information. Thus, the degree of difference between these organizations' definitions of materiality and those of regulatory bodies like the SEC (or regulatory-sanctioned bodies like the International Accounting Standards Board (IASB)) varies as well.

Showing wide variance, Table 5.1 summarizes the characteristics of the different definitions of materiality for these five organizations and the definition typical of regulatory bodies. CDP and SASB bear the closest resemblance to the regulatory definition. CDP hews closely to that of the IASB. SASB takes its definition directly from the SEC and U.S. case law, and thus is the only one of the five to imply the "total mix" of information.[28] For both, the reporting boundary is the company (SASB is focused only on companies, but CDP has a broader range of reporting entities which it does not explicitly reconcile with a definition of materiality created for public companies), the primary intended users are investors, and engagement is not part of the materiality determination process. However, this does not map seamlessly onto the regulatory definition. Both CDP and SASB see the act of reporting as a way to create positive social impact and improve a company's performance, emphasizing the importance of the long-term. None of these concerns are addressed in the regulatory definition.

Followed by AccountAbility's, GRI's definition of materiality is the furthest from the regulatory one. The latter does not match exactly with the regulatory definition on a single one of the eight characteristics. AccountAbility only matches on two: companies are the only preparing entity of interest and the company is the reporting boundary. The IIRC's definition is about halfway between the regulatory one and that of AccountAbility and GRI, falling somewhere between these definitions and those of CDP and SASB, as it is only focused on companies as a preparing entity but recognizes a larger boundary than the company itself. Although the primary users for the IIRC are providers of financial capital, the IIRC does not ground its definition in regulation, as do CDP and SASB. It also recognizes that other stakeholders

TABLE 5.1 Comparison of Materiality Definitions

	Regulatory Bodies (e.g., SEC, IASB)	AccountAbility	CDP	Global Reporting Initiative	International Integrated Reporting Council	Sustainability Accounting Standards Board
Preparing Entity	Public company	Company	Companies, supply chains, and cities	Companies, educational institutions, nonprofits, cities, government agencies	Companies	Primarily companies listed in the U.S.
Primary Unit of Analysis for Materiality Determination	Entity	Entity	Entity	Entity	Entity	Sector (industry)
Reporting Boundary	Company	Company	Company	Can be broader than the company	Can be broader than the company	Company
"Total Mix" Part of Determination	Yes	No	No	No	No	Implied
Intended User	"Reasonable Investor"	Shareholders and other stakeholders	Primarily shareholders	Primarily stakeholders but also shareholders		"Reasonable investor"
Covered by Regulation	Yes	No	No	No	No	Yes
Time Frame Specified	No	Yes (emphasis on long term)	Yes (emphasis on long term)	Yes (emphasis on long term)	Yes (short, medium, and long term)	Yes (emphasis on long term)
Engagement in Materiality Determination Process	No	Yes	No	Yes	Yes	No
Intended Social Impact	No	Yes	Yes	Yes	Indirectly yes	Indirectly yes
Company Intended to Benefit from Improved Performance	No	Yes	Yes	Yes	Yes	Yes

can find an integrated report useful—most likely those who want a holistic view of the company's performance and prospects. Also, unlike the regulatory definition, the IIRC regards engagement as part of the materiality determination process. Like all other voluntary standard setters, it sees reporting as a way of improving company performance, having a positive impact on society, and encouraging a longer-term perspective on the part of the company.

Much like the "Conceptual Frameworks" published by Financial Accounting Standards Board (FASB) and the IASB that establish the basic principles and elements of financial reporting,[29] the IIRC's International <IR> Framework (<IR> Framework) establishes the essential architecture for an integrated report. The standards and definition of materiality for the financial information in the report will come from IASB, U.S. Generally Accepted Accounting Principles (GAAP), or a local country GAAP. Because SASB, like the IIRC, is focused on investors, its definition of materiality is closer to their needs than that of stakeholders. However, because its definition is so grounded in a U.S. context and anticipates stakeholder engagement by sector and industry rather than by company, an integrated report may contain information on non-financial performance that goes beyond SASB's standards. If a "reasonable investor" does not see a particular stakeholder's issue as relevant it would not clear the materiality hurdle by the SEC's, and hence SASB's, definition. But if, in the company's judgment, the issue important to this stakeholder can affect its ability to create value for shareholders over the long term, the company's performance on this issue should be included in its integrated report. GRI's G4 Guidelines will be useful here. The IIRC and GRI are also more entity-specific than SASB, which is broken down by sector and then industry. CDP can be seen as a "subject matter expert" on certain environmental issues. Some of the standards contained in the Climate Change Reporting Framework can be included in SASB's standards[30] and the G4 Guidelines.[31]

AccountAbility's role is to provide guidance on the materiality determination process itself. Its focus is neither a general framework, like the IIRC, nor making recommendations on specific items to be reported, like CDP, GRI, and SASB. Companies interested in starting the journey towards integrated reporting should start with the <IR> Framework, using the SASB standards relevant to their industry, and the Climate Change Reporting Framework if environmental issues are material to them. They can then expand the reporting boundary as they see necessary and, through a process of engagement and the G4 Guidelines, provide whatever additional information on nonfinancial performance is appropriate. Because this will likely still leave a great deal of information of interest to stakeholders out of the integrated report, this information should be made available in other ways, such as in an online sustainability report.

AUDIENCE

As discussed in Chapter 2, the direct audience for, or "user" of, an integrated report is the "providers of financial capital." We also noted that while this typically signals providers of equity capital—investors—it should also include other types, like bondholders. In keeping with Holmes's call for a broad understanding of materiality, the <IR> Framework states in its section on "Materiality," "An integrated report should disclose information about matters that substantively affect the organization's ability to create value over the short, medium, and long term."[32] In doing so, it implies a definition of materiality rather than explicitly stating one. Also in keeping with Holmes's call for narrowing judgment, the <IR> Framework goes on to discuss a four-step process to determine what information is material.

1. "Identifying relevant matters based on their value to affect value creation . . . ,
2. Evaluating the importance of relevant matters in terms of their known or potential effect on value creation . . .
3. Prioritizing the matters based on their relative importance . . .
4. Determining the information to disclose about material matters."[33]

Narrowing down a long list to what ultimately passes the materiality threshold for inclusion in the integrated report demands the exercise of judgment to separate the "material" from the "immaterial." The firm's ability to determine what is and is not material through its senior management and those involved in governance[34] symbolizes its social agency. Since a given factor's relevance must be weighted by its importance to the company, "Judgment is applied in determining the information to disclose about material matters."[35] While the firm may undertake an involved stakeholder engagement process, it makes the ultimate decision as to what is material to its strategy. In doing so, it exercises judgment as to what is both important and relevant to the user audience, and of equally symbolic importance, what is *not* relevant or important enough to report.

According to the <IR> Framework, stakeholders are the indirect audience of an integrated report. "An integrated report benefits all stakeholders interested in an organization's ability to create value over time, including employees, customers, suppliers, business partners, local communities, legislators, regulators and policy-makers,"[36] it reads. Although not the direct audience, stakeholders can both influence what a firm determines is material (to the extent that their interests and actions affect providers of financial capital) and be members of the direct audience of report users (to the extent they are interested in a company's ability to create value over time). This is not the same as being interested in what the company is doing about issues that are material to them even if they are not determined to be material by the company.

More generally, it is common today for companies practicing integrated and/or sustainability reporting to distinguish between importance (or materiality) to the company and importance (or materiality) to society. This distinction is sometimes expressed through a "materiality matrix," a social construct whose meaning comes as much from how it is put together as its content. Too often, a misunderstanding about the difference between the entity and society levels of analysis muddles thinking on this subject.

Because we do not view society as an entity *per se*, and because materiality is an entity-specific concept, materiality cannot be defined for society. Society is a reified concept based on the agglomeration of entities that have more or less defined identities, such as NGOs, political organizations, employees, unions, communities, religious and civil society organizations, formal and informal networks, companies, and providers of financial capital. The different constituent parts of society which *are* entities can have their own views of materiality and how to determine it, just as a company can, does, and must. The firm can form its own *view* of what a stakeholder regards as material based on substantial input from that stakeholder or virtually none at all. However, the firm *cannot* determine what is material for the stakeholder any more than a stakeholder can determine what is material for the firm. By the same reasoning, one could also claim that the firm cannot determine what is material to the reasonable investor, to the providers of financial capital, and to the rest of the direct audience. The difference is that the law requires the firm to make this judgment regarding the "reasonable investor," but it does not address whether such a materiality determination is valid from a social construct point of view; firms are simply required to make this materiality determination.

While the fact that neither the firm nor its stakeholders can determine materiality for entities besides themselves seems obvious, the consequences of this distinction are enormous and often overlooked. Any attempt to identify what is material using an approach based on distinctions between what is "material to the company" and "material to society" confounds two very different concepts. The first is indeed materiality. The second is a firm's *perception* of what is important to society. Since society is not an entity with an identity, what the firm has really determined is not what is "material to society." Rather, it is reporting its own *perception* of what it thinks is important to society through a social construct based on an aggregation of its views about what is material to the stakeholders selected by the firm. How these stakeholders are chosen (and ignored), how their views are assessed, and the weightings the firm assigns to them in the aggregation function are part of the social construction process. The data modeling concept of "cardinality" applies here. As a social construct, the firm defines materiality in terms of its "one-to-one" entity relationship between the firm and the "providers of financial capital." Each party in this relationship is a defined entity, more or less. Between the firm and society, there exists a "one-to-many" relationship. "Many" is not an entity.

Because the company's stamp on "importance to society" is as strong as it is on "importance to the company," any stakeholder can argue that the company "did not get it right" in its determination of importance to society and, in doing so, cast doubt on the legitimacy of the company's assessment. This reflects the fundamental misunderstanding described in the previous paragraph. The firm is not—and should not think it is—providing an objective view of materiality from a stakeholder's, let alone society's, perspective. It is socially constructing its own view of what it thinks those stakeholders' views are. Stakeholders should recognize this for what it is, and they can attempt to change the company's perception if they do not agree with it.

In the same way that the firm cannot determine materiality for individual stakeholders, it cannot determine materiality for *other firms*—another indirect audience for an integrated report. In addition to suppliers and customers, other firms include competitors and potential competitors (who want to benchmark their performance against the firm's), potential acquirers (both strategic and financial buyers like private equity firms), and alliance or joint venture partners. While companies often include customers and suppliers in determining "importance to society," they almost never include other companies, thus making them unimportant in a discussion about materiality.

GOVERNANCE

Aside from AccountAbility, the IIRC places more importance on the role of corporate governance in determining materiality than do the other NGOs concerned with corporate reporting. In a background paper for its <IR> Framework, the IIRC stated:

Another unique feature of materiality for <IR> purposes is that the definition emphasizes the involvement of senior management and those charged with governance in the materiality determination process in order for the organization to determine how best to disclose its unique value creation story in a meaningful and transparent way.[37]

In the spirit of "narrowing of judgment," we think it possible to be more specific about the role of the board in determining materiality. In fact, we will argue that the responsibility for making this determination ultimately lies with the board and that, in order to fulfill its fiduciary responsibility, it *must* do so. However, in order to prescribe a more specific role for the board and to outline board tasks in the annual integrated reporting cycle, we must first review its basic, if often mischaracterized, role as an actor in the social construct of materiality.

In one of the most important business books of all time,[38] *The Modern Corporation and Private Property*,[39] Adolf Berle and Gardiner Means identified three broad privileges granted to corporations by the State:

1. The ability to limit liability, or to socialize losses,[40] while privatizing profits, thus attracting risk capital.[41]
2. The ability of corporations to own other corporations, allowing for concentration of control disproportionate to share of risk capital.[42]
3. The separation of ownership rights from control rights, enabling freely tradable shares.[43]

In summary, "The property owner who invests in a modern corporation so far surrenders his wealth to those in control of the corporation that he has exchanged the position of independent owner for one in which he may become merely recipient of the wages of capital . . . [Such owners] have surrendered the right that the corporation should be operated in their sole interest."[44] As noted at the beginning of this chapter, since society has granted corporations these special privileges, corporations have a moral, if not a civic, duty to think not only of profits, but also of the good of society.[45] This underpins the duty of corporations to not just "perform," but also to "report" material actions back to society beyond those that are profit-related.

The duty of a corporation to take society's interest into account in exchange for these special privileges is held, in trust, by the board of directors. Through the corporate privilege of personhood that is granted by society, a corporation arrives at its own legal identity, separate from its shareholders, directors, managers, employees, and stakeholders. As such, it has the capacity to survive many generations. In his book *Firm Commitment*, Professor Colin Mayer of Oxford University noted that the corporation's current decisions will have an impact long after the tenure of its current management and directors has expired, and, that consequently, the board is the appropriate trustee of the firm's intergenerational commitment.[46] This implies that director judgment must be informed by a keen sense of the social context within which the corporation is operating, further informing their oversight of the management team in formulating and implementing the company's strategy. It also implies that the board is responsible for taking a long-term view and ensuring that management is doing so as well to the extent it deems necessary.

In its 2003 version of *Redefining Materiality*, AccountAbility specifically stated in the section titled "Governing Materiality"[47] that each firm's board should define materiality within that firm's own context[48] and not that of its peers. Because the board's fiduciary responsibility is to the corporation itself rather than any particular stakeholder group—even investors[49]—it needs to assess how various stakeholders' interests affect the corporation. Doing so requires understanding the issues that are material to each stakeholder and reflecting on how this shapes what is material for the firm itself. We suggest adding a prior step to the four-step process recommended by the IIRC for determining materiality: "Identify stakeholders relevant to the corporation, their interests (including where they conflict), and the relative weight attached to each."

Our recommended first step is rarely done with any degree of rigor for two reasons. The first is the prevailing ideology that the fiduciary duty of directors requires them to place primacy on shareholders' interests. As we have noted, this is indeed ideology, not law, at least in the very Anglo-Saxon-influenced United States.[50] The second is that corporations and their boards are reluctant to define the relative importance of different members of the audience with great specificity. It is easier to say something general like, "We are committed to delivering excellent returns for our shareholders and we firmly believe that addressing stakeholders' interests further enables us to do so." While this sounds "nice" and is consistent with the emerging rhetoric in support of the "business case for sustainability," it ignores the fact that trade-offs often exist, particularly in the short term.[51] Since corporations often complain about the pressures for short-term performance imposed on them by the market, it is hard to reconcile this complaint with the breezy assertion of "doing well by doing good." Moreover, not only are there trade-offs between providers of financial capital and other stakeholders, there are trade-offs between one type of provider of financial capital and another (e.g., equity vs. debt), as well as between different stakeholders (e.g., those focused on an environmental issue vs. those focused on a social issue).

Today the use of a "materiality matrix" by some companies to communicate their view about the relative importance of different issues begs the question of just how differences in importance are determined. What all members of the audience want to know is the underlying weighting given to each stakeholder group and the company's view of how important an issue is to each group. Since materiality is binary and based on judgment, judgment must first be exercised in identifying which members of the audience really matter. Doing so requires the courage to recognize that some stakeholders will disagree with this judgment, perhaps vocally so. Attempting to evade this conflict through conciliatory vagaries like "we care about all of our stakeholders" not only clouds the company's capacity to determine its material issues, but it also inhibits the company's ability to benefit from the transformation function of corporate reporting.[52] Transformation requires stakeholder engagement and, as with every resource allocation issue, there are limits to the resources that can be devoted to this.

Determining the relative importance of different providers of financial capital and different stakeholders is ultimately a responsibility of the board. What does this mean in operational terms? We suggest that annually the board issue, as part of the company's integrated report, a forward-looking "Statement of Significant Audiences and Materiality." This statement will inform management, providers of financial capital, and all other stakeholders of the audiences the board believes are important to the survival of the corporation. While management can play a significant role in preparing this statement, it is ultimately a statement of the board, somewhat analogous to the annual financial audit. While management is deeply involved in the audit and, in the United States, the chief executive officer and chief financial officer must personally sign off on the adequacy of a company's internal control systems, it is the Audit Committee of the board that selects and engages the audit firm and signs off on the scope of the audit. The difference is that the audit statement is ultimately a responsibility of the board—not management.[53]

 ## MATERIALITY FOR INTEGRATED REPORTING

Evidence shows that the investor audience has a significant latent appetite for integrated reporting. The Statement of Significant Audiences and Materiality, when combined with the new tools we outline in the next chapter, may be a vehicle that accelerates the adoption of integrated reporting by this user audience. According to a 2014 Ernst & Young survey on "Tomorrow's Investment Rules," institutional investors want a clearer view of what is material and want it directly from the company.

> Materiality is a key concept that emerged from this survey. Investors were more likely to value information which came directly from the company itself rather than from third-party sources. In addition, among those that never consider ESG information in their decision-making process, the main reason for rejecting it was that they felt it was not material.[54]

When the board is very clear in its communication of what is material and what is not, and which audiences it feels are significant (and which are not), investors gain relevant guidance on how the board judges importance and its ability to exercise this judgment. Investors are looking for this guidance. The board's Statement of Significant Audiences and Materiality is a new venue through which the board can strengthen the social construction attribute of institutional symbolism. This symbolism, which makes clear what the company cares about and what it does not, is the foundation for the verity of the company's claims about its commitment to "sustainability." It is an important way in which the company avoids the charge of "greenwashing," but the company must also back up its claims about the audience and issues that are material and so included in their integrated report, with genuine resource commitments and stakeholder engagement, as discussed in the next chapter.

The board itself will determine the process for producing this statement using whatever tools and guidelines it chooses, while heeding the IIRC's guidance on concision in materiality. Selecting 10 audiences to include in the statement communicates more information than selecting 20, and selecting 5 audiences transmits more information than selecting 10. We suggest the following resources to aid the board in drafting its Statement of Significant Audiences and Materiality:

- The IIRC has established a *process* for determining materiality, which we have augmented as discussed above.
- SASB's rigorous, sector-specific, evidence-based standards are a good starting point for identifying ESG issues relevant to investors.

- GRI offers similar guidance regarding issues for stakeholders, and the board should determine which are material for the corporation itself.
- CDP provides the key perfomance indicators for reporting on climate, water, and forest issues that the board deems material.

In the previous chapter, we discussed more generally the way that the efforts of these four organizations are complementing each other in support of the integrated reporting movement. In the next chapter, we will discuss how the board's "Statement of Significant Audiences and Materiality" serves as the foundation for a management tool we call the "Sustainable Value Matrix."

 ## NOTES

1. Loss, Louis. *Securities Regulation.* New York: Little, Brown and Company, 1961.
2. "It is said that a fraudulent representation must be material to have that effect. But how are we to decide whether it is material or not? It must be by an appeal to ordinary experience to decide whether a belief that the fact was as represented would naturally have led to, or a contrary belief would naturally have prevented, the making of the contract." (Holmes, Oliver Wendell. "The common law." (1881) in Gutenberg Project version: [308] LECTURE IX. CONTRACT.- III. VOID AND VOIDABLE.) This is one of the first commercial law references to materiality. Later cases such as Basic Inc. v. Levinson, 485 U.S. 224, 108 S. Ct. 978, 99 L. Ed. 2d 194 (1988) and TSC Industries, Inc. v. Northway, Inc., 426 U.S. 438, 96 S. Ct. 2126, 48 L. Ed. 2d 757 (1976), as well as post-Securities Act regulations, arguably, stand on the shoulders of Holmes's legal construction of commercial materiality.
3. " . . . a showing of a substantial likelihood that, under all the circumstances, the omitted fact would have assumed actual significance in the deliberations of the reasonable shareholder. Put another way, there must be a substantial likelihood that the disclosure of the omitted fact would have been viewed by the reasonable investor as having significantly altered the 'total mix' of the information made available." TSC Industries, Inc. v. Northway, Inc., 426 U.S. 438, 96 S. Ct. 2126, 48 L. Ed. 2d 757 (1976) at 449.
4. The circularity of this [TSC v. Northway] definition leaves the question of what determines the "total mix" of information unanswered. Does it refer to all other material information except for the piece in question? If so, upon what basis was all this information judged to be material in the first place, since the "total mix" of information must be constructed one piece at a time? Was the first piece of information deemed material because it was important to a reasonable investor, and then all other information is judged in the

context of increasing amounts of information? Conceivably, whether a piece of information is material or not would be a function of how much other information is available. When little information is available, the relevance of an additional bit of information can be high. When a substantial amount of information is available, an additional piece may be less relevant. If the total mix of information also includes immaterial information, then the question arises regarding the basis on which the total mix is built.

5. The phrase "entity-specific" is used in the Financial Accounting Standards Board definition of materiality. "Information is material if omitting it or misstating it could influence decisions that users make on the basis of the financial information of a specific reporting entity. In other words, materiality is an entity-specific aspect of relevance based on the nature or magnitude or both of the items to which the information relates in the context of an individual entity's financial report. Consequently, the Board cannot specify a uniform quantitative threshold for materiality or predetermine what could be material in a particular situation." Financial Accounting Standards Board. Statement of Financial Accounting Concepts No. 8, p. 17, http://www.fasb.org/cs/BlobServer?blobkey=id& blobnocache=true&blobwhere=1175822892635&blobheader=application% 2Fpdf&blobheadername2=Content-Length&blobheadername1=Content-Dis position&blobheadervalue2=210323&blobheadervalue1=filename%3DCon cepts_Statement_No_8.pdf&blobcol=urldata&blobtable=MungoBlobs, accessed May 2014. For another discussion on materiality for nonfinancial information see, Eccles, Robert G., Michael P. Krzus, and George Serafeim. "A Note on Materiality for Nonfinancial Information." Harvard Business School Note N9-314-033, November 2013.

6. We would like to cite the work of Carla Edgley, Lecturer in Accounting and Finance Cardiff Business School, for her excellent compendium of sources on accounting materiality in her paper: Edgley, Carla. "A genealogy of accounting materiality." *Critical Perspectives on Accounting* (2013). All integrated reporting movement participants and materiality scholars will find this paper an excellent foundation for future research into the application of materiality beyond financial accounting into integrated reporting, as did we.

7. Also, nonfinancial reporting materiality is inherently less historical and more forward-looking than financial materiality. In Solomon, Jill, and Warren Maroun. "Integrated reporting: the influence of King III on social, ethical and environmental reporting." (ACCA, 2012), p. 8: "In practice, the materiality of sustainability-related information is notoriously difficult to establish. Placing a financial value on materiality for financial risks is a complex process but establishing materiality and materiality thresholds for traditionally 'non-financial' risks, which are hard to quantify, is far more challenging if even possible. . . . 'The string of corporate collapses over the past decade has led many stakeholders to question the relevance and reliability of annual financial

reports as a basis for making decisions about an organisation. Reports based largely on financial information do not provide sufficient insight to enable stakeholders to form a comprehensive picture of the organisation's performance and of its ability to create and sustain value, especially in the context of growing environmental, social and economic challenges. Sustainability reports have similarly suffered weaknesses, usually appearing disconnected from the organisation's financial reports, generally providing a backward-looking review of performance, and almost always failing to make the link between sustainability issues and the organisation's core strategy. For the most part, these reports have failed to address the lingering distrust among civil society of the intentions and practices of business. Stakeholders today want forward-looking information that will enable them to more effectively assess the total economic value of an organisation' (Mervyn King's Foreword, IRCSA 2011:1)." "At a meeting of key sustainability reporting role players, held at St James Palace by Prince Charles in 2009 [author Krzus attending], Mervyn King shared the realisation that came of age: 'Corporate reporting as we've been doing it for the last decade is no longer fit for purpose. With the complexity of reporting, nine out of ten people do not understand it. What you need is concise international language so that the trustee of your pension fund can make an informed investment about your money that is invested in that company, that it's going to sustain value creation in the long return. You cannot tell that by looking at a balance sheet or profit and loss statement. In the nature of things that is historical information. You're trying to look into the future when looking at sustained value creation within the completely changed world in which we operate. Climate change, ecological overshoot and overusing the natural assets of the planet—all these things are happening around the world.'" "Interview Summary Report." Compiled by Jess Schulschenk in collaboration with the Albert Luthuli Centre for Responsible Leadership at the University of Pretoria. Published by Ernst & Young South Africa. August 2012. p. 23.

8. New evidence indicates there may be significant differences in the meaning of materiality between countries. We entered "materiality" into the Google Correlate tool, and then subjectively selected the most relevant among the 30 most highly correlated search terms between January 2004 and April 2014. The most highly correlated, relevant terms for the USA were: income statement, balance sheet, sociocultural theory, and elasticity of demand, together having an approximate mean R^2 of 0.92. Results for India, U.K., Canada, Australia, and New Zealand showed a significant diversity in meaning, both from the U.S. and between each other, along with a general, and apparently significant, decrease in correlation. This suggests a need for future research into national differences in the perceived meaning of materiality. Non-USA results follow (approximate mean R^2 in parentheses). India (0.90):

accounting journal, positive words, account department, spending money, management roles. U.K. (0.85): subjective, definite, to analyse, discuss, a matrix, socially, normative. Canada (0.83): journal entry, the standard deviation, extrapolate, doubtful accounts, perceive, empathy. Australia (0.80): stakeholder analysis, behaviour change, critical appraisal, social learning theory, a firm. New Zealand (0.76): an organization, calculate standard deviation, an asset, the individual, a matrix.

9. Searle, John R. The Construction of Social Reality. New York: Simon and Schuster, 1995.

10. Badenhausen, Kurt. "Apple Dominates List of the World's Most Valuable Brands." *Forbes* online. November 6, 2013. Accessed online at http://www.forbes.com/sites/kurtbadenhausen/2013/11/06/apple-dominates-list-of-the-worlds-most-valuable-brands/ on May 1, 2014.

11. Loss continues: "Were any hard and fast rule to be laid down as to what constitutes fraud under the blue-sky law, the Oregon court has said, 'a certain class of gentleman of the J. Rufus Wallingford type . . . would lie awake nights endeavoring to conceive some devious and shadowy way of evading the law. It is more advisable to deal with each case as it arises." (Loss, "Securities Regulation." (1961), p. 1436.) "Common law deceit" used here as it refers to the broad body of case law and other governing prohibitions against lying, cheating or stealing in civil society, whereas "securities law" refers more specifically to prohibited deceptive practices as defined in the Securities Act of 1956, its successor Acts and implementing regulations, and to case law precedents related to this Act.

12. Holmes, William. "Materiality – Through the looking glass." *Journal of Accountancy,* 133, no. 2 (1972): 44-49.

13. International Integrated Reporting Council. "Materiality background paper for <IR>," pp. 2–8. http://www.theiirc.org/wp-content/uploads/2013/03/IR-Background-Paper-Materiality.pdf

14. In academic circles, the phrase "Westphalian Sovereignty" is sometimes summarized as "The religion of the prince is the religion of the place." Arguably, the source of the concept of "sovereignty," the Peace of Westphalia of 1648 was: "The end of the Thirty Years War brought with it the final end of the medieval Holy Roman Empire. Authority for choosing the religion of the political unit was given to the prince of that unit and not to the Hapsburg Emperor or the Pope. No longer could one pretend there was religious or political unity in Europe. Authority was dispersed to the various kings and princes, and the basis for the sovereign state was established." Russett, Bruce, Harvey Starr, and David Kinsella. *World Politics: The Menu for Choice.* Cengage Learning, 2005.

15. We will refer to the direct audience of integrated reporting as "users."

16. International Integrated Reporting Council. "The International <IR> Framework," p. 18. http://www.theiirc.org/wp-content/uploads/2013/12/13-12-08-THE-INTERNATIONAL-IR-FRAMEWORK-2-1.pdf

17. Berle, Adolf Augustus, and Gardiner Coit Means. *The Modern Corporation and Private Property*. Transaction Publishers, 1991 (10th version, original published in 1933). pp. 69, 120–121, 250–251.

18. The message about materiality and material issues in the European Union directive on disclosure of nonfinancial and diversity information is muddled. Section 3, LEGAL ELEMENTS OF THE PROPOSAL, Detailed Explanation of the Proposal, Nonfinancial information, states, "Article 1 (a) of the proposal will require certain large companies to disclose a statement in their Annual Report including material information relating to at least environmental, social, and employee-related matters, respect of human rights, anti-corruption and bribery aspects." However, the word "material" is not used in the text of amendments to either Article 46 or Article 36. Proposal for a DIRECTIVE OF THE EUROPEAN PARLIAMENT AND OF THE COUNCIL amending Council Directives 78/660/EEC and 83/349/EEC as regards disclosure of nonfinancial and diversity information by certain large companies and groups. http://www.ipex.eu/IPEXL-WEB/dossier/document.do?code=COM&year=2013&number=0207&extension=null&appLng=EN, accessed April 2014. (Site discontinued).

19. Securities and Exchange Commission. News, Press Releases, SEC Issues Interpretive Guidance on Disclosure Related to Business or Legal Developments Regarding Climate Change, http://www.sec.gov/news/press/2010/2010-15.htm, accessed April 2014.

20. Securities and Exchange Commission. "Commission Guidance Regarding Disclosure Related to Climate Change," 17 CFR Parts 211, 231 and 241 [Release Nos. 33-0106; 34-61469; FR-82], Securities and Exchange Commission, February 2, 2010, p. 27, http://www.sec.gov/rules/interp/2010/33-9106.pdf, accessed April 2014.

21. Ibid., p. 12.

22. Ceres was founded by a small group of investors in 1989 in response to the Exxon Valdez oil spill. The organization is an advocate for sustainability leadership. Ceres mobilizes a powerful network of investors, companies, and public interest groups to accelerate and expand the adoption of sustainable business practices and solutions to build a healthy global economy. Ceres. About Us, Who We Are, http://www.ceres.org/about-us/who-we-are, accessed April 2014.

23. The key findings of a February 2014 report by Ceres were (1) the SEC is not prioritizing the financial risks and opportunities of climate change as an important disclosure issue; (2) the SEC issued 49 comment letters that addressed the adequacy of climate change disclosure in 2010 and 2011, but only three comment letters in 2012 and none in 2013; (3) most S&P 500 climate disclosures in 10-Ks are very brief, provide little discussion of material issues, and do not quantify impacts or risks; (4) most S&P 500 companies that disclose via the CDP provide significantly more detailed information in

voluntary climate reporting compared to mandatory 10-K filings; and (5) a large number of companies fail to say anything about climate change in their annual filings with the SEC. Forty one percent of S&P 500 companies did not include any climate related disclosure at all in their 10-K filings in 2013. Ceres. Resources, Reports, *Cool Response: The SEC & Corporate Climate Change Reporting*, http://www.ceres.org/resources/reports/cool-response-the-sec-corporate-climate-change-reporting, accessed April 2014.

24. The SEC assumes the "rational investor" in its materiality guidance and rules, an assumption which should be questioned given recent research in behavioral economics. It is fair to assume that a reasonable investor is seen as making decisions based on classical microeconomic theory regarding perceptions of risk and return. In this theory, a "rational" man (or woman) has a linear utility function for the tradeoffs between risk and reward. However, a growing body of academic research in the field of behavioral economics is showing that the rational man or woman does not exist. Instead "behavioral man," specifically evidenced in investor and manager behaviors, has an S-shaped utility curve that is asymmetric about the origin. According to the branch of behavioral economics known as "Prospect Theory," actors in the domain of gains are somewhat more "risk averse" than explained by rational man theory. Conversely, investors and managers already in the domain of losses are significantly more risk seeking than explained by the rational model. Tversky, Amos, and Daniel Kahneman. "Advances in prospect theory: Cumulative representation of uncertainty." *Journal of Risk and Uncertainty* 5, no. 4 (1992): 297–323.) Barbara Black (2012) has pointed out the implications of this new research for federal securities regulation in her 2012 paper, "Behavioral Economics and Investor Protection," reframing the "reasonable investor": "The judicial view of a 'reasonable investor' plays an important role in federal securities regulation, and courts express great confidence in the reasonable investor's cognitive abilities. Behavioral economists, by contrast, do not observe real people investing in today's markets behaving as the reasonable investors that federal securities law expects them to be. Similarly, the efficient market hypothesis (EMH) has exerted a powerful influence in securities regulation, although empirical evidence calls into question some of the basic assumptions underlying EMH. Unfortunately, to date, courts have only acknowledged the discrepancy between legal theory and behavioral economics in one situation, class certification of federal securities class actions. It is time for courts to address the gap between judicial expectations about the behavior of reasonable investors and behavioral economists 'views of investors' cognitive shortcomings, consistent with the central purpose of federal securities regulation: protect investors from fraud." Black, Barbara. "Behavioral Economics and Investor Protection: Reasonable Investors, Efficient Markets." *Loyola University Chicago Law Journal*, 44 (2013): 1493–1509.

25. Ibid., pp. 21–27.

26. Ribstein, Larry. "The SEC, Global Warming, and the First Amendment." *Forbes*. February 1, 2010. http://www.forbes.com/sites/streettalk/2010/02/01/tools-streettalk-wordpress/

27. Hirji, Zahra. "Most US Companies Ignoring SEC Rule to Disclose Climate Risks." *Inside Climate News*. September 19, 2013. http://insideclimatenews .org/news/20130919/most-us-companies-ignoring-sec-rule-disclose-climate-risks, accessed April 2014.

28. SASB's reference to "total mix" is nuanced. "Materiality is a fundamental principle of financial reporting in the United States. The concept of materiality recognizes that some information is important to the fair presentation of an entity's financial condition and operational performance. Federal securities law seeks to protect individual investors by requiring publicly listed companies to disclose annual and other periodic performance information that would be necessary for a reasonable investor to make informed investment decisions. U.S. Federal law requires publicly listed companies to disclose material information, defined by the U.S. Supreme Court as information presenting 'a substantial likelihood that the disclosure of the omitted fact would have been viewed by the reasonable investor as having significantly altered the 'total mix' of information made available.' (TSC Indus. V. Northway, Inc., 426 U.S. 438 (1976)). Both U.S. and global companies that trade on U.S. exchanges are subject to Federal disclosure requirements. Regulation S-K, which sets the specific disclosure requirements associated with Form 10-K and other SEC filings, requires that companies describe known trends, demands and uncertainties that have a material impact on financial results in the Management's Discussion and Analysis of Financial Condition and Results of Operations (MD&A) section of Form 10-K." Sustainability Accounting Standards Board. "Approach, Materiality, Why is it Important?," http://www.sasb.org/materiality/important/, accessed April 2014.

29. "The International Financial Reporting Standards Framework describes the basic concepts that underlie the preparation and presentation of financial statements for external users." Deloitte. USGAAP*Plus*, Standards, Other pronouncements, Framework, *Conceptual Framework for Financial Reporting 2010*, http://www.iasplus.com/en-us/standards/other/framework, accessed April 2014. "Concepts Statements are intended to set forth objectives and fundamental concepts that will be the basis for development of financial accounting and reporting guidance. The objectives identify the goals and purposes of financial reporting. The fundamentals are the underlying concepts of financial accounting—concepts that guide the selection of transactions and other events and conditions to be accounted for; their recognition and measurement; and the means of summarizing and communicating them to interested parties." Financial Accounting Standards Board. Standards, Concepts

Statements, *Conceptual Framework for Financial Reporting*, http://www.fasb.org/jsp/FASB/Page/PreCodSectionPage&cid=1176156317989, accessed April 2014.

30. "The only direct reference we [SASB] have to CDP's work is through reference to the CDP questionnaire and the CDSB framework in several of our standards in the Non-Renewable Resource Sector." Andrew Collins, email correspondence with Robert Eccles, Mike Krzus, Tim Youmans, and Katie Schmitz Eulitt, April 23, 2014. Under the terms of a Memorandum of Understanding, SASB utilizes CDP's data as evidence for determining the materiality of climate change-related issues in certain industries. SASB also receives technical assistance in referencing CDSB protocols for disclosure of carbon emissions." http://www.sasb.org/approach/key-relationships/, accessed April 2014.

31. Under the terms of a Memorandum of Understanding between Global Reporting Initiative and the CDP, the organizations agreed to collaborate to avoid duplication of disclosure efforts. "[It] will improve the consistency and comparability of environmental data, making corporate reporting more efficient and effective and ease the reporting burden for the thousands of companies" that use CDP's climate change and supply chain programs and GRI Sustainability Reporting Guidelines. This will be achieved by allowing data points to be used in both reporting channels. The information provided through either channel can form parts of a sustainability report using GRI Guidelines and/or to answer parts of CDP questionnaires. A support document outlining how this can be applied will be published in early 2014. As with greenhouse gas emissions reporting, GRI and CDP strive for similar alignment related to water reporting. Both organizations will coordinate their technical processes in the coming months and years in order to help streamline the global water reporting approach. Global Reporting Initiative. About GRI, Alliances and Synergies, https://www.globalreporting.org/information/about-gri/alliances-and-synergies/Pages/CDP.aspx, accessed April 2014.

32. "The International <IR> Framework," Guiding Principles 3.17, p. 18.

33. Ibid., Guiding Principles 3.18, p. 18.

34. The International Integrated Reporting Council. "Materiality: Background Paper for <IR>," p. 2, http://www.theiirc.org/wp-content/uploads/2013/03/IR-Background-Paper-Materiality.pdf, accessed March 2014.

35. Ibid., p. 19.

36. "The International <IR> Framework," p. 7.

37. IIRC, Materiality: Background Paper for <IR>, p. 1.

38. "'In the time to come this volume may be proclaimed as the most important work bearing on American statecraft . . . and will mark a sharp turning point in fundamental, deep-thrusting thinking about the American State and American

civilization.'" Few books receive reviews like this in the *New York Herald Tribune* [Charles Beard, "'Who Owns—and Runs—the Corporations'," February 19, 1933, book review section], and still fewer that are academic research monographs. But so a book that was destined to establish a new field of scholarship was greeted with its publication in 1932. 'This book will perhaps rank with Adam Smith's Wealth of Nations as the first detailed description in admirably clear terms of a new economics epoch'" [Frank, Jerome and Norman Meyers, 1933, Yale Law Review, 42, 989–1000]. Mayer, Colin. *Firm Commitment: Why the Corporation is Failing Us and How to Restore Trust in It.* Oxford University Press, 2013, pp. 71–72.

39. Berle and Means. *The Modern Corporation and Private Property.*

40. The ability to limit liability, through bankruptcy protection, is common to sole proprietors, closely held companies, and individuals, as well as corporations. A key difference is that the corporation's control group (officers and directors) are able to socialize the losses on others' capital investment, not their own capital investment.

41. From American and English law, "the very existence of the corporation was conditioned on a grant from the state. This grant created the corporation and set it up as a separate legal person independent of any associates [investors and managers]," [also contemporarily termed "corporate personhood."] From this state granted personhood "privilege . . . flowed a limited liability of associates . . . a stockholder was not liable for any of the debts of the enterprise and he could thus embark a particular amount of capital in the corporate affairs without becoming responsible, beyond this amount, for the corporate debts." Berle and Means, *The Modern Corporation and Private Property*, pp. 120–121. Regarding the role of limited liability in attracting risk capital in Easterbrook, Frank H., and Daniel R. Fischel. "Limited liability and the corporation." U. Chi. L. Rev. 52 (1985): 89. p. 636, "Third, limited liability enables the transfer of securities on a trading market, ensuring liquidity. Absent limited liability, shares would be difficult to value because they would carry the potential of excess liabilities." The role of limited liability in attracting risk capital has also been shown mathematically in Merton, Robert C. "An Intertemporal Capital Asset Pricing Model," *Econometrica*, Vol. 41, No. 5 (Sep. 1973), which concludes on p. 885 that "An intertemporal model of the capital market has been developed which is consistent with both the expected utility maxim and the limited liability of assets [equities]."

42. Also derivative of corporate personhood, corporations can exert "Control Through a Legal Device. In the effort to maintain control of a corporation without ownership of a majority of its stock, various legal devices have been developed. Of these, the most important among the very large companies is the device of 'pyramiding.' This involves the owning of a majority of the stock of

one corporation which in turn holds a majority of the stock of another—a process which can be repeated a number of times. An interest equal to slightly more than a quarter or an eighth or a sixteenth or an even smaller proportion of the ultimate property to be controlled is by this method legally entrenched." Berle and Means, *The Modern Corporation*, p. 69.

43. "The separation of ownership from management and control in the corporate system has performed this essential step in securing liquidity. It is the management and 'control' which is now wedded to the physical property. The owner has no direct personal relation to it and no responsibility toward it. The management is more or less permanent, directing the physical property which remains intact while the participation privileges of ownership are split into innumerable parts ["dispersed ownership"]-" shares of stock"-which glide from hand to hand [as a "token"], irresponsible and impersonal . . . Most striking of all, a liquid token acquires a value purely and simply because of its liquidity." Berle and Means, *The Modern Corporation*, pp. 250–251. As cited above, the separation of ownership from control combined with personhood-derived limited liability enables the free trading of shares and liquid market for these shares.

44. Berle and Means, *The Modern Corporation*, p. 5.

45. Stout, Lynn (*The Shareholder Value Myth*, 2012) describes that the foundation of the "profit maximizing," thus stakeholder minimizing, corporate governance is the self-disproving view of social interaction symbolized by "Homo economicus": "Let us see how our friend Homo economicus stacks up against the list [of clinical sociopathic behaviors]. Lack of remorse (item 7)? Obviously; why would Homo economicus feel bad just because he hurt or misled another, if he advanced his own material welfare? Irresponsibility and reckless disregard for the safety of others (items 5 and 6)? Homo economicus feels responsible for, and cares about, no one but himself. Deceitfulness (item 2)? Homo economicus is happy to lie any time it serves his interests. Failure to conform to social norms with respect to lawful behaviors (item 1)? Whenever and wherever the police aren't around describes Homo economicus. Although Homo economicus is neither cranky nor impulsive—items 3 and 4—he has five of the seven characteristics on the list. Unburdened by pity or remorse, he will lie, cheat, steal, neglect duties, break promises—even murder—if a cold calculation of the likely consequences leads him to conclude that he will be better off. Like any sociopath, Homo economicus lacks a conscience." It is clear that most modern corporate board members are not Homo economicus, and it is within the norms of the modern corporate social construct to reciprocate back to society, beyond pure profit making. Stout, Lynn A. "Taking conscience seriously." *Moral Markets: The Critical Role of Values in the Economy*. Princeton University Press, Princeton (2007): 157–172.

46. Specifically, Mayer advocates a two-tier form of board governance called a "trust firm," somewhat similar to the German Board model (Franks, Julian R.

and Mayer, Colin, "Ownership and Control of German Corporations" (October 2001). *Review of Financial Studies*, Vol. 14, Issue 4, pp. 943–977, 2001.). Given that the trust firm is not (yet) the standard in the United States and other corporate domiciles, we feel that Mayer's "trust theory of the stratified Board" applies to today's current directors: ". . . the corporation is a rent extraction vehicle for the shortest term shareholders. The power of owners [controllers] with the shortest time horizon not only concentrates control and wealth amongst them and their agents, but also is the source of failure to account for the interest of any generation but their own. Competition may confer some benefits on their customers, but by focusing the horizon of the firm so closely on the near term, the wellbeing of all but the most immediate generation is disregarded. We should not therefore rely on competition to be the guardian of our offspring . . . [The corporation will have to turn to trustees who are the custodians of the firm's values] to restrain it from defaulting in the future. . . . Their presence changes the nature of the corporation from being a pure agency one, in which the directors act as agents of the shareholders, to a mixed trust arrangement in which the [board] acts in behalf of the designated stakeholders of the corporation." Mayer, *Firm Commitment*, pp. 240, 244–245. It is our belief that these stakeholders are the material and significant audiences that the firm defines and in its integrated reporting process.

47. Zadek, Simon, and Mira Merme. "Redefining Materiality." AccountAbility, http://www.accountability.org/images/content/0/8/085/Redefining%20Materiality%20-%20Full%20Report.pdf, accessed May 2014.

48. Findings from behavioral economics, previously cited in this chapter, may have implications for how boards determine materiality, by including consideration of whether the information would be perceived as positive or negative as they make judgments on materiality and significance. This is a major conceptual change since none of the discussion above considers valence as a factor in determining materiality.

49. "The Misleading Metaphor of Shareholder 'Ownership' . . . describes shareholders as 'owners' of corporations. As a legal matter, the claim that shareholders 'own' the corporation is obviously incorrect. Corporations are independent legal entities that own themselves; shareholders only own a security, called 'stock,' with very limited legal rights." [Footnote on p. 804: "This metaphor may have roots in the nineteenth century, when most corporations were closely held firms with only a single shareholder or a very small number of shareholders. In such firms, shareholders exercise far more control, and it may make more sense to think of them as owners."] "The Mythical Benefits of Shareholder Control." Stout, Lynn A., *Virginia Law Review*, Vol. 93, No. 3 (May, 2007), p. 804, http://www.jstor.org/stable/25050361.

50. "In other words, once again beyond legal requirements, the interests of others, including human rights, derive from those of the corporation's

shareholders. So the argument for shareholder value has been profoundly influential in shaping the laws and conventions that govern the conduct of our corporations. So elegant is the argument that I will employ it in coming to the exact opposite conclusion (pp. 31–32) . . . Shareholder value is an outcome not an objective. It should not drive corporate policy but be treated as a product of it. (p. 261)" Mayer, Colin. "*Firm Commitment: Why the Corporation is Failing Us and How to Restore Trust in It.*" (2013). Also see Stout, Lynn "*The Shareholder Value Myth: How Putting Shareholders First Harms Investors, Corporations, and the Public.*" (2012)

51. Eccles, Robert G. and George Serafeim. "The Performance Frontier: Innovating for a sustainable strategy." *Harvard Business Review* 91, no. 5 (2013).

52. "Corporate reporting serves another function, what can be termed the 'transformation function.' While the information function assumes no feedback from counterparties, the transformation function relaxes this assumption, allowing for engagement and activism from the counterparties. The counterparties receive and evaluate the information. Where they see opportunities to influence corporate behavior to their benefit, and potentially to the benefit of the corporation, they actively try to bring about change. This engagement, activism, and change process enables a company to transform. The transformation function does not assume that the information function is performed effectively. In many cases, counterparties engage and bring change under conditions of incomplete information. For example, NGOs like Global Reporting Initiative (GRI) and Transparency International (TI) engage with corporations to improve disclosure. Their engagement efforts are frequently exerted with incomplete, if any, information. It is natural to think, though, that counterparties will spend their efforts more productively if they are better informed." Eccles, Robert, and George Serafeim. "Corporate and Integrated Reporting: A Functional Perspective." Harvard Business School Working Paper, No. 14-094, April 2014.

53. Sarbanes-Oxley Act of 2002, PL 107-204, 116 Stat 745, Section 301, Paragraph 2: "RESPONSIBILITIES RELATING TO REGISTERED PUBLIC ACCOUNTING FIRMS. —The audit committee of each issuer, in its capacity as a committee of the board of directors, shall be directly responsible for the appointment, compensation, and oversight of the work of any registered public accounting firm employed by that issuer (including resolution of disagreements between management and the auditor regarding financial reporting) for the purpose of preparing or issuing an audit report or related work, and each such registered public accounting firm shall report directly to the audit committee."

54. E&Y. "Tomorrow's investment rules: a global survey." p. 2, http://www.ey.com/Publication/vwLUAssets/EY-Institutional-Investor-Survey/$FILE/EY-Institutional-Investor-Survey.pdf, accessed May 2014.

CHAPTER SIX

The Sustainable Value Matrix

N THE PREVIOUS CHAPTER, we suggested that the board exercise its responsibility to determine integrated reporting materiality through an annual "Statement of Significant Audiences and Materiality." This Statement forms the basis for the idea of the "Sustainable Value Matrix" (SVM), a tool that expands on the concept of a "materiality matrix." Like the materiality matrix, the SVM can be used for purposes of external reporting, stakeholder engagement, and resource commitment. It goes above and beyond this, however, in that the SVM can also be used to drive innovation to reduce or even reverse the tradeoffs that often exist between financial and nonfinancial performance. In doing so, it pushes the boundary of the Performance Frontier that represents the typical tradeoffs between financial and nonfinancial performance.[1] When companies see that fostering innovation is one of its benefits, the SVM will become an accelerator for integrated reporting,

 ## A SHORT HISTORY OF THE MATERIALITY MATRIX

While AccountAbility first articulated a formalized materiality determination process in their 2003 report, "Redefining Materiality,"[2] the materiality matrix

emerged, like many management innovations, in practice. For determining material issues, AccountAbility recommended a five-part materiality test embedded in a transparent process of stakeholder engagement, subjected to external assurance—with both the process and results under the direct responsibility of the board.[3] BP, one of the first companies to turn this test into a materiality matrix, used it to select and prioritize issues to include in its 2004 sustainability report.[4] Ford and BT followed, putting materiality matrices in their sustainability reports for 2004/2005 and 2006, respectively.[5]

While both AccountAbility and Global Reporting Initiative (GRI) originally saw the materiality matrix as a tool primarily for sustainability reporting, the process has evolved in practice to include interdependencies with financial information. AccountAbility observed an emerging commonality, stating, "These (matrices) were variations on the familiar matrix plots used in risk analysis, but with scales representing societal and business significance."[6] GRI took it a step further by prescribing the following: "The threshold for defining material topics to report should be set to identify those opportunities and risks which are most important to stakeholders, the economy, environment, and society, or the reporting organization, and therefore merit particular focus in a sustainability report."[7] In practice, however, the process continued to evolve, and companies did not always adopt all of GRI's guidance. For example, while GRI recommends the X-axis as "Significance of Economic, Environmental, and Social Impacts" and the Y-axis as "Influence on Stakeholder Assessments and Decisions,"[8] many firms choose to define the X-axis as "importance to the company" or something closely related.[9]

Ten years after their invention, materiality matrices are starting to follow certain trends. As the clarity with which companies define "materiality" varies, companies tend to use the term interchangeably with "importance." While the tool appears in many variations, they all share a basic design. One axis, typically the X-axis, arrays the importance of different sustainability issues from the company's perspective, while the Y-axis does the same from "society's" or the "stakeholders'" perspective. The effort to make the latter determination typically involves some form of stakeholder engagement. Issues considered highly important to both the company and its stakeholders are deemed "material" and form the focus of the report.

As the materiality matrix is built on the notion of materiality, its use implies that the company using it knows what *not* to report on—that is, it implies a certain amount of discipline in its determination process. The company and its audience, both of which have limited bandwidth for how much information they can consider, must focus on what is important for their decision-making purposes. As a concept, materiality provides a discipline for dividing information into categories of "material" and "not material." Sustainability or integrated reporting is one use of the materiality matrix. Stakeholder engagement, resource commitment, and, through the evolution to the SVM discussed in the next section, innovation, are three others.

In the early days of the matrix, GRI, AccountAbility, and subsequent others viewed stakeholder engagement as part of the process for constructing the matrix—*engagement for construction.*[10] It is through stakeholder engagement that companies determine how important or material something is to a stakeholder. The company must also decide how important or material the issue is to itself, the importance of which is a function of the nature of the issue, the ability of stakeholders to mobilize resources in support of the issue, and the impact this can have on the company—positive or negative. Once constructed, the materiality matrix can then be a platform for broader *engagement in use* with the company's stakeholders. Through it, the company can set the context for specific engagements so that each stakeholder sees its issue from the company's holistic perspective. Engagement for construction and engagement for use are analytically distinct. Engagement for use can help refine the company's understanding of differences in stakeholder perceptions on particular topics and in their expectations about what the company should be doing, as well as to facilitate collaboration on finding solutions to address issues of contention.

The materiality matrix can also inform resource commitments on the part of both the company and its stakeholders. From the company's perspective, issues it deems material to itself and its stakeholders logically deserve more resources (e.g., time, dollars, top management attention, and degree of stakeholder engagement) from a risk and opportunity perspective than immaterial issues. They become a key part of the company's strategy. From the stakeholder's perspective, the matrix can inform whether it should invest more (e.g., if its issue is rated low) or less (e.g., if its issue is rated high) resources in engaging with the company and mobilizing others to influence its decisions. Potential employees could use it to decide whether to work for the company. Customers may use it as a factor informing whether or not to buy its products. Suppliers could give the firm priority in times of shortages from high demand.

While reporting and resource commitment are analytically separate, a clear relationship exists between resource commitment decisions and external reporting, and it is indicative of the transformation function of corporate reporting. A company is more likely to report on topics to which it is devoting substantial resources. For example, a company may choose not to report on a material topic because it decides the litigation or competitive risk is too high. As noted in Chapter 4, while we are skeptical of this argument, it can be valid in certain circumstances.

 ## ISSUES WITH THE MATRIX

As materiality matrices are an emerging tool, research on their construction and use is limited. Even so, this and our own analyses make clear that most companies give only the most cursory explanation for how their matrix is put together. Yet it is this explanation that makes the materiality matrix most useful for the company's audience. In 2011, Framework LLC published "The Materiality Bridge," which examines the extent to which companies use materiality analysis as a tool for reporting and strategy by evaluating companies on *CR Magazine*'s list of 100 Best Corporate Citizens for 2010 and 2011 for evidence of materiality discussion in their most recent sustainability report.[11] Of the 100 companies, 51 conducted a formal materiality process to identify and prioritize sustainability issues, but only 13 produced a visual representation of the results.[12] An analysis of 195 GRI-based reports from Brazilian companies in 2013 found that 98 published materiality information in their sustainability reports.[13] Eighty-three of them disclosed which topics they considered material and 60 used a materiality matrix. Forty-three companies published between 5 and 10 material topics, with another 28 publishing between 11 and 20. Neither study examined how the matrix was constructed or used.

A 2011 report from Fronesys[14] reviewed the matrices of 31 companies to offer recommendations for how this management tool can be improved.[15] The most salient of these include the need for companies to disclose the underlying processes and scoring mechanisms used to create the matrix, to increase the level of detail in how they assess the impact of issues, and to review the results against peers in order to avoid inexplicable anomalies. Although the report also covers variance in the axis labels and the range of constituencies along the stakeholder and company axes, it focuses mainly on the scoring of issues and how they compare across companies.[16] Two metrics are developed to analyze these issues. The first, "Issue Coherence Level (ICL)," measures how the same issues are scored by different companies.[17] The second, "Materiality Convergence," assesses the overlap between companies and stakeholders concerning the importance of a given issue.[18]

Fronesys's analysis assumes that there is enough underlying similarity in how materiality matrices are constructed that this kind of aggregate analysis, particularly the ICL, can be done—an assumption whose validity is undermined by significant discrepancies in matrix construction. As we will discuss, the following aspects are subject to variation: how the X- and Y-axes are defined (and even which is X and which is Y); whether there is only a "present" or also a "future trend" aspect to either axis; how issues are defined, identified, and ranked; the degree and nature of engagement for determining issues and their weightings; and, for the stakeholder axis, how various stakeholders are weighted to get to a single dimension of "stakeholders"—or even "society." Comparing matrices across companies is also directly contrary to our treatment of materiality in the previous chapter. What is material for a firm is entity-specific and must be determined by that firm and ratified by its board of directors.

A comparison of two companies in the same industry, Ford and Daimler, illustrates the impact of these differences. Each has a fairly sophisticated approach to its materiality matrix. (Appendix 6A, "Comparing Ford and Daimler's Materiality Matrices," discusses each firm's matrix in some detail.) The two car companies use inverse definitions of each other's X- and Y-axes, and Daimler defines each simply in terms of "importance," implying the present. In contrast, Ford incorporates a future dimension into the company axis of "current and potential." It also uses yet another framing for the stakeholder axis, basing it not on magnitude but on acceleration ("increasing concern"). Important differences in the process and degree of explanation used to identify issues and their importance for both the company and stakeholders also exist. When the very definitions of each axis and the processes used to identify and rank issues differ, the resulting matrices will be different as well. This is certainly the case with Ford and Daimler.

While the companies' use of different issue descriptions and format for placing those issues in the matrix makes it harder to compare the two, distinctions can be made. For Daimler, customer satisfaction (in the top right-hand corner), (see Figure 6A.2) integrity and compliance, attractiveness as an employer, training and professional development, innovation and development, and business partner integrity management all rank very high. These or rough equivalents do not appear in Ford's High Impact, High Concern box. Ford is more concerned with public policy issues, water, sustainability of its supply chain, and the company's financial health. Not surprisingly, climate change issues rank high for both companies. Because of the entity-specific nature of materiality, we deduce that the differences between the issues identified in these two close competitors' materiality matrices is largely a function of differences in their definition of significant audiences.

 ## THE CURRENT STATE OF MATERIALITY MATRICES

To better understand how companies currently construct and use materiality matrices, we examined those of 91 companies (see Appendix 6B for our methodology and the list of companies reviewed). We define a materiality matrix as a diagram having two axes, populated with named issues, where their location on the matrix (or scoring) is evident.[19] Based on this analysis, we examined current practice in terms of five aspects of materiality matrix construction and use: stakeholder identification and engagement, dimension definition and label, issue identification and description, issue scoring, and interactivity.

Stakeholder Identification and Engagement

We observed substantial variation in how stakeholder identification and engagement is done and the degree to which each is explained. Only 12% of our sample explains the identification process to any extent, yet 87% do so for the stakeholder engagement process (albeit with substantially varying degrees of detail).[20] In cases where it was possible to ascertain the number of stakeholder groups (63%), the average was 7.9. The most common stakeholder groups named were customers, communities, employees, suppliers, investors, media, government, and nongovernmental organizations (NGOs). Most companies name the high-level stakeholder groups, but few identify the specific stakeholders that comprise them. An exception, Volkswagen, provides an additional "Stakeholder dialogues" report as part of its 2012 sustainability report, which names the individual stakeholder, the stakeholder cluster, and the geographical context.[21] University of St. Gallen is part of the "Science" stakeholder group and the European Union geography, whereas the Federation of German Industries, a domestic geographical group, is part of the "Politics and Government Agencies" stakeholder group.

Stakeholder identification methods are limited and, across our sample, no consistent method was used. Dow established a Sustainable External Advisory Council, which "provides for open dialogue between Dow's business leaders and independent external thought leaders" and whose purpose is to help identify stakeholders who "can drive, block or shape the discourse around sustainability."[22] Carlsberg Group, on the other hand, uses GRI G3 guidelines to identify a prioritized list of eight external and internal stakeholder groups.[23]

While stakeholder engagement methods primarily include interviews, surveys, discussion groups, and media scanning, the depth with which companies pursue such engagement is uneven. Some merely conduct informal discussions or surveys. Others create thorough processes or consult with outside groups to devise methods for engagement. Staples Australia, for example, sent out a questionnaire that was "completed by over 400 stakeholders including associates, customers, suppliers, sustainability professionals and community stakeholders," asking them "which sustainability issues were the most important for us to address."[24] Daiwa House, Japan's largest homebuilder, disaggregated its six stakeholder groups and ordered the priority of the top five issues for each group.[25] Although Daiwa House did not explain the process of aggregating the stakeholder priorities in creating the matrix, its disaggregation allows the viewer to compare the level of issue importance across groups—a level of transparency rarely seen. Kepco, the largest electric utility in South Korea, provides a chart showing its different stakeholder groups, its responsibility to these groups, and the channels it uses to engage with them (Figure 6.1).[26]

Issue Identification and Description

Both the number of material issues and their descriptions varied immensely between companies. The average number of issues included in the matrices we reviewed was 23, with a range from 7 to 69. Companies used different formats such as color, symbols, size of dot, and arrows when presenting issues in the matrix. Symbols or colors were used to denote certain themes, mostly along the environmental, social, and governance dimensions.[27] For example, Thomson Reuters uses different symbols for the categories Community, Workplace, Environment, and Marketplace, whereas Enel uses three different colors for the categories "Business and governance," "Environmental management," and "Social."[28] Another 5.5% of the sample varied the size of the issue dot, which most often represented the degree of control the company had over the issue.[29] Finally, 4.4% of matrices included an arrow either in place of the dot or next to the dot to show how the issue's importance had increased or decreased in the previous years or how it was predicted to change in the future. For example, UBS uses up or down arrows to signify whether an issue is likely to increase or decrease in relevance to UBS stakeholders and significance to UBS's performance.[30]

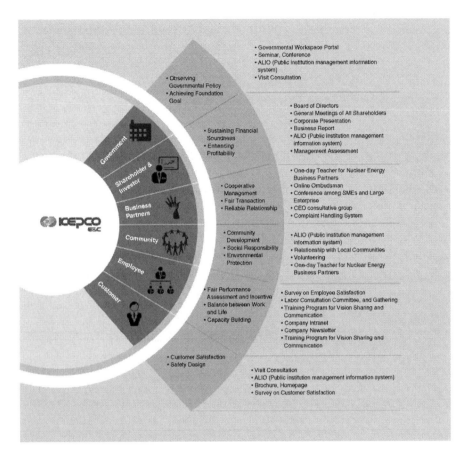

FIGURE 6.1 Stakeholder Engagement at Kepco

Source: Kepco. *Kepco 2012 Sustainability Report,* http://www.kepco-enc.com/
webzine_business-kopec/sr_2012_e.pdf, p. 20, accessed May 2014.

Dimension Definitions and Labels

Most companies (88%) use the X-axis for the company dimension and the
Y-axis for the society or stakeholder dimension. The remaining 12% simply
reversed them. Most companies also adhere closely to GRI's recommendation of
labeling the company axis as "Significance to the company/organization" and
the society or stakeholder as "Significance to stakeholders,"[31] but very few
explain the meaning of "significance" on either axis. For the company
dimension, significance is typically defined in terms of impact on strategy,

financial performance, and sometimes reputation. The Norwegian petroleum company Statoil defines the company dimension clearly, saying, "The impact on Statoil was assessed based on factors such as potential financial impact, reputational impact, environmental and social impact, corporate strategy and key operations and industry comparison and standardisation."[32]

Because the stakeholder dimension contains diverse stakeholders with different interests, it is even harder to define, let alone know, what it means in the aggregate. As with the company dimension, its meaning depends upon what data are used and how different data are aggregated. One of the better explanations for this dimension comes from the Danish food producer Danisco: "In our matrix we rank the issues not only based on the number of stakeholders that raise the issue, but also the level of interest or concern that any one stakeholder group may have. Items that are of high concern to our most important stakeholders, customers, and employees may rank high on the interest continuum."[33]

Although far less frequent, some axis definitions add other elements to "significance" or "importance." The most common additional element, although relatively atypical (found in only 12% of the population studied) and with substantial variation itself, is to include a component of time on the company axis. For example, Nestlé labels its X-axis "Current or increasing impact on Nestlé," while Ball Corporation's is "Current or potential impact on Ball."[34] Clearly, "increasing" and "potential" are different ideas; the first is already happening and the second is something that might happen. In either case, no explanation is given regarding how the present and future were weighted in evaluating an issue from the company's perspective. Furthermore, the time dimension is rarely defined or quantified. Ford is one exception: "Though we consider possible impacts and importance out to 10 years, three to five years is the timeframe in which Ford can make meaningful changes in our own actions based on our internal planning and production cycles."[35] Still, the company did not explain its weightings between present and future.

Issue Scoring

What type of data and methodology are used to score the issues? The more information provided on how issues are scored, including both the type of data and the methodology used to collect and aggregate it, the more useful the matrix becomes for the reader. Without this information, the reader only learns the company's point of view about the relative significance of each issue. While useful, it is equally, if not more, useful to understand *how* the company came to this point of view. As with the above aspects of constructing a materiality matrix, most companies provide little to no explanation about how issue scoring is done, with only 8% providing even a modicum of explanation. Generally, little to nothing is said about the algorithms used to score an issue.

Regardless of the algorithms used, companies vary in terms of the precision with which issues are placed in the matrix. Three basic methods were observed: (1) numerical labels on the axis (e.g., 1 through 5), (2) word labels (e.g., high, medium, and low), and (3) no labels (with implied low to high).[36] For each, companies create cells in the matrix or used "isobars" to represent materiality "boundaries."

Still, some companies clearly articulate their scoring method and provide qualitative interpretation. UBS, with axis units of 1–100, breaks down the scoring into five different areas.[37] Royal DSM uses a numerical scoring system along the axis and segments its matrix into four quadrants with different descriptions.[38] However, no companies in our sample explicitly state how their stakeholders are weighted or how their views are aggregated on the Y-axis.[39]

Interactivity

Finally, we examined creative ways in which the company was leveraging online tools, a topic discussed more generally in Chapter 8. On their websites, companies can address some of the limitations we observed in the above aspects by making their materiality matrix more interactive. Some have an interactive materiality matrix that provides the user with an additional layer of data. These typically appear on the company's website with "clickable" issue points that direct the user to a page that explains the issue in more depth and details the company's response. Clicking on the issue "resource scarcity" on the German chemical company BASF's materiality matrix, for example, takes the user to a page addressing BASF's different strategies for resource efficiency and renewable raw materials.[40] Other interactive matrices allow the user to change the perspective along one or multiple dimensions. Cisco, for example, has an interactive materiality matrix that allows the user to populate the matrix with only one issue category (Society, Environment, or Governance) or based on the level of control the company had over the issue (High, Moderate, or Low).[41] Campbell's Soup, on the other hand, allows the user to populate the matrix with one of four different issue categories.[42]

Uses of the Matrix

As with the construction and presentation of the matrix itself, in our study of 91 companies we found substantial variation in the relative emphasis companies accord to reporting, stakeholder engagement, and resource commitment, and the degree to which the company explains how it uses the matrix for these purposes. In most cases, its main implied use is for the sustainability or integrated report, yet very few companies clearly link the entries in the matrix to the content of the report. Exceptions include Samsung Life Insurance and GS Engineering and Construction, which provide page numbers for the material issues prioritized in the matrix.[43] Similarly, companies rarely discuss engagement in use and, as described above, we noted tremendous variation in the amount of disclosure about engagement for construction. From an audience perspective, the most opaque use of the matrix by companies is for resource commitment decisions. One exception is Mountain Co-op's explanation of its materiality analysis: "At MEC, we use materiality analysis in two ways: to inform sustainability strategy by highlighting issues that matter to stakeholders and the organization, and to inform reporting to ensure transparent communication about material issues. By understanding what is material to our organization and our stakeholders, we can prioritize our strategy and our report accordingly."[44] This simple statement makes clear that the company believes more emphasis should be put on reporting about issues that have significant resource commitments.

FROM THE MATERIALITY MATRIX TO THE SUSTAINABLE VALUE MATRIX

We applaud the work companies and NGOs have done to develop the idea of a materiality matrix. It is an important contribution to helping companies develop sustainable strategies and work with their stakeholders to develop a sustainable society. However, we believe it is time to take the logical next step of improving the rigor by which this matrix is created and used. Evidence of the need for this is our analysis of the 91 matrices discussed above. We propose that it is time to shift from the "Materiality Matrix" to the "Sustainable Value Matrix (SVM)."

"Sustainable Value Matrix" is more than a mere change in terminology. Our rationale for why a "Sustainable Value Matrix" is a more appropriate term than "Materiality Matrix" is grounded in the discussion of the previous chapter, particularly the idea that materiality only has meaning from the perspective of the entity that determines it. A firm cannot define the materiality of others—be they companies or other stakeholders. Thus, only one dimension, conventionally the X-axis, is "about" materiality, and we call this axis "Materiality to the Firm."

A sustainable strategy is one which enables a company to create value for its shareholders over the long term while contributing to a sustainable society. This involves recognizing what is *material* to investors from the company's perspective and, in its view, what is *significant* to society. Those stakeholders that are not significant and the issues they represent are absent from the company's "Statement of Significant Audiences and Materiality." The SVM and its supporting disclosures can be a visual representation of this Statement.

We call the stakeholder dimension, typically the Y-axis, "Society's Issue Significance." It is *not* "materiality to society." While specific stakeholders have their own view of materiality, society as a whole does not. To recall the "cardinality" concept from the previous chapter: between the firm and society, there exists a "one-to-many" relationship, not the one-to-one entity relationship required for materiality. Many is not an entity. The Y-axis is the firm's representation of the aggregated views of its chosen stakeholders as reified in the concept of "society." Through a process it designs, the firm determines the relevant (and irrelevant) stakeholders,[45] how it will engage with them to get their views, other methodologies for gathering data, and the algorithm for aggregating these data into one measure on this dimension for this issue. In truth, the most accurate label for the Y-axis is "The Firm's Perception of the Significance of Its Chosen Stakeholders' Interests Aggregated as 'Society.'"

However, we choose to shorten this mouthful to "Society's Issue Significance." This view is influenced by the firm's own perception of its role in society because this determines the stakeholders it chooses to engage with and the weightings it gives in aggregating their views. Thus it is not and *should not* be construed as an "objective" or "accurate" view of the relative importance society attaches to issues.[46] It is about how important the company thinks issues are to society *from its perspective,* as grounded in the board's "Statement of Significant Audiences and Materiality," which identifies the relevant stakeholders and their relative importance.[47]

Highlighting the binary nature of materiality, the SVM is a literal matrix with defined cells, not necessarily of equal size, and thresholds (Figure 6.2).

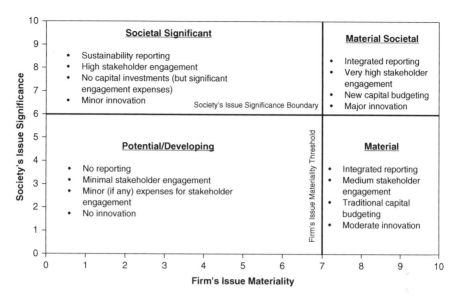

FIGURE 6.2 The Sustainable Value Matrix

(The inset "A Hypothetical SVM for a Pharmaceutical Company" provides a hypothetical example of the SVM for a pharmaceutical company.) Each cell has reporting, stakeholder engagement, resource commitment, and innovation attributes. The company has the responsibility and, consequently, must have the courage to be clear about which issues it considers to rise above the materiality and significance thresholds and which do not. The firm, as represented by its board, must first decide the "Firm Issue Materiality Threshold," which identifies the threshold for material issues, and then the "Society's Issue Significance Boundary," which identifies the boundary for stakeholder issue significance. Where to place each line is completely at the firm's discretion. It simply must do so and be clear about the methodology it uses to make this decision, which starts with the "Statement of Significant Audiences and Materiality."

The Four Cells

The "Material Societal Issues" cell contains the issues that the company has determined are most relevant for the stakeholders it considers most significant given the corporation's objectives. All of these issues should be the responsibility of line management and should be included in the company's integrated report. They also require high levels of stakeholder engagement and resource commitment. Often issues in which there is a tradeoff between meeting the objectives of providers of financial capital and stakeholders, the issues in this cell are those with the greatest need for major innovation. Specifically, a type of "open innovation" through stakeholder engagement can allow a company to simultaneously improve financial and nonfinancial performance. These major innovations are typically high risk, requiring substantial capital commitments, and long time frames before they pay off.[48] In its integrated report, the company should explain its efforts and expectations for stakeholder engagement, resource commitment, and innovation.

Because they are highly important to sustainable value creation—especially for the audience of shareholders—issues in the "Material Issues" cell should also be included in the company's integrated report. While the company deems them less significant for stakeholders, a medium degree of engagement is appropriate because of the opportunities they provide for moderate innovation regarding sustainability issues.[49] In general, resource commitments will be less than in the above cell, but they can still be significant.

In contrast, the issues in the "Societal Significant Issues" cell are not material for sustainable value creation. Still, a company cannot completely ignore civil society even if it does not deem these issues, at least for now, critical to its strategy. As such, these issues require a modest resource commitment and offer only minor opportunities for innovation for sustainability. Because the company has acknowledged the importance of these issues, however, it should practice high levels of stakeholder engagement and transparent sustainability reporting about them outside of its integrated report. These issues can be managed through a "sustainability program" being led by the "sustainability group," perhaps under the direction of a Chief Sustainability Officer. They are not the responsibility of line management.

The final cell, labeled "Potential/Developing Issues," includes topics that can and should be largely ignored—at least for now. There is no need to report on them and it would be a mistake to do so, as this will only create clutter and distract the audience from the issues the company deems are significant. Consequently, little effort should be made in stakeholder engagement and minimal resources should be committed to these issues. Innovation is largely irrelevant in this cell. Even if opportunities exist, the resources are best committed elsewhere.

The transformative power of the SVM is a product of the exercise of governance judgment, evidenced by clearly displaying this binary treatment of materiality and significance, drawing clear lines to inform reporting, stakeholder engagement, resource commitment decisions, and opportunities for innovation. By being clear on what it sees as material and significant and what is not, the company establishes credibility and legitimacy. It avoids charges of "greenwashing" that can legitimately be made when a company says "we care about everything and everybody."

Yes, such demarcations can lead to conflict. Stakeholders unhappy with the placement of their issue(s) in a company's SVM may choose to try to influence them to change it. That is their right. It is also the company's obligation to engage—although not necessarily agree—with them. The SVM is the basis for a more meaningful conversation between a company and all of its stakeholders within the now-clarified framework of how the corporation sees its role in society. While the general quality of integrated reports being produced today is fair, however, there is substantial room for improvement in how companies communicate their views on materiality—an issue addressed in the next chapter on the quality of integrated reporting.

A Hypothetical SVM for a Pharmaceutical Company

Although clearly no company has produced an SVM, we can make this idea more concrete with an "as if" example for a hypothetical pharmaceutical company example (Figure 6.3). We say "as if" since this example violates the fundamental tenet of the SVM, which is that it is an entity-specific social construction. However, using data from other sources, we can illustrate what such a matrix might look like for a pharmaceutical company, with a corresponding "as if" analysis recognizing that it is not from an actual company's perspective. The 43 issues in this SVM are taken directly from the Sustainability Accounting Standards Board (SASB)[50] (Table 6.1). We used their Materiality Map™ to determine the value on the X-axis, setting the "Firm's Issue Materiality Threshold" line at SASB's cutoff point for materiality. The values on the Y-axis are the averages of a survey of eight partners at the Boston Consulting Group who are experts on the pharmaceutical industry, as a simulation of the stakeholder engagement process.[51] In keeping with the spirit of exercising discipline in drawing the "Society's Issue Significance Boundary," we set it at 6.0, on a 1–10 scale.

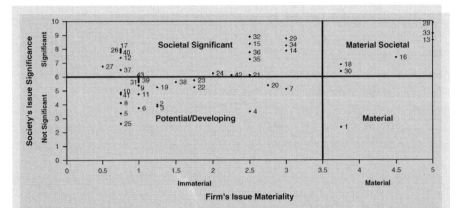

FIGURE 6.3 A Hypothetical Sustainable Value Matrix for a Pharmaceutical Company

Of the list of 43 issues (Figure 6.3), only 6 appear in the "Material Societal Issues" cell and they are either in the "Social Capital" or "Business Model and Innovation" SASB issue categories. This makes intuitive sense for a pharmaceutical company. Climate change risk (issue number "1") is the only entry in the "Material Issues" cell. This may suggest that the company perceives this issue as more significant than it believes stakeholders do. Or, it could be that this hypothetical firm is heavily weighting new Securities and Exchange Commission and European Union regulatory guidance on climate change when determining materiality. The "Societal Significant" cell is heavily populated by "Leadership and Governance" topics regarding the company's products, along with a significant number of "Social Capital" and "Business Model and Innovation" issues. Except for climate change risks, all issues in the "Environment" category appear in the "Potential/Developing Issues" cell, consistent with the perceived relatively low impact a pharmaceutical company has on the environment. Finally, while no Human Capital category issues were considered material by the firm, the firm perceives that its stakeholders think that "employee health and safety" as well as "retention and recruitment" are significant ("Societal Significant" cell), and that the remaining five other human capital issues are not significant to stakeholders.

TABLE 6.1 SASB Pharmaceutical Issues

Number	Issue	Category	Cell
1	Climate change risks	Environment	Material
2	Environmental accidents and remediation	Environment	Potential/Developing
3	Water use and management	Environment	Potential/Developing
4	Energy management	Environment	Potential/Developing
5	Fuel management and transportation	Environment	Potential/Developing
6	GHG emissions and air pollution	Environment	Potential/Developing
7	Waste management and effluents	Environment	Potential/Developing
8	Biodiversity impacts	Environment	Potential/Developing
9	Communications and engagement	Social Capital	Potential/Developing
10	Community development	Social Capital	Potential/Developing
11	Impact from facilities	Social Capital	Potential/Developing
12	Customer satisfaction	Social Capital	Societal Significant
13	Customer health and safety	Social Capital	Material Societal
14	Disclosure and labeling	Social Capital	Societal Significant
15	Marketing and ethical advertising	Social Capital	Societal Significant
16	Access to services	Social Capital	Material Societal
17	Customer privacy	Social Capital	Societal Significant
18	New markets	Social Capital	Material Societal
19	Diversity and equal opportunity	Human Capital	Potential/Developing
20	Training and development	Human Capital	Potential/Developing
21	Recruitment and retention	Human Capital	Societal Significant
22	Compensation and benefits	Human Capital	Potential/Developing
23	Labor relations and union practices	Human Capital	Potential/Developing
24	Employee health, safety, and wellness	Human Capital	Societal
25	Child and forced labor	Human Capital	Potential/Developing

(continued)

TABLE 6.1 (*Continued*)

Number	Issue	Category	Cell
26	Long-term viability of core business	Business Model and Innovation	Societal Significant
27	Accounting for externalities	Business Model and Innovation	Societal Significant
28	Research, development, and innovation	Business Model and Innovation	Material Societal
29	Product societal value	Business Model and Innovation	Societal Significant
30	Product life cycle use impact	Business Model and Innovation	Material Societal
31	Packaging	Business Model and Innovation	Potential/Developing
32	Product pricing	Business Model and Innovation	Societal Significant
33	Product quality and safety	Business Model and Innovation	Material Societal
34	Regulatory and legal challenges	Leadership and Governance	Societal Significant
35	Policies, standards, codes of conduct	Leadership and Governance	Societal Significant
36	Business ethics and competitive behavior	Leadership and Governance	Societal Significant
37	Shareholder engagement	Leadership and Governance	Societal Significant
38	Board structure and independence	Leadership and Governance	Potential/Developing
39	Executive compensation	Leadership and Governance	Potential/Developing
40	Lobbying and political contributions	Leadership and Governance	Societal Significant
41	Raw material demand	Leadership and Governance	Potential/Developing
42	Supply chain standards and selection	Leadership and Governance	Societal Significant
43	Supply chain engagement and transparency	Leadership and Governance	Potential/Developing

Data Source: Sustainability Accounting Standards Board. SASB Materiality Map™, http://sasb.s3-website-us-east-1.amazonaws.com/, accessed May 2014.

NOTES

1. Eccles, Robert G. and George Serafeim. "The Performance Frontier: Innovating for a sustainable strategy." *Harvard Business Review* 91, no. 5 (May 2013): 50–60.
2. Fronesys, "Materiality Determination: Analysing who, what and how," October 2011, p. 3. This report summarizes the results of detailed analyses of the materiality matrices of 31 companies. A full version of the report is available for purchase from Fronesys.
3. The report recommended a five-part materiality test: (1) Direct, short-term financial impacts, (2) Policy-based performance, (3) Business peer-based norms, (4) Stakeholder behavior and concerns, and (5) Societal norms (regulator and nonregulatory). AccountAbility. Research, Organizational Accountability, http://www.accountability.org/images/content/0/8/085/Redefining%252520Materiality%252520-%252520Full%252520Report.pdf p. 4, accessed May 2014.
4. BP, "Making the Right Choices," *Sustainability Report 2004*, http://www.bp.com/liveassets/bp_internet/globalbp/STAGING/global_assets/downloads/S/Sustainability_Report_2004.pdf, accessed May 2014.
5. Ford, "Our Route to Sustainability," *Sustainability Report 2004/5*. http://corporate.ford.com/doc/2004-05_sustainability_report.pdf, accessed May 2014. BT, "Social and Environmental Report," 2006. http://www.btplc.com/betterfuture/betterbusiness/betterfuturereport/pdf/2006/2006Environmentalreport.pdf, accessed May 2014.
6. AccountAbility. "The Materiality Report," http://www.accountability.org/images/content/0/8/088/The%20Materiality%20Report.pdf, accessed May 2014, p. 20. The report analyzed the approaches and experiences of Anglo American, Ford Motor Company, The Gap Inc., Hydro Tasmania, Nike, Novozymes, BP Plc, BT Group Plc, and Telefonica. "The Materiality Report," p. 7. For an example of a risk analysis matrix, see PricewaterhouseCoopers, "A practical guide to risk assessment," December 2008, p. 28, Figure 5. Risk analysis can be defined as "a systematic process for identifying and evaluating events (i.e., possible risks and opportunities) that could affect the achievement of objectives, positively or negatively. Such events can be identified in the external environment (e.g., economic trends, regulatory landscape, and competition) and within an organization's internal environment (e.g., people, process, and infrastructure). When these events intersect with an organization's objectives—or can be predicted to do so—they become risks." p. 5.
7. Global Reporting Initiative. Reporting, G3.1 and G3 Guidelines, Guidelines Online, https://www.globalreporting.org/resourcelibrary/GRI-Technical-Protocol.pdf, accessed May 2014. GRI calls the material issue selection process the "prioritization step": "The methodology applied in the

Prioritization step varies according to the individual organization. Specific circumstances such as business model, sector, geographic, cultural and legal operating context, ownership structure, and size and nature of impacts affect how an organization prioritizes the topics and Aspects it covers in its sustainability report. What is important, given this variation, is the need for an organization to develop a rational process, the ability to document it, and the ability to replicate the process in subsequent reporting cycles."

8. Ibid.
9. Mark McElroy, the founder and executive director of the Center for Sustainable Organizations, critiqued this formulation of the matrix, arguing that it "amounts to a perversion of the idea of materiality in sustainability reporting, because it essentially cuts out consideration of what are arguably *the most* material issues: the broad social, economic and environmental impacts of an organization, regardless of how they relate to a particular business plan or strategy." "Are Materiality Matrices Really Material?" http://www .sustainablebrands.com/news_and_views/articles/are-materiality-matrices-really-material, accessed December 2013. In the Technical Protocol for GRI3.1, released in the 2011, the X-axis was changed to "significance to the organization." https://www.globalreporting.org/resourcelibrary/GRI-Technical-Protocol.pdf, accessed May 2014.
10. Framework LLC, "State of Integrated Reporting," 2013, p. 5 and Fronesys, "Materiality Futures," 2011, p. 7.
11. Framework LLC, "The Materiality Bridge," 2011.
12. The visual representation could be a matrix, chart, or diagram. Framework LLC, "The Materiality Bridge," 2011. p. 2.
13. Report Sustentabilidade, "Materiality in Brazil: How companies identify relevant topics," 2013. http://www.reportsustentabilidade.com.br/research-materiality-in-brazil.pdf, accessed May 2014.
14. Fronesys describes itself as a Digital Economy advisory service. Their focus is on research, consulting, and training in four core areas, Innovation and entrepreneurship, Sustainability, Big Data and Smart Cities and Digital skills. Fronesys. About, http://www.fronesys.com/blog/about.html, accessed May 2014.
15. Fronesys, "Materiality Futures," 2011, p. 8. The companies were selected for inclusion using Corporateregister.com, Framework: CR (now known as Framework LLC) materiality analysis and Internet search engines. Each company selected had a published materiality matrix with at least three degrees of granularity per axis and with individual issues identified and positioned in the matrix. The 31 companies identified each had a published materiality matrix with at least three levels of granularity per axis and with individual issues identified and positioned within the matrix.

16. NGOs were the most common constituency for the stakeholder axis, whereas Management/experts were the most common constituency for the company axis. Fronesys, "Materiality Futures," 2011. pp. 10–11.

17. "This is calculated by averaging the distance of all points on an issue chart from the average materiality point. Using this approach, if all companies have agreed on the position an issue takes along the company axis, and their stakeholders have similarly agreed on the position the issue takes along the stakeholder axis, then the Issue Coherence Level (ICL) would be zero. On the other hand a totally random distribution would result in an ICL of about 4." Fronesys, "Materiality Futures," 2011. p. 14. The study finds that "economic stability/recession" has the greatest coherence level, while "biodiversity" has the least.

18. "If the company and its stakeholders agreed on the materiality ranking for every issue considered then there would be perfect convergence and all the issue points would sit on an x=y straight line. To measure materiality convergence, Fronesys proposes the statistical parameter known as the average residual (R^2), as defined in figure 8, where R^2 is, in effect, a measure of divergence form the x=y line." Fronesys, "Materiality Futures," 2011. p. 16.

19. For instance, China Mobile has a materiality matrix which was excluded because it does not properly label issue location. It provides a matrix populated with unlabeled dots, with a list of material issues given below the matrix. However, none of these issues are scored and it is not possible to correlate them with the dots on the matrix. China Mobile Limited. *2012 Sustainability Report*, http://www.chinamobileltd.com/en/ir/reports/ar2012/sd2012.pdf, p. 6, accessed May 2014.

20. The company's reporting and website were evaluated for explanations of the stakeholder identification process and stakeholder engagement process.

21. Volkswagen. *Sustainability Report 2012*, http://sustainability-report2012 .volkswagenag.com/fileadmin/download/11_Stakeholder_Dialoge_e.pdf, accessed May 2014.

22. Dow. *2012 Annual Sustainability Report*, http://www.dow.com/sustainability/ pdf/35865-2012%20Sustainability%20Report.pdf, pp. 41, 43, accessed May 2014. See also for more background on the SEAC: Eccles, Robert G., George Serafeim, and Shelley Xin Li. "Dow Chemical: Innovating for Sustainability." Harvard Business School Case 112-064, January 2012. (Revised June 2013.)

23. Carlsberg Group. CSR, Materiality Analysis, http://www.carlsberggroup .com/csr/ReportingonProgress/overview/Materialityanalysis/Pages/Mater iality Matrix.aspx, accessed May 2014.

24. Staples. Staples Soul, Reporting Approach, Materiality Analysis, http://www .staples.com/sbd/cre/marketing/australia_soul/staples-soul-reporting-approach .html#id_ra2, accessed May 2014.

25. Daiwa. *Daiwa House Group Annual Report 2012*, http://www.daiwahouse.com/english/groupbrand/ar/pdf/daiwahouseAR2012E_2.pdf, p. 145, accessed May 2014.

26. Kepco. *Kepco 2012 Sustainability Report*, http://www.kepco-enc.com/webzine_business-kopec/sr_2012_e.pdf, p. 20, accessed May 2014.

27. Enel. Sustainability, Responsibility, Materiality Matrix, http://www.enel.com/en-GB/sustainability/our_responsibility/materiality_matrix/, accessed May 2014.

28. Thomson Reuters. The Knowledge Effect, Materiality Matrix, http://blog.thomsonreuters.com/index.php/materiality-matrix/, accessed May 2014.

29. Other uses included "Global Sustainability Significance." Mountain Equipment Co-op. MEC's 2013 Materiality Matrix, http://www.mec.ca/media/Images/pdf/accountability/MEC_2013_materiality_matrix_v2_m56577569831501444.pdf, accessed May 2014 and "Pressure from stakeholders." Braskem. Annual Report 2012, http://rao2012.braskem.com/media/pdf/RAB12_PDF_completo_in.pdf, accessed May 2014.

30. UBS. About us, Corporate responsibility, Our approach, Materiality assessment, https://www.ubs.com/global/en/about_ubs/corporate_responsibility/commitment_strategy/materiality-matrix.html, accessed May 2014.

31. The three most common labels on the X-axis were "relevance to" (26%), "impact on"(23%), and "importance to" (20%). The three most common labels on the Y-axis were "importance to" (34%), "relevance to" (16%), and "significance to" (9%).

32. Statoil. *Annual Report 2012*, Sustainability Report, http://www.statoil.com/AnnualReport2012/en/Download%20Center%20Files/01%20Key%20downloads/20%20Sustainability%20Report%202012/Sustainability.pdf, p. 51, accessed May 2014.

33. Danisco. *2010/2011 Sustainability Report*, http://cdn.danisco.com/uploads/tx_tcdaniscofiles/danisco_sustanability_report_2010-11_04.pdf, p. 20, accessed May 2014.

34. Nestlé. Creating Shared Value, What is CSV, Materiality, http://www.nestle.com/csv/what-is-csv/materiality, accessed May 2014. Ball Corp. Sustainability, Our Approach, Priorities, https://www.ball.com/materiality/, accessed May 2014.

35. Ford, Sustainability 2013/2013, http://corporate.ford.com/microsites/sustainability-report-2012-13/blueprint-materiality-analysis.

36. Numerical (14.3%), Labels (60.4%), No labels (25.3%).

37. UBS. E: 0–19. Relevant to a limited number of stakeholders and no current impact on UBS performance. D: 20–39. Relevant to a group of stakeholders and minor current impact on UBS performance. C: 40–59. Relevant to groups of stakeholders and limited current impact on UBS performance. B: 60–79. Relevant to most (including all key) stakeholder groups and relative current

impact on UBS performance. A: 80–100. Relevant to all stakeholders and direct current impact on UBS performance.

38. DSM. *Royal DSM Integrated Annual Report 2012.* http://annualreport2012 .dsm.com/downloads/DSM-Annual-Report-2012.pdf, accessed May 2014. The upper right quadrant is "Prioritize," the upper left is "Actively monitor and communicate," the bottom left is "low priority," and the bottom right is "actively manage."

39. Although Daimler acknowledges the complexity of aggregating stakeholders' views in producing the Y-axis in its 2012/2013 materiality matrix, it only provides a one-sentence explanation for how this as done: "In addition, weighted averages were calculated for what in some cases were divergent interests among individual stakeholder groups. These averages (weighted) were incorporated into the matrix in an aggregate form." Daimler. *Sustainability Report 2012,* About this report, Materiality matrix, http://sustainability.daimler.com/reports/daimler/ annual/2013/nb/English/7520/materiality-matrix.html, accessed December 2013. Deloitte recommends using decision science to calculate the stakeholder weighting: "Given today's immature state of knowledge on ESG valuation impacts, decision science methods are a powerful tool that can help managers develop a single scale and structure some of the complexity involved in ESG topics, including the subjective biases of multiple stakeholders. Using these methods can augment the credibility of ESG materiality determination and can allow business leaders to better defend their decisions about ESG management, investment and disclosure on matters of value to their myriad stakeholders." Decision science can be used to weight and aggregate the scores of individual stakeholder groups, as well as incorporate the importance of a time dimension in these issues. Using such methods can increase the transparency of the scoring process, and provide an objective measure, which acknowledges the differences in stakeholder groups. Deloitte. "Disclosure of long term business value; What matters?" http://www .deloitte.com/assets/Dcom-UnitedStates/Local%20Assets/Documents/us_scc_ materialitypov_032812.pdf, accessed May 2014.

40. BASF. Sustainability, Identification and Management of Sustainability Issues, Materiality analysis, http://www.basf.com/group/corporate/en/sustainability/ management-and-instruments/global-materiality-matrix, accessed May 2014. For other examples, see the following. Vodafone. Sustainability, Our vision and approach, Material issues, http://www.vodafone.com/content/sustainability/ our_vision_and_approach/managing_sustainability/material_issues.html, accessed May 2014. Fraport. Connecting Sustainability – Report 2012, Sustainability Management, Sustainability Strategy, http://sustainability-report.fra-port.com/sustainability-management/sustainability-strategy/#wesen, accessed May 2014.

41. Cisco. 2013 Corporate Social Responsibility Report, http://www.cisco.com/ assets/csr/pdf/CSR_Report_2013.pdf, accessed May 2014.

42. Campbell Soup Company. *2013 Corporate Social Responsibility Report*, http://csr.campbellsoupcompany.com/csr/pages/success/materiality-analysis.asp#.UvGgNRBdVQF. Inactive link as of May 2014. The four stakeholder categories were "Customer/Consumer"; "Stakeholder Relations and Community"; "Workplace"; and "Environment and Supply Chain."

43. Samsung Life Insurance. *2010-2011 Samsung Life Insurance Sustainability Report*, http://www.samsunglife.com/companyeng/pdf/2010_2011_SR_eng_full_page.pdf, accessed May 2014. The Corporate Library. GS E&C Integrated Report, http://public.thecorporatelibrary.net/Sustain/sr_2011_313140.pdf, accessed May 2014.

44. Mountain Equipment Co-op.

45. Most companies use a fairly high-level classification of stakeholders into broad groups like employees, customers, suppliers, and NGOs. But there are nuances within each and decisions made about how to construct the sample for each stakeholder group. The situation is especially complicated with NGOs. The company may not always know which NGO is the most "legitimate" one for representing society's interest on a particular topic. Conversely, identifying an NGO as a stakeholder in constructing the matrix and in ongoing engagement processes can confer legitimacy on the NGO, raise questions about why the company selected a particular NGO and not another, or both. For a thorough discussion of some of the nuances in identifying, selecting, and engaging with stakeholders see Wheeler, David, Heike Fabig, and Richard Boele. "Paradoxes and Dilemmas for Stakeholder Responsive Firms in the Extractive Sector: Lessons from the Case of Shell and the Ogoni." *Journal of Business Ethics* 39 (September 2002): 297–318.

46. We observed this already in our comparison of Ford's matrix and Daimler's matrix. We saw that the same issues were given different scores along each company's materiality matrix, underlining the fact that the Y-axis is not an objective measure of importance to society but the company's *judgment* of an issue's significance to society.

47. This approach has already been adopted by a few companies which name the Y-axis either "society" or "societal interest." See the following. Cisco. Petrobas, Investor Relations, Sustainability Report, http://investidorpetrobras.com.br/en/governance/sustainability-report/relatorio-de-sustentabilidade-detalhe-4.htm), accessed May 2014. DSM.

48. Eccles and Serafeim explain that this is not for the faint of heart, "Addressing the most significant trade-offs between financial and ESG performance—challenges that are often unsolved in a sector—requires major, organization-wide innovation: entirely new products, processes, and business models that improve performance in 'bundles' of material issues. Developing a single product or process innovation to address a specific issue may be part of the solution but in and of itself won't shift the performance frontier for the

company as a whole." Furthermore, they add, ". . . major innovations often require substantial investments whose benefits will not be seen for years to come. If a company expects shareholders to commit for the long term in order to receive those benefits, it needs to provide them with information that justifies their investments. Combining ESG and financial performance information in a single document [an integrated report], as Natura did, is an effective way to do this." Eccles and Serafeim. "The Performance Frontier," pp. 54 and 58.

49. Eccles and Serafeim note that minor to moderate innovation may not be enough. "While minor innovations, such as efficiency improvements, can nudge a downward-sloping performance frontier up a bit, only major innovations in products, processes, or business models can shift the slope from descending to ascending." The authors continue, "If your firm's performance in an area—say, energy use or labor practices—falls short of industry benchmarks, getting it up above par is a first priority. At the very least it will mitigate your risks, since stakeholders tend to focus on industry laggards in campaigns aimed at increasing corporate ESG performance. Many improvements, such as reducing manufacturing waste, involve minor or moderate innovations that can enhance efficiency and, therefore, financial performance. Those sorts of innovations are increasingly necessary (but not sufficient) to ensure competitiveness." Ibid., pp. 53–54.

50. Sustainability Accounting Standards Board. Approach, Materiality, SASB Materiality Map™ http://www.sasb.org/materiality/sasb-materiality-map/, accessed May 2014.

51. Martin Reeves, email correspondence with Robert Eccles, April 17, 2014. We are deeply grateful to Martin Reeves, Senior Vice President of the Boston Consulting Group and head of their Strategy Institute, and seven of his partners for taking the time to fill out the survey, which provided data for the Y-axis.

Comparing the Ford and Daimler Materiality Matrices

WHILE THE 3 × 3 matrix displayed on Ford's website on December 30, 2013 (Figure 6A.1), is similar in structure to its first public effort in 2005, changes are evident. The number of issues in the matrix increased from 34 to 61, issue definitions have become more detailed and elaborate, issue trends from previous materiality analyses are noted, and the matrix has increased interactivity.[1] The High Impact, High Concern issues in the top right-hand corner of the matrix are included in the company's printed summary report, the issues in the three adjacent boxes are reported on the web, and those in the remaining five boxes are not covered in detail through any type of reporting. The website has an "interactive" feature whereby the user can click on a box to see which issues it contains.[2] The High Impact, High Concern box shows 14 issues in seven categories (Figure 6A.1) and for each issue, the user can scroll down to see a definition/description, comments, trend analysis, and hyperlinks to other pages on Ford's website that provide a more detailed discussion and information on Ford's strategy in relation to the issue.[3]

Without going into great detail, Ford provides a reasonably clear view of how it developed its 2012/2013 matrix. The company defines "material information" as "that which is of greatest interest to, and which has the

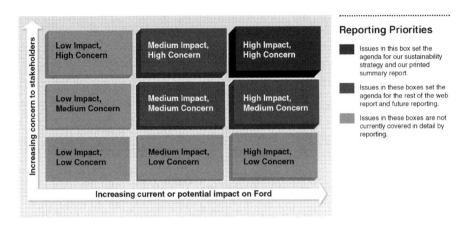

FIGURE 6A.1   Ford's Materiality Matrix

Source: Ford. Sustainability 2011/12, Our Blueprint for Sustainability, Overview of the Analysis Process, http://corporate.ford.com/microsites/sustainability-report-2012-13/blueprint-materiality-analysis, accessed December 2013.

potential to affect the perception of, those stakeholders who wish to make informed decisions and judgments about the Company's commitment to environmental, social and economic progress."[4] It also emphasizes, "materiality as used in this Sustainability Report does not share the meaning of the concept for the purposes of financial reporting."[5]

Ford provides a general description of how issues are identified and ranked for both the company and stakeholder axes with no supporting analytical detail. For the company axis, Ford notes the frequency with which issues are raised in its policies, business strategy, and performance tracking tools, and the Annual Report or Form 10-K. Ford does not explicitly say how it defines "current or potential impact" on the X-axis, but it does note that it considers "possible impacts and importance out to 10 years."[6] For the stakeholder dimension, Ford analyzes summaries of stakeholder engagement sessions as well as documents representing broader stakeholder views.[7] The company does not explain how this analysis was aggregated into a single stakeholder dimension, but it does note that extra weight was assigned to "investors and multi-stakeholder inputs, as they are the key audiences of our reporting."[8]

A Ceres Stakeholder Committee that included representatives of non-governmental organization (NGOs), socially responsible investment organizations, and a supplier company reviewed Ford's analysis. On Ford's website, the

TABLE 6A.1 Ford's High Impact, High Concern Issues

14 material issues have been identified at this level
SUSTAINABILITY VISION AND MANAGEMENT
Sustainability vision, governance, and management
PUBLIC POLICY
GHG/fuel economy regulation
GOVERNANCE
Human rights strategy
CLIMATE CHANGE
Low-carbon strategy
Vehicle GHG emissions
Electrification strategy
WATER
Water strategy – local community impacts
Water strategy – water impacts of products
Water strategy – water impacts of operations
OPERATIONS
Environmental management
SUPPLY CHAIN SUSTAINABILITY
Human rights in the supply chain
Supplier relationships
Sustainable raw materials
Supply chain environmental sustainability

Source: Ford. Sustainability 2011/12, Our Blueprint for Sustainability, Overview of the Analysis Process, http://corporate.ford.com/microsites/sustainability-report-2012-13/blueprint-materiality-analysis, accessed December 2013.

company reported the Committee's detailed recommendations and noted what type of data assurance, if any, had been done on each issue.[9]

Ford's competitor, Daimler, also produced a materiality matrix (Figure 6A.2) for its 2012 "Sustainability Report."[10] Like Ford, Daimler updates the matrix every two years and indicates the degree of assurance provided on various issues. Compared to Ford, Daimler reversed the X-axis (determined through stakeholder engagement) and Y-axis (determined through the company's Sustainability Office and Board Sustainability

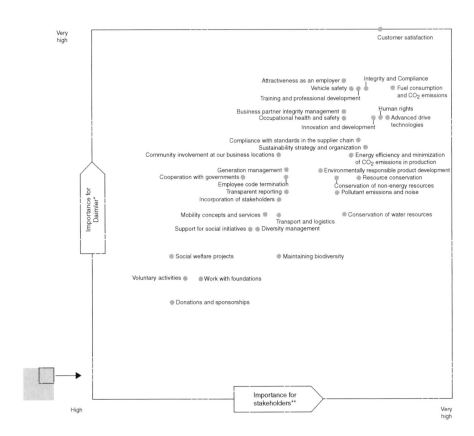

FIGURE 6A.2 Daimler's Materiality Matrix
Source: Daimler. *Sustainability Report 2012.*

Committee). Rather than using boxes to separate issues, the Daimler matrix only presents issues that score between "High" and "Very high" along each axis.[11] Daimler's matrix also contains no interactive features. Both companies are similar in that they use documents and stakeholder engagement to identify and weight issues, although Daimler provides more detail on the process—as on the stakeholder axis, starting with an annual "Daimler Stakeholder Dialogue" held in Stuttgart, Germany, and organized into different working groups by topic (e.g., environmental protection and human rights).[12]

In its 2011 Sustainability Report, Daimler includes a materiality analysis process chart (Figure 6A.3) showing the process by which their matrix is constructed. Daimler also conducted its first online survey, which "was open

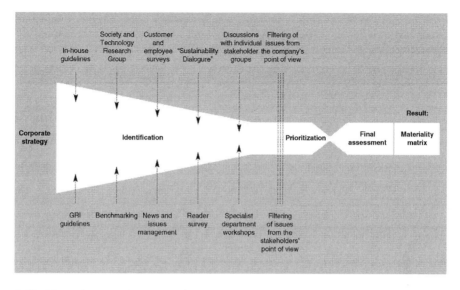

FIGURE 6A.3 Daimler Materiality Matrix Construction Process
Source: Daimler. *Sustainability Report 2011.*

for all interested stakeholders to participate in online at daimler.com during a four-week period between November 15 and December 14, 2012."[13] Some 700 responses were received. Like Ford, Daimler attaches greater weight to some stakeholder groups (e.g., shareholders, customers, suppliers, employees, and NGOs) than others (which are not named).[14] However, also like Ford, no analytical detail is provided about how these weightings resulted in issue placement on the Y-axis.

 NOTES

1. A review was conducted of Ford's materiality matrices from 2004/2005 to 2012/2013, excluding the 2009/2010 matrix, which was unavailable.
2. Ford updates this analysis every two years.
3. Ford. Sustainability 2011/12, Our Blueprint for Sustainability, Overview of the Analysis Process, http://corporate.ford.com/microsites/sustainability-report-2012-13/blueprint-materiality-analysis, accessed December 2013.
4. Ibid.
5. This clarification of materiality in the sustainability context was not added until Ford's second materiality matrix was constructed for its 2006/2007

sustainability report. In its 2011/12 Sustainability Report, Ford significantly updated its materiality analysis using the three steps recommended by AccountAbility: (1) identify the material business issues, (2) prioritize these issues, and (3) review the analysis. In the first step, Ford reviewed a variety of company documents (e.g., on policies, business strategy, and performance tracking tools, and the Annual Report and Form 10K); got comments from external stakeholders (customers, communities, investors, and NGOs); reviewed summaries of stakeholder engagement sessions held by the company; and reviewed documents that represented stakeholder views more broadly (e.g., GRI's G3 Guidelines, the Ceres Roadmap to Sustainability, and reports from socially responsible and mainstream investors). Ibid.

6. Ibid.
7. These documents included the Ceres Roadmap for Sustainability (http://www .ceres.org/resources/reports/ceres-roadmap-to-sustainability-2010/view, accessed May 2014), reports on consumer trends and attitudes, and reports from socially responsible and mainstream investors. Ibid.
8. Ibid.
9. Ford. Sustainability 2012/13, Our Blueprint for Sustainability, Assurance, http://corporate.ford.com/microsites/sustainability-report-2012-13/review-assurance#fn01, accessed December 2013.
10. Daimler. *Sustainability Report 2012*, About this report, Materiality matrix, http://sustainability.daimler.com/reports/daimler/annual/2013/nb/English/ 7520/materiality-matrix.html, accessed December 2013.
11. Daimler's first materiality matrix that appeared in its 2011 Sustainability Report had more clearly defined "high," "very high," and "extremely high" categories. Daimler 360, Facts on Sustainability 2011, http://sustainability .daimler.com/daimler/annual/2013/nb/English/pdf/DAI_2011_sustainability_ en.pdf, p 11, accessed December 2013.
12. Daimler. *Sustainability Report 2012*.
13. Ibid.
14. The Daimler materiality analysis was further advanced and has significantly changed since 2011-12. In order to be even more transparent and precise, the Sustainability Report 2013 illustrates the results of materiality analysis using a table instead of a matrix. At the core of the analysis was an open stakeholder survey with over 800 responses received. In addition, sustainability dialogues to discuss issues from a qualitative perspective were organized in Germany and international markets. In 2013, Daimler's analysis of sustainability topics from the company's point of view reflects the evaluation by Daimler's Board of Management, Sustainability Board and Sustainability Office. For more information see, Daimler. Sustainability Report 2013, http://sustainability.daimler. com/reports/daimler/annual/2014/nb/English/7520/materiality-analysis .html, accessed June 2014.

Methodology for the Materiality Matrices Review

W E STUDIED THE MATERIALITY matrices of 91 companies as published on their websites, restricting our search for matrices to those that had been published or updated since 2010 in order to provide the most accurate review of current practice. An initial group of 16 companies was identified from an Internet search, which we supplemented with companies identified through four other sources. Framework LLC's 2011 report "The Materiality Bridge" was the source of 10 companies. The 2011 Fronesys report "Materiality Futures" was the source of 14 companies. RobecoSAM provided proprietary data from its Corporate Sustainability Assessment of 2000 firms.[1] This is a representative sample of the Standard & Poor's (S&P) Global Broad Market Index since the sample is based on a geographical and sector mix that closely mirrors the S&P broader universe of approximately 10,000 companies. RobecoSAM evaluated these companies for evidence of a materiality process description, a materiality matrix, or a discussion of materiality issues. We identified 42 companies from their study as having materiality matrices and included them in our review. Finally, from the analysis of integrated reports in Chapter 7, we were able to identify an additional nine companies to include in our review.

The materiality matrix was located either separately on the company's website or in one of its reports (annual, sustainability, or integrated). We evaluated both the materiality matrix itself and the surrounding text or links. Our analysis followed three broad categories: stakeholders, matrix construction, and purpose and use.

Stakeholders

▪ Does the company explain how it identified its stakeholder groups?
▪ Does the company explain the stakeholder engagement process?
▪ How many stakeholder groups did the company engage with?

Matrix Construction

▪ How is the X-axis labeled?
▪ How is the Y-axis labeled?
▪ Does either label have a time element (e.g. current/increasing/future)?
▪ How many issues are included in the materiality matrix?
▪ Are the issues defined or explained?
▪ Are the issues themed by color or symbol?
▪ Does the company alter the size of the issue dot?
▪ Are arrows used to show the movement of issues over time on the materiality matrix?
▪ Is the matrix interactive?
▪ Is the scoring method for issues explained?
▪ What is the scale used on the axis? (numerical/categorical/none)

Purpose and Use

▪ Does the company use the matrix for reporting purposes or management purposes? (The text surrounding the materiality matrix was examined for any reference to the matrix as a tool for reporting or as a tool for management purposes. Management purposes could include either stakeholder engagement or resource allocation.)

The list of companies, the source used to identify the company, the year the matrix was published, and a link to the matrix are provided in Table 6B.1.

TABLE 6B.1 Company Materiality Matrices Reviewed

Company	Source	Year	Link
Acciona	RobecoSAM	2012	http://annualreport2012.acciona.com/media/31795/Annual_Report_2012.pdf
ASAHI GLASS CO LTD	RobecoSAM	2013	http://www.agc.com/english/csr/book/pdf/pdf/agc_report_2013e.pdf, p. 20
AT&T	Framework LLC "State of Integration"	2010	http://www.att.com/gen/corporate-citizenship?pid=24331
ATLAS COPCO AB	RobecoSAM	2012	http://www.atlascopco.com/microsites/images/atlas%20copco%20annual%20report%202012_tcm17-3522782_tcm411-3526280.pdf
Ball Corp	Framework LLC "State of Integration"	2011	https://www.ball.com/materiality/
BANCO DO BRASIL	RobecoSAM	2012	http://www45.bb.com.br/docs/ri/ra2012/eng/ra/06.htm
BASF	Internet search	2013	http://www.basf.com/group/corporate/en/sustainability/management-and-instruments/global-materiality-matrix
Bayer	Fronesys	2013	http://www.annualreport2013.bayer.com/en/homepage.aspx
BMW	Fronesys	2012	http://www.bmwgroup.com/e/0_0_www_bmwgroup_com/verantwortung/svr_2012/nachhaltiges_wirtschaften.html
Braskem	Internet search	2012	http://rao2012.braskem.com/media/pdf/RAB12_PDF_completo_in.pdf
BT GROUP PLC	RobecoSAM	2013	https://www.btplc.com/betterfuture/betterbusiness/betterfuturereport/report/strat/mat.aspx
CAIXABANK SA	RobecoSAM	2011	http://multimedia.lacaixa.es/lacaixa/ondemand/criteria/gri/2011/indicadores_gri_ing/files/assets/downloads/publication.pdf
Campbell's	Framework LLC "State of Integration"	2013	http://csr.campbellsoupcompany.com/csr/pages/success/materiality-analysis.asp#.UvGgNRBdVQF

(Continued)

TABLE 6B.1 (Continued)

Company	Source	Year	Link
Carlsberg	Internet search	2011	http://www.carlsberggroup.com/csr/ReportingonProgress/overview/MaterialityAnalysis/Pages/MaterialityMatrix.aspx
CEMIG	Integrated report evaluation	2010	http://www.cemig.com.br/es-es/la_cemig/Documents/Relatrio%20Cemig%202010%20(Ingles)%20(Baixa).pdf
Cisco	Framework LLC "State of Integration"	2013	http://www.cisco.com/assets/csr/pdf/CSR_Report_2013.pdf
COCA-COLA HELLENIC BOTTLING	RobecoSAM	2012	http://integratedreport.coca-colahellenic.com/
Daimler	Fronesys	2013	http://sustainability.daimler.com/reports/daimler/annual/2013/nb/English/7520/materiality-matrix.html
DAIWA HOUSE INDUSTRY CO	RobecoSAM	2012	http://www.daiwahouse.com/english/groupbrand/ar/pdf/daiwahouse AR2012E_2.pdf
Danisco	Fronesys	2011	http://cdn.danisco.com/uploads/tx_tcdaniscofiles/danisco_sustanability_report_2010-11_04.pdf
Deloitte	Internet search	2013	http://public.deloitte.com/media/0565/5-reporting-process.html
Deutsche Telekom	Fronesys	2012	http://www.cr-report.telekom.com/site13/strategy-management/stakeholder-involvement/stakeholder-expectations#atn-1341-1679,atn-1341-1678
DOOSAN HEAVY INDS & CONSTR	RobecoSAM	2012	http://org-www.doosan.com/doosanheavy/attach_files/report/english/2012_report.pdf
DOOSAN INFRACORE CO	RobecoSAM	2012	http://org-www.doosan.com/doosaninfracore/attach_files/csr_report 2012%20Doosan%20Infracore%20Integrated%20Report_en.pdf

Company	Source	Year	URL
Dow Chemical	Framework LLC "State of Integration"	2012	http://www.dow.com/sustainability/pdf/35865-2012%20Sustainability%20Report.pdf
DURATEX SA	RobecoSAM	2012	http://www.duratex.com.br/ri/en/download/Duratex_RA_12.pdf
EDP ENERGIAS DE PORTUGAL SA	RobecoSAM	2012	http://www.edp.pt/en/sustentabilidade/partesinteressadas/Pages/partesinteressadas.aspx
ELECTROLUX AB	RobecoSAM	2012	http://annualreports.electrolux.com/2012/en/sustainability/valuechain/materialitymappingp/materiality-mapping.html
ENAGAS SA	RobecoSAM	2012	http://www.enagas.es/cs/StaticFiles/ENAGAS/Informe_Anual_2012/en/Annual_ReportWEB_2012/pubData/source/Annual_Report_2012.pdf
Enel	Internet search	2012	http://www.enel.com/en-GB/sustainability/our_responsibility/materiality_matrix/
Eni	Fronesys	2012	http://www.eni.com/en_IT/sustainability/reporting-system/materiality-analysis/materiality-analysis.shtml
Eon	Fronesys	2012	http://www.eon.com/en/sustainability/approach/stakeholder-management/materiality-analysis.html
Ford	Fronesys	2013	http://corporate.ford.com/microsites/sustainability-report-2012-13/blueprint-materiality-analysis
Fraport	RobecoSAM	2012	http://www.fraport.com/en/sustainability/sustainability-management/strategy-and-goals/wesentlichkeitsmatrix.html
Friends Life	Fronesys	2012	http://www.friendslife.com/crreport/overview/material-issues.jsp
GECINA	RobecoSAM	2012	http://www.gecina.fr/fo/fileadmin/user_upload/docs_finance/Rapport%20Document%20reference/2013/RSE-EXPERT_VA.pdf

(Continued)

TABLE 6B.1 (Continued)

Company	Source	Year	Link
GRUPO DE INVERSIONES SURAMER	RobecoSAM	2012	http://www.gruposuramericana.com/en/Annual%20Reports/Annual_Report_2012.pdf
GRUPO NUTRESA SA	RobecoSAM	2012	http://www.gruponutresa.com/es/webfm_send/274
GS ENGINEERING & CONSTRUCTN	RobecoSAM	2011	http://public.thecorporatelibrary.net/Sustain/sr_2011_313140.pdf
Heineken	Framework LLC "State of Integration"	2012	http://www.sustainabilityreport.heineken.com/overview/brewing-a-better-future/where-to-now.html
Heinz	Internet search	2011	http://www.heinz.com/CSR2011/about/materiality_analysis.aspx#
IND DE DISENO TEXTIL SA	RobecoSAM	2012	http://www.inditex.com/investors/investors_relations/annual_report
Intel	Framework LLC "State of Integration"	2012	http://csrreportbuilder.intel.com/PDFFiles/CSR_2012_Full-Report.pdf
Kemira	RobecoSAM	2012	http://www.kemiraannualreport2011.com/sustainability-performance/our-approach/materiality-matrix
Kepco	Internet search	2012	http://www.kepco-enc.com/webzine_business-kopec/sr_2012_e.pdf
KONINKLIJKE KPN NV	RobecoSAM	2013	http://www.kpn.com/v2/static/annualreport-2012/english/pdf/sr/kpn-csr-2012-complete.pdf
KT CORP	RobecoSAM	2012	http://file.kt.com/kthome/eng/social/csrReport/csr03/SR_eng_2013_full.pdf
Lassila & Tikanoja	Integrated report evaluation	2012	http://www.lassila-tikanoja.fi/annualreport2012/PDF/LT_Annual_Report_2012%20-%20suojattu.pdf
Lemminkäinen	Integrated report evaluation	2012	http://www.lemminkainen.com/Global/Investors/Annual-reports/Annual%20report%202012.pdf

Maersk	Integrated report evaluation	2012	http://www.maersk.com/Sustainability/Documents/Maersk_Sustainability_Report_2012.pdf
Mars	Internet search	2011	http://www.mars.com/global/about-mars/mars-pia/our-approach-to-business/defining-our-approach.aspx
Miller-Coors	Internet search	2012	http://www.millercoors.com/GBGR/Brewing-for-Good/Materiality-Map-Information.aspx
Mountain Equipment Co-Op	Internet search	2013	http://www.mec.ca/media/Images/pdf/accountability/MEC_2013_materiality_matrix_v2_m565775698315011444.pdf
NATURA COSMETICOS SA	RobecoSAM	2012	http://natura.infoinvest.com.br/enu/4381/RA_NATURA_2012_ENG_Final.pdf
NESTE OIL OYJ	RobecoSAM	2012	http://www.nesteoil.com/default.asp?path=1,41,12079,12082,17615
Nestlé	RobecoSAM	2013	http://www.nestle.com/csv/what-is-csv/materiality
NOBEL BIOCARE HOLDING AG	RobecoSAM	2012	http://corporate.nobelbiocare.com/Images/en/2012_AnnualReport_final_3_tcm269-61852.pdf
Novozymes	Integrated report evaluation	2013	http://www.unglobalcompact.org/system/attachments/62021/original/NovozymesReport2013_COP.pdf?1391154433
OMRON CORP	RobecoSAM	2010	http://www.omron.com/about/csr/pdf_inquiry/pdf/report_2010/report_e2010.pdf
OUTOKUMPU OY	RobecoSAM	2012	http://reports.outokumpu.com/en/2012/sustainability/reporting-on-sustainability/focus-on-material-issues/
Petrobras	Fronesys	2012	http://investidorpetrobras.com.br/en/governance/sustainability-report/relatorio-de-sustentabilidade-detalhe-4.htm
PWC	Internet search	2013	http://www.pwc.co.uk/corporate-sustainability/materiality.jhtml

(Continued)

TABLE 6B.1 (Continued)

Company	Source	Year	Link
ROYAL DSM NV	RobecoSAM	2012	http://annualreport2012.dsm.com/downloads/DSM-Annual-Report-2012.pdf
RSA INSURANCE GROUP PLC	RobecoSAM	2012	http://www.rsagroup.com/rsagroup/dlibrary/documents/35403_RSA_CR_Report_03May.pdf
SAIPEM SPA	RobecoSAM	2012	http://saipemcsr2012.message-asp.com/en/reporting/methodology-and-reporting-criteria
Samsung	Internet search	2013	http://www.samsung.com/us/aboutsamsung/sustainability/sustainabilityreports/download/2013/2013_Sustainability_Report.pdf
SAMSUNG LIFE INSURANCE CO	RobecoSAM	2011	http://www.samsunglife.com/companyeng/pdf/2010_2011_SR_eng_full_page.pdf
SAP AG	RobecoSAM	2010	http://archive.sapsustainabilityreport.com/2010/be-heard
Siemens	Internet search	2013	http://www.siemens.com/sustainability/en/sustainability-at-siemens/materiality.htm
Singapore Exchange (SGX)	Integrated report evaluation	2103	http://files.shareholder.com/downloads/ABEA-69RPAC/295439418 2x0x686021/68D2ADDE-5720-4A19-8903-7D5E33E38069/Singapore_Exchange_Annual_Report_2013.pdf
SK HYNIX INC	RobecoSAM	2012	http://www.skhynix.com/inc/pdfDownload.jsp?path=/ko/sustainable/sustain/2012SK_hynix_en.pdf
SK TELECOM CO LTD	RobecoSAM	2012	http://www.sktelecom.com/en/social/list_persist_report.do
Staples (Australia)	Framework LLC "State of Integration"	2012	http://www.staples.com/sbd/cre/marketing/australia_soul/staples-soul-reporting-approach.html#id_ra2

Company	Method	Year	URL
State Street	Framework LLC "State of Integration"	2012	http://www.statestreet.com/better/documents/2012/StateStreet_CR2012_Report.pdf
Statoil	Integrated report evaluation	2012	http://www.statoil.com/AnnualReport2012/en/Download%20Center%20Files/01%20Key%20downloads/20%20Sustainability%20Report%202012/Sustainability.pdf
SWISSCOM AG	RobecoSAM	2013	http://report.swisscom.ch/sites/all/themes/swisscom/pdf/Swisscom_AR_2013_EN.pdf
Symantec	Framework LLC "State of Integration"	2013	http://www.symantec.com/corporate_responsibility/topic.jsp?id=priority_issues
TELECOM ITALIA SPA - NEW	RobecoSAM	2012	http://www.telecomitalia.com/tit/en/sustainability/our-approach/hot-topics/our-materiality-matrix.html
Telefonica	Internet search	2012	http://annualreport2012.telefonica.com/informe-sostenibilidad/analisis-de-materialidad/matriz-de-materialidad.html
TELENET GROUP HOLDING N.V.	RobecoSAM	2011	http://corporate.telenet.be/_webdata/materiality_matrix_0.pdf
The HSH Group	Integrated report evaluation	2012	http://www.hshgroup.com/en/~/media/Files/HSHGroup/Investor_Relations/Financial_Results/2012/Annual_Report/AR_2012_C15.ashx
Thomson Reuters	Internet search	2012	http://blog.thomsonreuters.com/index.php/materiality-matrix/
TUV Rhineland	Fronesys	2011	http://www.tuv.com/media/geschaeftsbericht/2011/new_en/pdf_6/TUV_CR11_Sustainability_EN.pdf
UBS	Internet search	2013	https://www.ubs.com/global/en/about_ubs/corporate_responsibility/commitment_strategy/materiality-matrix.html

(Continued)

TABLE 6B.1 (*Continued*)

Company	Source	Year	Link
UPM-KYMMENE CORP	RobecoSAM	2012	http://www.upm.com/EN/RESPONSIBILITY/Principles-and-Peformance/gri/Documents/UPM%20annual%20report%202012.pdf
USINAS SIDERURGICAS DE MINAS	RobecoSAM	2011	http://www.usiminas.com/irj/servlet/prt/portal/prtroot/pcd!3aportal_content!2fusiminas!2fcomum!2fconteudo!2fiviews!2fbr.com.su.i.iview.JAI_iView_Publica_do_KM/prtl_est/Corporativo/RelatorioDeSustentabilidade/2011/eng/ra/14.htm
Vodaphone	Fronesys	2013	http://www.vodafone.com/content/dam/sustainability/pdfs/vodafone_sustainability_report_2012_13.pdf
Volkswagen	Fronesys	2012	http://annualreport2012.volkswagenag.com/managementreport/value-enhancingfactors/csrandsustainability.html
WESTPAC BANKING	RobecoSAM	2011	http://www.westpac.com.au/docs/pdf/aw/WestpacGroup_2011_Annual_Review.pdf
Wipro	Fronesys	2012	http://www.wipro.com/Documents/GRI_2011_12.pdf
YIT	Integrated report evaluation	2012	http://vuosikertomus2012.yit.fi/en/corporate-responsibility/responsibility-our-way-working/materiality-matrix

NOTE

1. Special thanks to Cecile Churet and RobecoSAM for providing these data.

CHAPTER SEVEN

Report Quality

I N CHAPTER 3, WE identified company adoption of integrated reporting as the key indicator of momentum. In Chapter 2, however, we also discussed the difference between a "combined report" and a truly "integrated" report. In Chapter 6, we described how greenwashing occurs when companies are insufficiently disciplined in their development of what we call the Sustainable Value Matrix (SVM). It is not solely the absolute number of companies practicing integrated reporting, but the quality of adoption that matters. How thorough and comparable these integrated reports are begins with the quality of frameworks for integrated reporting and standards for reporting on non-financial information. Although companies may achieve a truly integrated report by other means, the effectiveness with which they apply these frameworks and standards will determine how useful these reports are to investors.

To assess report quality, we analyzed 124 listed companies' self-declared integrated reports in the context of the "Consultation Draft of The International <IR> Framework" (Consultation Draft), published in July 2013.[1] Sourced from Global Reporting Initiative (GRI) website via its "Sustainability Disclosure Database" on October 17, 2013, 100 were English-language reports of the 135 non-South African companies that had made this declaration. To these, we added the reports of the largest 24 South African listed companies by revenue. The analysis team began its work on October 8, 2013, and completed it on March 14, 2014. During that period, the team held numerous conference calls to discuss the research and analysis. Over 400 hours were spent coding the data template for each of these 124 reports, with an additional 500 hours spent aggregating and analyzing these data.[2]

While it may seem counterintuitive to use a framework that did not exist at the time of report preparation to analyze reports, this approach allows us to gauge whether, even at this early stage of the movement, companies were intuitively following the principles of integrated reporting as articulated in December 2013's "The International <IR> Framework" (<IR> Framework). If company practice matches the framework's suggestions, it both validates the framework and suggests that it is not unreasonably difficult to apply.[3]

In comparing company reports with the Consultation Draft, scoring was done based on its seven Content Elements, its Six Capitals, and seven Special Factors, for a total of 20 factors. Each factor was scored from 0 (lowest) to 3 (highest), meaning the maximum score a report could receive was 60. Sub-scores were calculated for each of the Content Elements, Six Capitals, and Special Factors. While some degree of subjectivity is inevitable in scoring narrative data, numerous steps were taken to ensure that the coding was done as consistently and reliably as possible across reports and coders. Appendix 7A contains a full explanation of the methodology used.

We had no expectations of report quality prior to our analysis, but the results pleasantly surprised us. With admittedly substantial variation, these 100 companies were, on average, doing a fair job. The 24 South African companies fared noticeably better, likely due to the fact that they had at least two years of experience producing an integrated report thanks to King III and the Integrated Reporting Committee of South Africa's 2011 Discussion Paper (IRC of SA Discussion Paper), and that, because of these pushes, they had been learning how to improve based on audience feedback and observing practices of other companies. However, some areas of noticeable weakness appeared in both samples. Discussed below, these included outlook in the Content Elements and materiality, connectivity of information, and stakeholder engagement in Special Factors.

THE SIX CAPITALS

The <IR> Framework places great emphasis from both an integrated reporting and integrated thinking perspective on how companies use the six capitals

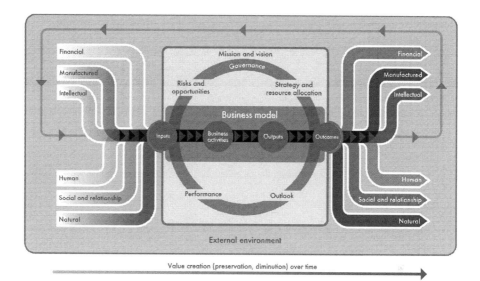

FIGURE 7.1 "The International <IR> Framework" Value Creation Process
Source: International Integrated Reporting Council. "The International <IR> Framework,"
p. 13, http://www.theiirc.org/international-ir-framework/, accessed April 2014.

(financial, manufactured, natural, human, intellectual, and social and relationship) "to create value over the short, medium and long term."[4] Although previously discussed in Chapter 2, this is illustrated again in Figure 7.1.[5]

For all six capitals, the average score for the 124 companies was 2.0, with 25 of them receiving a 3 on all six capitals. For each capital, a majority of the companies received a 2 or 3 rating: financial (85.5%), manufactured (67.7%), natural (82.2%), human (83.1%), intellectual (71.8%), and social and relationship (80.7%). South African companies averaged 2.3, while the average score for the other companies was 2.0. We consider the disclosures made by CEMIG,[6] Lassila & Tikanoja,[7] Singapore Stock Exchange,[8] Inditex,[9] Telekom Slovenije,[10] and AngloGold Ashanti[11] to be excellent examples of reporting on each of the capitals.

There was not a great deal of variation in the average score by type of capital—a range of .33 from lowest to highest (Figure 7.2). Likely due to the fact that 17 of these companies were in financial services, manufactured capital received the lowest (1.83) score. It is simply not relevant for the sector. Human capital and natural capital received the highest scores at 2.16 and 2.15, respectively, suggesting that most companies see them as important to their value creation process.[12] Intellectual capital also ranked low (1.93). Although

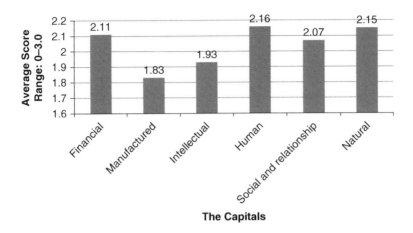

FIGURE 7.2   Average Score by Capital

admittedly difficult to measure, the same is true for human capital, suggesting that many companies did not see it as an important capital.

With a total average of 2.29 vs. 1.98 for the rest of the sample, South African companies scored higher on all six capitals. The difference was especially large for manufactured (2.29 vs. 1.72) and intellectual capital (2.29 vs. 1.84). The former is a result of a high percentage of South African companies (54%) relying on manufactured capital due to the fact that they operate in the energy, food and beverage, metal products, mining, pharmaceutical, and telecommunications sectors.[13]

 CONTENT ELEMENTS

The average score for the seven content elements we evaluated was 2.1, about the same as for the six capitals, with 25 companies receiving a 3 on all seven. Again, a majority of companies received a 2 or 3 rating for each content element: organizational overview and external environment (86.3%), governance (83.1%), risks and opportunities (71.8%), strategy and resource allocation (78.2%), business model (78.2%), performance (86.3%), and outlook (71.8%). We consider the disclosures made by Banco do Brasil,[14] Umicore,[15] Kumba Iron Ore,[16] Aviva,[17] BAE Systems,[18] Société Générale de

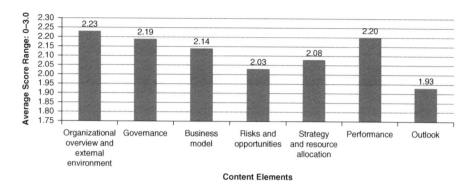

FIGURE 7.3 Average Score by Content Element

Surveillance,[19] and Syngenta[20] to be excellent examples of reporting on each of the content elements.

In the average score by content element, a difference of .30 from lowest to highest (Figure 7.3), little variation was noted. Opportunities and risks (2.03) and future outlook (1.93) were the two lowest scores. These low scores may indicate the inherent lack of clarity in discussing future-oriented issues and the accompanying anxiety companies have in doing so—especially in litigious environments.

South African companies scored higher on all content elements. With a total average of 2.35 vs. 2.06 for the rest of the sample (a difference similar to that of the scores on capitals), governance (2.50 vs. 2.11) had the highest score, virtually tied with organizational overview and external environment (2.46). Given how integrated reporting in South Africa came out of the King III code for corporate governance, the governance score is not surprising. Even in South African companies' two lowest-scoring elements, risks and opportunities (2.29 vs. 1.97) and outlook (2.21 vs. 1.86), their absolute score was still higher than that of the other sample.

When we supplemented this simple quantitative analysis by comparing the intention in the <IR> Framework with the patterns we saw in company practice, we found that even when the company described a particular content element in a fulsome way, the information was often scattered throughout many different parts of the report. Terminological inconsistencies were also rife. Thus, while companies received fairly high scores by each factor on average, nearly all of these reports needed substantial improvement in terms of the <IR>

Framework's Guiding Principles on the connectivity of information and report presentation:

> The connectivity of information and the overall usefulness of an integrated report is enhanced when it is logically structured, well presented, written in clear, understandable and jargon-free language, and includes effective navigation devices, such as clearly delineated (but linked) sections and cross-referencing. In this context, information and communication technology can be used to improve the ability to search, access, combine, connect, customize, re-use or analyse information.[21]

While a small number of the reports we studied were "logically structured, well presented, written in clear, understandable and jargon-free language," very few succeeded in providing "effective navigation devices, such as clearly delineated (but linked) sections and cross-referencing." Almost none used information and communication technology "to improve the ability to search, access, combine, connect, customize, re-use or analyse information." As a result, deciphering how "the pieces fit together" in these integrated reports required more energy than necessary.

Organizational Overview and External Environment

While the <IR> Framework asks, "What does the organization do, and what are the circumstances under which it operates?"[22] and explains what the answer to this question should include, it intentionally does not prescribe a format for the report.[23] We found no consistent approach in how companies provided this information. It was often mixed with other content elements, like business model and/or performance-related information like financial results, which in some cases were about financial capital. Moreover, when an organizational overview was provided, it appeared in different places. For example, the company might include a link in its online integrated report to another part of the company's website—such as "Corporate Profile," "Who We Are," "About Us," or a "snapshot"—where the user would still have to search for the information of interest.

Governance

The <IR> Framework asks, "How does the organization's governance structure support its ability to create value in the short, medium and long term?"[24]

In contrast to organizational overview, most companies discussed governance in a single, well-defined section of their report. This is likely due to the fact that most countries have codes and regulations regarding corporate governance that define it as a topic. Nevertheless, we found substantial variation in how companies treated the issue. Some used very lengthy sections of their report—dozens of pages—providing many details about the various elements of corporate governance, such as executive compensation. Longer sections sometimes contained discussions about risk but usually did not address those risks that come from pursuing opportunities. Other companies had very short sections with little detail. Many factors explain this variation in length, from the impact of mandated reporting requirements, companies taking a compliance-only, tick-the-box approach, and simply not knowing how best to discuss this element. Rarely did this discussion explicitly include time frames.

Business Model

The <IR> Framework asks, "What is the organization's business model?"[25] As depicted in Figure 7.1, how the organization creates value over the short-, medium-, and long-term is at the core of the <IR> Framework. The <IR> Framework emphasizes that effectiveness and readability can be enhanced by explicit identification of its key elements, a simple diagram with accompanying explanation of these elements' relevance to the organization,[26] a narrative flow that is logical given the particular circumstances of the organization, and identification of critical stakeholder dependencies and important factors affecting the external environment.[27]

As a Guiding Principle, most business model discussions would benefit from increased "connectivity of information." While some companies combined the description of their business model with a discussion of performance, we did not find a single case in which the company explicitly defined the relationship between its business model and short-, medium-, and long-term value creation. As with governance, we noted substantial variation in the depth with which companies discussed their business model, although we did not find a single example in which a company used the <IR> Framework's recommended features for enhancing effectiveness and readability. Even at the business unit level, some had detailed descriptions that included a discussion of the company's market and strategy, and how the capitals were used in the resource allocation process. Rarely, however, did a company explicitly link the capitals to the capital input/activities/output/capital impact process.

Risks and Opportunities

The <IR> Framework asks, "What are the specific risks and opportunities that affect the organization's ability to create value over the short, medium and long term, and how is the organization dealing with them?"[28] Relevant risks and opportunities are those that affect the availability, quality, and affordability of the capitals the company needs to create value over different time frames.[29] A comprehensive discussion about either risks or opportunities was rare in the reports we analyzed. On the whole, the discussion was even more scattered in the report, especially for opportunities, than it was for organizational overview and external environment. This could often be attributed to differences in how companies frame these topics. When companies saw risk and opportunity as two sides of the same coin, they discussed them, including their interdependencies, together. Otherwise, opportunities were covered in a variety of places, such as the outlook section (itself a content element) or in discussion relevant to one of the capitals, such as R&D investments. Perhaps driven by regulatory reporting requirements, it was more common for risks to be a stand-alone section. Still, they were also covered in such sections as materiality, governance, or even in a general "About This Report" or "About Us" section.

Strategy and Resource Allocation

The <IR> Framework asks, "Where does the organization want to go and how does it intend to get there?"[30] Answering this question includes a statement of strategic objectives for the short-, medium-, and long-term; what the company is doing to accomplish them; resource allocation plans for implementing this strategy; and how it will measure achievements and target outcomes over different time frames.[31] We found strategy and resource allocation to be one of the most diffuse of the content elements, as it never appeared as a separate section or even as the main topic of a well-defined section by another name. The topics in this content element were typically covered in discussions about the company's business model and performance. Companies varied in the extent to which they were explicit about the six capitals when discussing resource allocation. In some cases, one or more of the capitals was described, but the company was not explicit about the use of this capital as a resource.

Performance

The <IR> Frameworks asks, "To what extent has the organization achieved its strategic objectives for the period and what are its outcomes in terms of effects on the capitals?"[32] This includes both qualitative and quantitative information such as indicators with respect to targets and opportunities, with explanations of their significance, implications, and the methods and assumptions used in compiling them; the organization's positive and negative effects on the six capitals; the nature of its relationships with key stakeholders and how the organization has responded to their legitimate needs and interests; and linkages between past and current performance, and between current performance and outlook.[33] For the most part, the reports we reviewed would be better categorized as "combined reports" rather than "integrated reports." They included the anticipated information on financial and operating performance, often presented well through summaries earlier in the report and with more detail and accompanying explanation. Sometimes later in the report, detail included the business unit or even product level.

Although typically framed as "sustainability" or "corporate social responsibility" performance, all reports contained information on nonfinancial performance, with the capitals discussed more in the background than foreground. The degree of detail regarding nonfinancial performance varied widely, as did how prominently it was displayed. For a relatively small number of companies, a modest amount of forward-looking information—targets or projections—was presented in the context of past performance, both financial and nonfinancial. Noticeably lacking in nearly all reports were explanations of how financial and nonfinancial performance related to each other—a grave oversight considering the centrality of "connectivity" as an idea. Also lacking in virtually all reports was any explanation of how past performance and other factors would contribute to future value creation considered for the short-, medium-, and long-term.

Outlook

The <IR> Framework asks, "What challenges and uncertainties is the organization likely to encounter in pursuing its strategy, and what are the potential implications for its business model and future performance?"[34] As the company's view on anticipated future changes, outlook should be built on sound and transparent analysis about changes in the external environment in the short-, medium-, and long-term; what effect these will have on the organization; and how the organization is currently equipped to respond to critical challenges and uncertainties that are likely to arise.[35]

Although a few came close, virtually no company provided all of the information suggested by the <IR> Framework. Further evidence that this was the weakest of the content elements is that only 25 companies scored a 3, compared to 45–50 for all the others. Various formats were used to present the company's view on outlook. Some companies had a specific outlook section, although titles and level of detail varied. Others provided this information throughout the report, sometimes down to the business unit level. A few companies combined performance and outlook into a single section. Companies varied substantially in exactly what information they regarded as important for this element. It was fairly common for companies to discuss trends and challenges. Although less common, a number of companies identified challenges and uncertainties. Probably due to liability and competitive concerns, most companies did not provide targets, forecasts, projections, or even scenarios.

SPECIAL FACTORS

The average score for the seven Special Factors we evaluated was 1.68 (2.09 for South African companies vs. 1.58 for all other companies). Significantly lower overall than for the six capitals and content elements, this category also had the largest range from high to low of .92 (Figure 7.4), with only 11 companies receiving a 3 on all seven factors. Concomitantly, a smaller percentage of companies had a score of 2 or 3 for each special factor: material

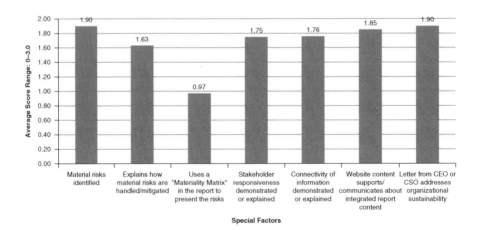

FIGURE 7.4 Average Score by Special Factor

risks identified (62.1%), explained how material risks are handled/mitigated (54.0%), used a materiality matrix (34.5%),[36] stakeholder engagement demonstrated and explained (60.5%), connectivity of information demonstrated or explained (68.6%), and letter from chief executive officer (CEO) or chief sustainability officer (CSO) addressing organizational sustainability (67.7%). The one exception was website content supporting the integrated report (92.9%). We consider disclosures made by Wärtsilä,[37] DSM,[38] SAP,[39] American Electric Power,[40] and BS Financial Group[41] to be excellent examples of reporting on each of the special factors.

These data suggest that the "Guiding Principles" part of the <IR> Framework will be the most challenging to follow. Connectivity of information demonstrated or explained, the key to producing an integrated report rather than a combined report, received a score of 1.76. Only 25 companies received a score of 3 on this item. Stakeholder engagement demonstrated and explained also scored fairly low at 1.75.[42] Although identification of material risks received a score of 1.90, explanation of how material risks are handled or mitigated received a score of 1.63, and use of a materiality matrix only got a score of .97 based on the fact that most companies (nearly 60%) did not have one in their report—although some did on their website.

A comparison between South African companies and the rest of the population casts the lower scores on special factors into even sharper relief. In contrast to the rest of the sample (scored at 1.58), the average for the South African companies was 2.09—a much bigger spread than for the six capitals and content elements. Furthermore, some of the greatest differences in all of the factors occurred in special factors. The most striking disparity was in providing a materiality matrix (1.71 vs. 0.79). South African companies were also much better at explaining how material risks were handled or mitigated (2.08 vs. 1.52), showing connectivity of information (2.33 vs. 1.62), and using their website to support their integrated report (2.33 vs. 1.74). Some of these differences could be due to use of the IRC of SA Discussion Paper, which contained an in-depth discussion of materiality. Despite the fact that the term "connectivity" is not overtly mentioned, South African companies scored much higher here. Similarly, for the CEO/CSO letter, South African companies scored 2.21 in contrast to the rest of the sample's 1.83, which is also not covered in the IRC of SA Discussion Paper. Interestingly enough, there was virtually no difference between South African (1.79) and non-South African companies (1.74) on stakeholder engagement demonstrated or explained, although stakeholders received substantial discussion in the IRC of SA Discussion Paper.

Materiality

The treatment of materiality in the <IR> Framework has been covered extensively in Chapter 5. Since most companies discussed materiality as a risk factor, we focused our analysis accordingly. Although not high in an absolute sense, the materiality scores indicated that companies on average did a better job identifying their material risks than they did in explaining how they handled or mitigated them. Some discussed material risks at the business unit level. The very low score for use of a materiality matrix indicates that disclosure about the process companies used for identifying material risks was generally poor, even if some did discuss the relationship between stakeholder engagement and the identification and management of material risks. Disclosure was even poorer when it came to explaining the company's definition of materiality or if and how it was making progress in managing these risks.

Stakeholder Engagement

Stakeholder relationships are one of the Guiding Principles in the <IR> Framework: "An integrated report should provide insight into the nature and quality of the organization's relationships with its key stakeholders, including how and to what extent the organization understands, takes into account, and responds to their legitimate needs and interests."[43] Different from the actual quality of stakeholder engagement itself, we measured the quality of *disclosure* about stakeholder engagement. However, we hypothesize that these are closely related to each other; stakeholders will challenge a company that makes excessive claims about its degree of stakeholder engagement.

Other than use of a materiality matrix, stakeholder engagement was, along with connectivity of information, ranked the lowest of the special factors. It was also the only category in which there was no discrepancy between South African companies and the rest of the sample. However, as discussed in the previous chapter, there is a close relationship between stakeholder engagement and identifying material issues. Nearly 90% of the companies receiving the highest score for stakeholder engagement also received the highest score for identifying material risks (Table 7.1). In contrast, 75% of the companies that received the lowest score for stakeholder engagement also scored the lowest for identifying material risks.

Companies that scored high in both categories typically disclosed on them in the same section of their report. Various formats were used to disclose stakeholder engagement, including tables and graphics. Some companies were explicit about following certain standards (e.g., AA1000 from AccountAbility)

TABLE 7.1 Stakeholder Engagement and Identifying Material Risks

		Stakeholder Engagement Demonstrated and Explained				
		3	2	1	0	Total
Material Risks Identified	3	34 (88%)	14 (39%)	4 (14%)	1 (5%)	53
	2	1 (3%)	12 (32%)	10 (34%)	1 (5%)	24
	1	3 (9%)	9 (24%)	13 (45%)	3 (15%)	28
	0	0 (0%)	2 (5%)	2 (7%)	15 (75%)	19
	Total	38 (100%)	37 (100%)	29 (100%)	20 (100%)	124

or best practice frameworks (e.g., from GRI).[44] In a few cases, companies only provided positive information about the outcomes of stakeholder engagement, raising the question of whether they were following the <IR> Framework's Guiding Principle of Reliability and completeness: "A complete integrated report includes all material information, both positive and negative."[45]

Providing further support for the previous chapter's argument that constructing the SVM and getting its full value requires effective stakeholder engagement, we also found a strong relationship between company publication of a materiality matrix and its level of stakeholder engagement (Table 7.2). Nearly three-quarters of the companies that received the highest score on the materiality matrix scored the highest on stakeholder engagement—in contrast to only 16% among companies that did not include a materiality matrix in their integrated report. This suggests that producing a materiality matrix enhances disclosure about stakeholder engagement, likely because stakeholder

TABLE 7.2 Stakeholder Engagement and the Materiality Matrix

		Company Uses a "Materiality Matrix" in the Report to Present the Risks				
		3	2	1	0	Total
Stakeholder Engagement Demonstrated and Explained	3	19 (73%)	4 (24%)	3 (38%)	12 (16%)	38
	2	4 (15%)	11 (64%)	1 (12%)	21 (29%)	37
	1	3 (12%)	1 (6%)	4 (50%)	21 (29%)	29
	0	0 (0%)	1 (6%)	0 (0%)	19 (26%)	20
	Total	26 (100%)	17 (100%)	8 (100%)	73 (100%)	124

engagement is an important element of constructing the matrix and thus often discussed when the matrix is presented.

Connectivity of Information

While all of the Guiding Principles are important, for us "Connectivity of information" lies at the heart of integrated reporting. It is through showing connectivity, or the relationships between different aspects of corporate performance, that a report transitions from a "combined report" to an "integrated report." According to the <IR> Framework, "An integrated report should show a holistic picture of the combination, interrelatedness, and dependencies between factors that affect the organization's ability to create value over time."[46] This requires integrated thinking to facilitate the connectivity of information flow into internal reporting, analysis, and decision-making so that the results are reflected in the external integrated report.[47]

As it is difficult to achieve in a paper format and almost equally hard to evaluate, connectivity of information received a fairly low score for the entire sample. To trivialize the concept, connectivity of information refers to the notion that "everything is related to everything else." This is illustrated in Figure 7.5, which shows that the explanation of connectivity of information in the <IR> Framework includes all of the six capitals and substantive content elements (except for Basis of preparation and presentation and General reporting guidance). Thus, a company has to make choices about what connections to make and in what priority and sequence. Since all content elements are related to each other, the company can justifiably discuss the others when focusing on any specific one. In fact, as shown in Figure 7.6, in

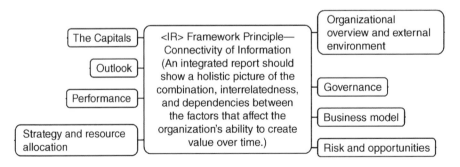

FIGURE 7.5 Connectivity of Information, Content Elements, and the Capitals

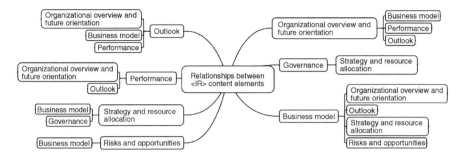

FIGURE 7.6 Relationships of the Content Elements to Each Other in the International <IR> Framework

discussing each content element, the <IR> Framework explicitly refers to many other elements. If the integrated report were organized by content element, each of which discusses other relevant content elements, this would lead to substantial repetition and would violate the Guiding Principle of Conciseness.[48] However, the same problem would exist if the report were organized in another way. Since a paper report proceeds in a linear fashion in spite of many interrelationships among different pieces of information in the report, there will always be a tradeoff between concision and connectivity. The solution, we will argue in Chapter 9, is to use information technology as a way of assuaging the limitations of a paper format presentation.

We found the most common attempt to provide connectivity to be in the discussion of the company's business model, risks and opportunities or, to a lesser extent, in strategy and resource allocation. The rarest instance of all—and, to us, the "Holy Grail" of integrated reporting—was a clear articulation of how performance in one dimension affected performance on another. Major obstacles to this include understanding these cause-and-effect relationships and having the data to test hypotheses about them, the latter further limited by the lack of standards. In order to ascertain their robustness, these relationships must be tested across a number of firms.

Website Content

Focused on the content of an integrated report and the relationship between integrated reporting and integrated thinking, the <IR> Framework has relatively little to say about the different channels and formats for providing or gathering information and for stakeholder engagement. That is, the Internet and the role of technology are not addressed in great detail. In its discussion defining the meaning of an integrated report, the <IR> Framework merely notes that the integrated report can be an "entry point" to more detailed information, such as the use of hyperlinks for web-based reports.[49]

Since the next chapter is devoted to corporate reporting websites, here we will merely identify some of the ways in which the companies in our sample were leveraging the Internet. For the most part, they were quite modest, much like the examples in the previous chapter. PDF reports always included a link to the company's website, but specific topics in most of these PDF reports were not linked to exact sections of the website where the content was discussed in greater detail.[50] In some cases, the online version of the integrated report included links to supplementary information, like more detailed data or further explanation of a topic. This sometimes helped to illustrate the connectivity of different pieces of information. A few companies enabled users to construct their own custom report by choosing which sections of the integrated report to assemble. Although this feature was not available at the individual data item level, in some cases the user could download data in blocks. Finally, some companies put their materiality matrix on their website. Some *only* put it on their website. A few included the interactive capabilities discussed in the previous chapter. One of the most interesting examples, discussed in more detail in the next chapter, was SAP's completely digital integrated report, which enables the audience to better comprehend the company's view on the connectivity of different types of performance information.

CEO Letter

Although the <IR> Framework says virtually nothing about a letter from the CEO or any other company official, we studied this item as a proxy for integrated thinking. To what extent was integrated thinking reflected in the opening letter from a senior company official that always accompanies an annual or integrated report? Although not always signed by the CEO, every report we examined contained some type of letter. Some letters were signed by the Chairman of the Board or even the CSO. When the latter was the case, it gave the impression that the integrated report had evolved out of a sustainability report rather than a financial report. Putting aside the fact that very few of these letters explicitly used the term "integrated report" or "integrated reporting," the general quality of integrated thinking demonstrated in these letters was poor.

Although better letters attempted to explain how "CSR" or "sustainability" was core to the company's strategy and/or beliefs (i.e., not a stand-alone initiative), these assertions were rarely supported by much information. Those who made this statement sometimes claimed that by being a more sustainable company, they would contribute to a more sustainable society. This too appeared in general terms with little data to back up the claim from a company or society perspective. Some letters accomplished even less than this, mentioning "sustainability programs" or "CSR initiatives" without any attempt to link them to the core strategy and operations of the company. Since these opening letters set the tone for the reader, they are a strong signal of just how integrated the report really is. Conversely, the quality of the letter will be a function of the quality of the integrated report. That said, regardless of the letter's quality and that of the integrated report it accompanies, these paper documents are only one way in which the company communicates to its audience. These must be viewed in the broader context of how companies are using the Internet for their corporate reporting websites, the subject of the next chapter.

ASSURANCE

Although the integrated reporting movement is still in its early stages, the issue of whether and how to perform an integrated audit or assurance opinion has already emerged. The traditional audit opinion on the financial statements is a form of "positive" assurance that proclaims everything was done right. To the extent nonfinancial information has an audit opinion, it almost always receives a negative assurance opinion, which roughly translates to "we couldn't find anything seriously wrong." A financial audit opinion is largely binary. The company either gets a clean audit opinion or it does not (a "qualified opinion"), and the latter is rare because of the negative signal it sends to the market. Generally, the company and its auditor work hard to make sure the audit opinion is a clean one.[51]

For nonfinancial information, degrees of assurance range from self-assurance (the company says, "Trust me."), through limited assurance (from an accounting firm or other service provider), to full assurance (positive). Although rare, full assurance almost always comes from a Big Four accounting firm. Limitations on a full assurance opinion for nonfinancial information include the lack of measurement, reporting, and auditing standards. In addition, two other significant challenges are acquiring or developing the capabilities necessary to provide assurance on nonfinancial information and litigation risk, especially in the United States.[52] Very few companies have even come close to having a positive assurance opinion on an entire integrated report, although Philips appears to be making progress toward that objective (see inset "Assurance on the Philips Annual Report").

Roughly half of the firms (55%) had some type of assurance opinion on their nonfinancial information, of which three-quarters (76%) came from a Big Four accounting firm. The others were typically from a boutique sustainability consulting firm. In our sample, we did not find any example in which there was a single audit opinion for both financial and nonfinancial information. In some cases, the same audit firm provided both opinions; in others, two different firms did.

Assurance on the Philips Annual Report

Assurance on nonfinancial information has been evolving since Philips published its first integrated report in 2008. The company and its independent auditor, KPMG, faced two significant hurdles: the "quality of the internal control systems within the company for both financial and environmental, social, and governance (ESG) data, and the creation of global standards for measuring and reporting nonfinancial information."[53] Table 7.3 provides insights into progress made by Philips and KPMG in resolving the controls and standards issues.

TABLE 7.3 Assurance on Nonfinancial Information at Philips

Year	Scope[54]	Criteria[58]	Standard[55]	Opinion[57]
2008	Limited assurance	GRI G3	ISAE 3000	Does not appear to be unfairly stated
2009	Limited assurance	GRI G3	ISAE 3000	Does not appear to be unfairly stated
2010	Limited assurance	GRI G3	ISAE 3000	Nothing came to our attention
2011	Limited assurance	GRI G3.1	ISAE 3000	Nothing came to our attention
2012	Reasonable assurance	GRI G3.1	ISAE 3000	Fairly presented
2013	Reasonable assurance	GRI G4	ISAE 3000	Presents fairly

The "Scope" and "Opinion" columns are inextricably linked. Scope refers to the type of procedures performed in order to support the level of opinion provided. For example, evidence to support a limited assurance engagement is typically obtained primarily through analytical procedures and inquiries, whereas a combination of procedures, such as inspection, observation, confirmation, recalculation, reperformance,[58] analytical procedures, and inquiry are generally used to obtain reasonable assurance.

The progression from limited assurance (2008–2011) to reasonable assurance (2012 and 2013) suggests that KPMG has concluded that controls over Philips's nonfinancial reporting systems had become more effective as a result of investments made by the company to improve internal controls, processes, and nonfinancial reporting systems, which provided a higher level of data quality.

Consistent reference over the six-year period to GRI Guidelines as the "Criteria" against which the Philips's disclosures were measured and KPMG's use of International Standard on Assurance Engagements (ISAE) 3000[59] over the same time frame is an indication that rigorous and institutionally legitimate standards for measuring and reporting nonfinancial information exist. To be clear, KPMG was not providing assurance on the Philips integrated report as a whole. Their assurance was applicable only to the disclosure of information made in compliance with GRI Guidelines.

If GRI Guidelines meet the suitable criteria test of ISAE 3000, then there is a possibility that the international accounting firms might eventually view "The International <IR> Framework" as furnishing appropriate criteria for the provision of limited and reasonable assurance. The question, admittedly a large and challenging one, is "Will 'The International <IR> Framework' be accepted by corporations and accounting firms as institutionally legitimate and therefore suitable criteria for an ISAE 3000[60] assurance engagement?"

 ## NOTES

1. International Integrated Reporting Council. "Consultation Draft of the International <IR> Framework," http://www.theiirc.org/consultationdraft2013/, accessed April 2014. The Consultation Draft was used because "The International <IR> Framework" had not been published by the time we started our data collection process.

2. Chapter 7 could not have been written without Liv Watson, Director of New Markets at Workiva (formerly WebFilings), Brad Monterio, Managing Director at Colcomgroup, and David Colgren, President and CEO at Colcomgroup. We are deeply grateful to them for their time, effort, and sense of humor during this intense project. These three individuals executed all of the data collection and we worked closely with them in analyzing the data and writing this chapter.

3. Although we used the Consultation Draft to develop the coding scheme, we used the "The International <IR> Framework" as the basis for analyzing the results.

4. International Integrated Reporting Council. The International <IR> Framework, p. 5, http://www.theiirc.org/international-ir-framework/, accessed April 2014.

5. Ibid., p. 13.

6. CEMIG (Brazil), 2012 Annual and Sustainability Report. This is an example of "Financial capital." The discussion of "Financial capital" resembles disclosures typically found in the U.S. Securities and Exchange Commission Form 10-K. Under a major caption of "Capital Resources and Liquidity," the capital intensive nature of the business and liquidity requirements are presented in terms of cash generated through operational activities, net cash consumed through investment and financing activities, and a discussion titled "Raising Capital and Debt Management Policy," http://www.cemig.com.br/en-us/the_cemig/Documents/2012_annual_sustainability_report.pdf, accessed March 2014.

7. Lassila & Tikanoja (Finland), Annual Report 2012. This is an example of "Manufactured capital." The report describes how the company uses its physical assets to help customers reduce waste volumes, extend the useful lives of properties, recover materials, and decrease the use of raw materials and energy. The report addresses initiatives such as reducing electricity, heating or water consumption, collecting and transporting waste for recovery, and providing secondary raw materials to industrial customers. http://www.lassila-tikanoja.fi/annualreport2012/, accessed March 2014.

8. Singapore Stock Exchange (Singapore), Annual Report 2013. This is an example of "Intellectual capital." One page with a graphic and narrative describes Singapore Stock Exchange as a full-service exchange with world-class trading and clearing platforms for securities and derivatives products. Among other points, the narrative specifically covers a range of issuer services, promotes its trading engine as the world's fastest, and highlights their ability to offer a range of real-time price information for securities and derivatives markets. http://investorrelations.sgx.com/annuals.cfm, accessed March 2014.

9. Inditex (Spain), Annual Report 2012. This is an example of "Human capital." A 23-page section, "Commitment to People," is an in-depth discussion of corporate programs and actions to develop self-sufficient and responsible staff, and strengthen links with the community through a wide range of social investment programs. https://www.inditex.com/en/investors/investors_relations/annual_report, accessed March 2014.

10. Telekom Slovenije (Slovenia), Annual Report 2012. This is an example of "Social and relationship capital." The company explains in detail its communications with stakeholder groups such as employees, shareholders, suppliers, communities, media, and governmental and nongovernmental organizations. In addition to creating long-term value for shareholders, the company sees itself as being operated for the benefit of employees, the wider community, and other stakeholders. http://porocilo.telekom.si/en/, accessed March 2014.

11. AngloGold Ashanti (South Africa), Integrated Report 2012. This is an example of "Natural capital." Mining transforms the earth and the company's report section "Responsible Custodianship of Water and Land" focuses on reducing raw water consumption and improvement in integrated water management practices and discharge water quality. It includes a discussion of the importance of land and land use in exploration, mining, and biodiversity, as well as the choices involved in digging a mine and mitigating the effects of tailings facilities, stockpiles, and waste rock dumps to avoid sensitive areas, within the constraints of economics and geology. http://www.aga-reports.com/12/, accessed March 2014.

12. Another potential factor is that many of the South African companies used Global Reporting Initiative's Guidelines and these cover topics like human and natural capital.

13. "Manufactured capital" is composed of physical objects (as distinct from natural physical objects) that are available to an organization for use in the production of goods or the provision of services. International <IR> Framework, p. 11. The sector breakdown of the South Africa companies was seven mining (30%), seven financial services (30%), two telecommunications (8%), one each from energy (4%), food and beverage (4%), media (4%), metal products (4%), pharmaceutical (4%), retail (4%), textiles and apparel (4%), and one conglomerate (4%).

14. Banco do Brasil (Brazil), Annual Report 2012. This is an example of the Content Element "Organizational overview and external environment." The "Corporate Profile" section of the annual report includes an overview of mission, values, vision, market environment, growth potential of the loan portfolio, strategic relationships, technology platforms, and area of banking operations. http://www45.bb.com.br/docs/ri/ra2012/eng/downloads/BB_AR_2012.pdf, accessed March 2014.

15. Umicore (Belgium), Annual Report 2012. This is an example of the Content Element "Governance." Umicore's "Corporate Governance Review" includes detailed sections on the corporate governance framework, corporate structure, shareholders, the Board of Directors, Executive Committee, relevant information in the event of a takeover bid, conflicts of interests, auditor selection, corporate Code of Conduct, market manipulation, and insider trading and compliance with the 2009 Belgian Code on Corporate Governance. http://www.umicore.com/reporting/statements/governance/corporate-governance-review/, accessed March 2014.

16. Kumba Iron Ore (South Africa), Integrated report 2012. This is an example of the Content Element "Risks and opportunities." A four-page section begins with a brief discussion of their risk management approach, roles and responsibilities, and risk management process, including identification, analysis and controls, mitigation initiatives, and reporting and monitoring. The report

identifies each key risk with a description of the root cause, potential impacts, and risk mitigation actions. http://www.kumba.co.za/reports/kumba_ar2012/integrated/pdf/integrated_report.pdf, accessed March 2014.

17. Aviva (United Kingdom), Corporate responsibility report 2012. This is an example of the Content Element "Strategy and resource allocation." Aviva uses graphics and brief contextual narrative to describe its business model, the company's strategic objectives, and how sustainability principles are incorporated into the strategy and delivery of products and services. The report includes a forward-looking discussion of opportunities and risks affecting the business. http://www.aviva.com/library/reports/2012cr/docs/full-report.pdf, accessed March 2014.

18. BAE Systems (United Kingdom), Annual Report 2012. This is an example of the Content Element "Business model." The business model is discussed with the context of a section titled "Strategic Review." In addition to the business model, the "Strategic Review" includes CEO commentary, key performance indicators, and a strategy overview. A business model graphic has four components: customer focus, program execution, financial performance, and responsible behavior. Each component in the matrix is linked to more detailed discussions in the report and additional links take the reader to further information about markets and opportunities, reporting segments, key resources, and governance. http://bae-systems-investor-relations-v2.production.investis.com/~/media/Files/B/BAE-Systems-Investor-Relations-V2/Annual%20Reports/BAE-annual-report-final.pdf, accessed March 2014.

19. Société Générale de Surveillance (SGS) (Switzerland), Corporate Sustainability Report. This is an example of the Content Element "Performance." SGS covers performance in several sections of their annual report. Tables and other graphics in a section titled "Our Performance" present various metrics used to assess progress across five key components: excellence, people, integrity, environment, and community. A separate in-depth narrative on each of the foregoing components provides insights into different aspects of performance. http://www.sgs.com/~/media/Global/Documents/Technical%20Documents/Reports/Policies/sgs_sustainability_report_ST_en_12.pdf, accessed March 2014.

20. Syngenta (Switzerland), Annual Review 2012. This is an example of the Content Element "Outlook." Syngenta does not present a separate section on Outlook. The company provides stakeholders with a glimpse into future innovation, growth prospects, and new products in its discussion of "Performance." For example, the discussion of soybeans—the world's primary source of vegetable protein—includes anticipated accomplishments in disease resistance and herbicide tolerance in 2015 and 2020. http://www.syngenta.com/global/corporate/SiteCollectionDocuments/pdf/publications/investor/2013/annual-report-2012/syngenta-annual-review-2012-english.pdf, accessed March 2014.

21. "The International <IR> Framework," p. 17.

22. Ibid., p. 5.
23. This element includes the organization's mission and vision; culture, ethics, and values; ownership and operating structure; and key quantitative information like the number of employees, revenues, and other significant changes from a prior period. It also describes the industries and countries in which the company operates; micro- and macro-economic conditions; customer demands and competitors; and significant aspects of the legal, commercial, social, environmental, and political context. "The International <IR> Framework," pp. 24–25.
24. Important aspects of governance include the company's leadership structure (including the skills and diversity of the leadership team); specific processes used to make strategic decisions and monitor the culture of the organization; particular actions by those charged with governance to monitor the strategic direction of the organization and its approach to risk management; whether the company's governance practices exceed minimum legal requirements; and how remuneration and incentives are linked to value creation. "The International <IR> Framework," p. 5.
25. "The International <IR> Framework," p. 5.
26. Although we found some effective infographics that illustrated business models (with some even linking them to strategic priorities), the information was not consumable because it was unstructured. How does one get data out of an infographic except to manually rekey or scrape that data?
27. "The International <IR> Framework," pp. 25–27.
28. Ibid., p. 5.
29. Risk and opportunity assessment includes the specific circumstances in which something would come to fruition, recognizing that this involves a degree of uncertainty. Citing the Guiding Principle of "Materiality," low probability events that could have large consequences should be discussed. The company should also discuss what it is doing to identify and mitigate risks, and identify and take advantage of opportunities. "The International <IR> Framework," p. 27.
30. "The International <IR> Framework," p. 5.
31. In addition, factors that differentiate a company—which are the source of competitive advantage—should be discussed, including the role of innovation, how the organization develops and exploits intellectual capital, and the extent to which the embedding of social and environmental issues in company strategy is a source of competitive advantage. Finally, the company should explain if and how stakeholder engagement had a role in the formulation of the company's strategy and resource allocation plans. "The International <IR> Framework," pp. 27–28.
32. "The International <IR> Framework," p. 5.
33. To the extent possible, quantitative key performance indicators (or narrative explanations when not possible) showing positive and negative relationships ("connectivity") between financial performance and the other capitals should

be provided. Finally, the company should explain the impact regulations have had or could have on performance, including the performance implications of noncompliance. "The International <IR> Framework," p. 28.

34. "The International <IR> Framework," p. 5.

35. The "Outlook" discussion should also include the implications of anticipated changes in financial performance, accomplishing strategic objectives, and the availability, quality, and affordability of the capitals. This may involve forecasts, projections, and sensitivity analyses. Finally, the organization should take into account legal and regulatory requirements and how these might change. "The International <IR> Framework," pp. 28–29.

36. The company received a score of 0 if the materiality matrix was on its website but not in the PDF integrated report itself. When there was a materiality matrix in the report, the company got a 1, 2, or 3 based on the quality and effectiveness of the matrix.

37. Wärtsilä (Finland), Annual Report 2012. This is an example of the Special Factors of "Material risks identified," "Explained how material risks are handled/mitigated," and "Used a materiality matrix." The report presents information about material issues as a "heat map," which indicates whether a risk or opportunity is new, increasing, decreasing, or static. It also identifies property and casualty insurance coverage. A detailed matrix discusses individual risks with linkage to a five-tier (low to high) colored-coded profile, policies and guidelines addressing each risk, and the management group responsible for management and mitigation. http://www.wartsilareports.com/en-US/2012/ar/frontpage/, accessed March 2014.

38. DSM (Netherlands), Integrated Annual Report 2012. This is an example of the Special Factor "Stakeholder responsiveness demonstrated and explained." The company's views on stakeholder engagement begin, "DSM believes and invests in a strategic and pro-active dialogue with its key stakeholders not only to share thoughts and views, but also to deepen the company's insights into governmental, societal and customer trends, drivers and needs." A materiality matrix indicating how issues are prioritized by society and the business is presented. DSM's views on the role of business in society includes a paragraph or two on critical issues such as water management, food safety, and dialogue throughout the company's value chain. A graphic with supporting narrative explains how the company engages with seven stakeholder groups and how the company responds to stakeholder interests. http://www.dsm.com/content/dam/dsm/cworld/en_US/documents/integrated-annual-report-2012.pdf?fileaction=saveFile&wcm_dsn=http://www.dsm.com, accessed March 2014.

39. SAP (Germany), Integrated Report 2012. This is an example of the Special Factor "Connectivity of information demonstrated or explained." To the best of our knowledge, SAP is the only company that published the entire integrated report in an online version. SAP uses an interactive graphic to demonstrate

how material issues and ESG performance are linked to overall financial performance. In addition, the linked narratives within the connectivity graphic weave a thread from, for example, strategic objectives and critical issues to the environmental and societal context in which SAP operates. http://www .sapintegratedreport.com/2012/en/key-facts/connecting-financial-and-non-financial-performance.html, accessed March 2014.

40. American Electric Power (United States) 2013 Corporate Accountability Report. This is an example of the Special Factor "Website content supporting the integrated report." Our evaluation criteria focused on access from the integrated report to other communications, financial information, and other supporting areas of the corporate website. The online AEP integrated report includes clearly labeled tabs guiding the user to a high-level overview, strategy, opportunities and risks, performance, engagement, and videos. The website includes links to other reports published by AEP such as those provided to GRI, CDP, coal supplier survey, and Clinton Global Initiative. AEP also developed an interactive iPad app for their 2013 Corporate Accountability Report. http:// www.aepsustainability.com, accessed March 2014.

41. BS Financial Group, Sustainability Report 2012. This is an example of the "Special Factor Letter from CEO or CSO addressing organizational sustainability." This is the first time that BS Financial Group published financial and sustainability information in a single document. The CEO message is brief and would benefit from more detail; however, the content presents a clear understanding on the CEO's belief that environmental, economic, and social performance are inextricably linked. http://eng.bsfng.com/02/0103.jsp, accessed March 2014.

42. Thirty-eight companies received a score of "3" on Stakeholder engagement demonstrated and explained.

43. "The International <IR> Framework," p. 17. Through stakeholder engagement, the company learns how different stakeholders perceive value and what is important to them; identifies material matters, including risks and opportunities; and becomes aware of trends that could become significant and affect materiality in the future. Stakeholder engagement is an ongoing process that is accomplished through day-to-day contact with employees and customers and through focus on particular issues, such as planning a facility expansion in a local community. Stakeholder engagement contributes to integrated thinking (and vice versa) and assures a sense of stewardship on the part of the company for the capitals it uses to create value. pp. 17–18.

44. GRI G4 Sustainability Reporting Guidelines "Reporting Principles and Standard Disclosures" and "Implementation Manual" provide comprehensive guidance for the preparation of sustainability reports by organizations, regardless of their size, sector, or location. The guidelines make it clear that the determination of materiality and stakeholder engagement are

inextricably linked. https://www.globalreporting.org/reporting/g4/Pages/default.aspx, accessed April 2014. Since its founding in 1995, Account-Ability has been on the frontlines of providing guidance on stakeholder engagement and materiality for nonfinancial information. Both topics have been addressed in several AccountAbility publications including, AA1000 AccountAbility Principles Standard 2008 (http://www.accountability.org/standards/aa1000aps.html), AA1000 Assurance Standard 2008 (http://www.accountability.org/standards/aa1000as/index.html), AA1000 Stakeholder Engagement Standard (http://www.accountability.org/standards/aa1000ses/index.html), Guidance for Reporting Organisations Seeking Assurance to AA1000AS 2008 (http://www.accountability.org/about-us/publications/guidance-for-1.html) and "Redefining Materiality II: Why It Matters, Who's Involved and What it Means for Corporate Leaders and Boards," http://www.accountability.org/about-us/news/announcements/redefining-materiality-ii.html. All AccountAbility URLs accessed April 2014.

45. "The International <IR> Framework," p. 22.

46. Ibid., p. 16.

47. Connectivity involves showing how all the Content Elements are related to each other from a system perspective, such as relationships between the capitals, how the company's strategy adapts to new risks and opportunities, and how the organization's strategy and business model are adapting to a changing external environment. Connectivity includes explaining the relationships between past, present, and anticipated future performance; showing the relationship between different types of performance, such as customer satisfaction and revenue growth, and investment in human capital and market share; providing both quantitative and qualitative information, such as narrative explanations for KPIs; consistency between important internal metrics and those reported externally; consistency between all of the company's external communications; and having a well-structured and well-presented integrated report that is free from jargon. "The International <IR> Framework," pp. 16–17.

48. "The organization seeks a balance in its integrated report between concision and the other Guiding Principles, in particular completeness and comparability. "The International <IR> Framework," p. 21.

49. "The International <IR> Framework," p. 8.

50. Often the link in the report only took the user only to the company website, requiring a significant amount of navigation to find specific integrated reporting-related content. In other cases, the link led to the PDF file of the report for download and it was not interlinked to other content on the website. Which part of the company's website a link took the reader to varied, such as "About Us," "Investor Relations," or "Sustainability."

51. Qualified auditors' reports can take one of several forms. The independent auditor may issue an adverse opinion (the financial statements, taken as a whole, do not conform to international or U.S. accounting principles), a disclaimer of opinion (no expression of an opinion), a limitation of scope (the auditor could not perform all necessary procedures or tests), an "except for" opinion (a specific departure from international or U.S. accounting principles), and other modifications including a going concern or a change in accounting principles. The U.S. Securities and Exchange Commission will not accept financial statements with an auditors' report that disclaims an opinion, expresses an adverse opinion, includes an "except for" qualification due to a departure from GAAP or a qualification with respect to the scope of the audit. U.S. Securities and Exchange Commission. Division of Corporation Finance. *Staff Reporting Manual*, Section 4200, Accountants' Reports, http://www.sec.gov/divisions/corpfin/cffinancialreportingmanual.shtml, accessed April 2014.

52. There are several major challenges to providing an opinion on the nonfinancial information contained in an integrated report. One, developing a global set of credible standards for measuring and reporting nonfinancial information which are viewed as the equivalent of International Financial Reporting Standards and U.S. Generally Accepted Accounting Standards for accounting and reporting. Two, developing rigorous methodologies for providing positive assurance on nonfinancial information similar to audits of financial statements. Three, integrating standards and assurance methodologies for financial and nonfinancial information in a way that provides a "true and fair view of an organization's sustainability," which in the case of assurance on an integrated report means taking into account the extent to which the company is meeting the needs of other stakeholders in order to be able to continue creating value for its shareholders. In addition, once assurance goes beyond the financial statements and notes to include the Guiding Principles and Content Elements of "The International <IR> Framework," a much broader range of professional capabilities becomes necessary. None of the major accounting firms are even close to possessing these capabilities, although some are working to develop them. Finally, litigation risk is a hot topic in the auditing profession, especially in the litigious United States. Today, the debate centers on the audits of financial statements, especially when what is perceived to be an audit failure is confounded with a company's bankruptcy, or when major fraud, especially in top management, is detected. The global debate must be expanded to include liabilities that will emerge from giving as much prominence to nonfinancial information as to financial information. Legislators and regulators will have to address this topic in a reasoned and responsible way. Ultimately, laws and regulations must balance the need to punish incompetence and malfeasance while creating an environment that encourages the accounting firms to make

the investments necessary to provide high-quality assurance on nonfinancial information. Eccles, Robert G., Michael P. Krzus, and Liv A. Watson. "Integrated Reporting Requires Integrated Assurance." *Effective Auditing for Corporates: Key Developments in Practice and Procedures*, edited by Joe Oringel, 161–177. London: QFINANCE Key Concepts, Bloomsbury Information Limited, 2012.

53. Eccles, Robert G. and Daniela Saltzman. "Integrated Assurance at Philips Electronics N.V." Harvard Business School Case 412-054, Revised May 6, 2013.

54. A reasonable assurance engagement is one in "which the practitioner reduces engagement risk to an acceptably low level in the circumstances of the engagement as the basis for the practitioner's conclusion. The practitioner's conclusion is expressed in a form that conveys the practitioner's opinion on the outcome of the measurement or evaluation of the underlying subject matter against criteria." In a limited assurance engagement, "the practitioner reduces engagement risk to a level that is acceptable in the circumstances of the engagement but where that risk is greater than for a reasonable assurance engagement as the basis for expressing a conclusion in a form that conveys whether, based on the procedures performed and evidence obtained, a matter(s) has come to the practitioner's attention to cause the practitioner to believe the subject matter information is materially misstated. The nature, timing, and extent of procedures performed in a limited assurance engagement is limited compared with that necessary in a reasonable assurance engagement but is planned to obtain a level of assurance that is, in the practitioner's professional judgment, meaningful. To be meaningful, the level of assurance obtained by the practitioner is likely to enhance the intended users' confidence about the subject matter information to a degree that is clearly more than inconsequential." International Federation of Accountants. International Standard on Assurance Engagements (ISAE) 3000 Revised, Assurance Engagements Other than Audits or Reviews of Historical Financial Information, https://www.ifac.org/publications-resources/international-standard-assurance-engagements-isae-3000-revised-assurance-enga, accessed March 2014.

55. "Suitable criteria exhibit the following characteristics: (a) Relevance: Relevant criteria result in subject matter information that assists decision-making by the intended users. (b) Completeness: Criteria are complete when subject matter information prepared in accordance with them does not omit relevant factors that could reasonably be expected to affect decisions made on the basis of that subject matter information by the intended users. Complete criteria include, where relevant, benchmarks for presentation and disclosure. (c) Reliability: Reliable criteria allow reasonably consistent measurement or evaluation of the underlying subject matter including, where relevant, presentation and disclosure, when used in similar circumstances by different practitioners. (d)

Neutrality: Neutral criteria result in subject matter information that is free from bias as appropriate in the engagement circumstances. (e) Understandability: Understandable criteria result in subject matter information that can be understood by the intended users. The suitability of criteria for a particular engagement depends on whether they reflect the above characteristics. The relative importance of each characteristic to a particular engagement is a matter of professional judgment. Further, criteria may be suitable for a particular set of engagement circumstances, but may not be suitable for a different set of engagement circumstances. For example, reporting to governments or regulators may require the use of a particular set of criteria, but these criteria may not be suitable for a broader group of users. Criteria can be selected or developed in a variety of ways. For example, they may be: Embodied in law or regulation, Issued by authorized or recognized bodies of experts that follow a transparent due process, Developed collectively by a group that does not follow a transparent due process, Published in scholarly journals or books, Developed for sale on a proprietary basis, and Specifically designed for the purpose of preparing the subject matter information in the particular circumstances of the engagement." Ibid.

56. Ibid.
57. "In a reasonable assurance engagement, the conclusion shall be expressed in a positive form. In a limited assurance engagement, the conclusion shall be expressed in a form that conveys whether, based on the procedures performed and evidence obtained, a matter has come to the practitioner's attention to cause the practitioner to believe that the subject matter information is materially misstated." Ibid.
58. "Reperformance" is when the auditor executes procedures or controls that were originally performed by the company.
59. The U.S. Public Company Accounting Oversight Board promulgated AT Section 101, Attest Engagements, which is substantively the same as ISAE 3000. http://pcaobus.org/Standards/Attestation/Pages/AT101.aspx, accessed March 2014.
60. ISAE 3000 is the international standard for providing assurance on nonfinancial information of all types. For example, ISAE 3000 is used to guide an assurance engagement on a GRI report, see Table 7.3, Assurance on Nonfinancial Information at Philips. The question we ask is will the international accounting firms accept the <IR> Framework as "suitable criteria" (see endnote 55) to assess whether an organization's integrated report adheres to the guidance provided by the International Integrated Reporting Council. International Federation of Accountants. International Standard on Assurance Engagements (ISAE) 3000 Revised, Assurance Engagements Other than Audits or Reviews of Historical Financial Information, https://www.ifac.org/publications-resources/international-standard-assurance-engagements-isae-3000-revised-assurance-enga, accessed May 2014. For additional information, see endnotes 54–57.

Methodology for Analyzing 124 Company Integrated Reports

W E ANALYZED 124 REPORTS—24 from South African companies and 100 from companies in other countries. Reports were selected if they were:

1. Self-declared to be an integrated report
2. Published by a company of any size listed on a stock exchange
3. Published in 2013 (for the 2012 fiscal year)
4. Published in English
5. Publicly available
6. Available for download in a PDF format

Companies producing the report could be from any geographic region and industry sector, and they could use any reporting framework. Reports meeting our criteria were sourced from Global Reporting Initiative's (GRI) Sustainability Disclosure Database[1] on October 17, 2013.

The analysis team used the "Consultation Draft of The International <IR> Framework"[2] (Consultation Draft) issued in July 2013 as the basis for developing the evaluation methodology, recognizing that all of the reports analyzed were published prior to the release of "The International <IR> Framework"[3]

(<IR> Framework) in December 2013. Twenty factors were used for scoring reports. Seven of these came from the Consultation Draft's "Content Elements." Even though the Consultation Draft was used for our report assessment, the Content Element names are the same as those later used in the <IR> Framework.

- Organizational overview and external environment
- Governance
- Business model
- Risks and opportunities
- Strategy and resource allocation
- Performance
- Outlook

The Consultation Draft's "Six Capitals" (financial, manufactured, natural, intellectual, human, and social and relationship) were also used as scoring factors in the analysis.

In addition to the 13 factors from the Consultation Draft, we added the following seven "Special Factors" that we created:

- Identifies material risks
- Explains how material risks are handled/mitigated
- Uses a "Materiality Matrix" in the report to present the risks
- Demonstrates or explains stakeholder engagement
- Demonstrates or explains connectivity of information
- Website content supports/communicates integrated report content
- Letter from CEO or CSO (Chief Sustainability Officer) addresses organization's sustainability

Our category of "Special Factors" was similar to the Consultation Draft's "Guiding Principles," with several exceptions. We felt that some principles ("Conciseness," "Reliability and completeness," and "Consistency and comparability") would be difficult to assess in a reasonably objective manner. We also felt that "Strategic focus and future orientation" was largely repeated in the content elements of "Risks and opportunities," "Strategy and resource allocation," and "Outlook." We strictly followed the Consultation Draft's six capitals, and all of its Content Elements except for "Basis of preparation and presentation" and "General reporting guidance," both of which are very broad categories that would have been difficult to assess, particularly as their components overlapped with some of the Guiding Principles, like "Materiality."

Because of materiality's importance, we subdivided it into three Special Factors: (1) whether material risks were identified in the reports, (2) whether there was an explanation of how these risks would be mitigated, and (3) whether the company included a materiality matrix within the report. Two other Special Factors considered were "Stakeholder engagement" and "Connectivity of information" (matching the Consultation Draft). Because of the growing importance of the Internet in corporate reporting, we also assessed the company's website to see if it supported its integrated report. Finally, as an indicator of whether the company regarded sustainability as core to its strategy or merely a program, we examined the letter from the Chairman, CEO, or other senior executive to see whether the commentary described the company's goals and objectives in the broader context of sustainability issues confronting the organization. We considered it to be a reflection of "the tone at the top" and whether sustainability was being embedded into the business strategy or simply viewed as a bolted-on initiative.

The scoring process was based on a scale of 0–3, with 0 the lowest and 3 the highest number of points awarded for each factor. The maximum score per report across all factors is 60 points (20 factors scored at 3 points each). Every reasonable effort was made to ensure that scoring was as objective as possible, but some degree of subjectivity was inevitable. An inter-rater reliability of 80% was established to maximize consistency of scores across analysts. To accomplish this, each analyst scored the same five reports, and scores from each analyst were compared for each factor and evaluated for their inter-rater reliability. Scoring was consistent at least 80% of the time. Reports were distributed across the team to balance the workload and each analyst initially scored each report on the 20 factors. Once all reports had been scored, each analyst reviewed scores again and, in some cases, made adjustments to scores based on individual factors where appropriate. All averages, totals, correlations, charts, and graphs were generated from these data.

 ## NOTES

1. Global Reporting Initiative. Excel Spreadsheet of Sustainability Disclosure Database, Discover the Database, What's Included, http://database.global-reporting.org/search, accessed October 2013.

2. International Integrated Reporting Council. "Consultation Draft of the International <IR> Framework," http://www.theiirc.org/consultationdraft2013/, accessed April 2014.

3. International Integrated Reporting Council. The International <IR> Framework, p. 5, http://www.theiirc.org/international-ir-framework/, accessed April 2014.

CHAPTER EIGHT

Reporting Websites

TODAY, COMPANIES USE THEIR websites for a multitude of purposes: to market their products, advertise, engage with customers and employees, post important information on a real-time basis, enhance their image, and reinforce their brand—not to mention to sell products themselves. In comparison, how a company uses its website for corporate reporting purposes is fairly narrow. Because it is an increasingly significant channel through which the company can communicate with shareholders and other stakeholders, however, it is an important one. By capitalizing on their reporting websites, companies can move beyond the paper constraints of an integrated *report* in order to create a platform for the company's integrated *reporting*—a more multidimensional, interactive, and engaging form of communication. In the previous chapter, we saw that most companies producing integrated reports were doing little to support these documents online in a way that would make the information they contain more useful and usable. While the Internet has the potential to dramatically enhance integrated reporting and integrated thinking, it can also do so for more traditional corporate reporting. To the extent this is happening, it is reasonable to expect that large companies have the resources to do so.

To assess how the world's most sophisticated companies are leveraging the Internet for corporate reporting purposes, we studied the websites of the largest 500 companies in the world: the "Global 500."[1] The list came from *Fortune* for fiscal years that ended on or before March 31, 2013. While size is not equal to sophistication, we reason that it is a good proxy. Furthermore, a few statistics indicating the economic significance of these companies give them, in our view, a responsibility to be effective in communicating their performance to shareholders and other stakeholders through both reports and websites. Their revenues ranged from $467.2 billion for the number-one-ranked Royal Dutch Shell to $24.1 billion for Ricoh at number 500. Market capitalization ranged from number 11-ranked (in revenues) Chevron's $ 504.8 billion to 309-ranked (in revenues) Alliance Boots at $17.0 million.[2] In 2012, their revenues totaled $24.3 trillion, and they had profits of $1.9 trillion. Their market cap of $21.9 trillion represented 42% of the global market cap of the world's approximately 46,000 listed companies. This tremendous economic power is concentrated in a very small number of companies, and even within this elite group, there is also a high degree of concentration. The top 100 represent 48%, 43%, and 32% of the revenues, profits, and market cap, respectively, of these 500 companies.[3]

Based upon detailed studies of over 100 companies' websites,[4] including some of the best examples of how integrated reporting companies are using their websites, we developed an inventory of items to cover general website characteristics (e.g., did the company have a separate website focused on the corporation itself or was it part of its e-commerce websites, as under an "About Us" tab), how the website was being used for financial reporting (e.g., how many years of annual reports were available online and whether reports provided in different languages), and how the website was being used for sustainability reporting (e.g., does the company provide information about sustainability on their website such as a report and how difficult it was to find it). Only 24 of these companies were practicing integrated reporting.

 METHODOLOGY

The data collection exercise proved challenging[5] due to the vast variation in structure, functionality, and presentation of websites. Approximately 75% of the companies on our list were headquartered outside the United States. Consequently, we encountered language barriers and cultural differences, such as lower use of social media in China compared to the United States and Europe. This may be explained by China's comparatively lower percentage of Internet users and the growing use of social media services unique to China that would not appear on the English version of the site.[6] Determining which languages were covered on a site was sometimes difficult due to the number of languages and alphabets used by some companies. In some cases, the website did not offer an English version and we relied on Google Translate.[7] While we initially sought an automated method for gathering the data, we found that it had to be done by hand and carefully checked.[8] We created a template for coding up the features of each company's website, and the data were then transferred into a spreadsheet.

The last step in the data collection and preparation process was to create a set of logical categories for grouping the individual features (shown in Appendix 8.A).[9] The categories we created were Financial Transparency (amount and quality of financial information), Sustainability Transparency (amount and quality of sustainability information), Connectivity (easy and obvious linkages of related parts of the website to each other),[10] Interactivity (features to engage the user), and Utility (features to make the website as usable and user-friendly as possible).[11] The raw score for each company was aggregated by category and converted to a Z-Score, which was then normalized between 1 and 100.[12]

 ## WEBSITE CATEGORY ANALYSIS

Table 8.1 shows the average category scores by sector. Technology & Communications has the highest score of 61 (Healthcare is 59 and Resource Transformation is 58) and Infrastructure the lowest score of 40. The high scores may be a result of companies in these industries needing to have high-quality websites in general. Technology & Communications companies attempt to differentiate commodity products through branding and Healthcare companies need to educate consumers and build trust. Resource Transformation companies are necessary, but highly controversial, and need to ensure their license to operate.

For the separate categories, Connectivity shows the least variation across sectors ranging from Consumption (51) to Services (42). Utility has the widest range in scores by sector, from 64 for Healthcare to 32 for Infrastructure. This could be due to the fact that Consumption companies need to have much more useful websites for selling their products in comparison to Infrastructure companies. Financial Transparency, Sustainability Transparency, and Interactivity all have virtually the same range in scores across sectors.

Total Score by region saw more variation, with Europe highest at 67 and Asia lowest at 35 (Table 8.2). However, this comparison may be somewhat

TABLE 8.1 Global 500 Reporting Website Categories by Sustainability Accounting Standards Board (SASB) Sector

SASB Industry	Number of Companies	Financial Transparency	Sustainability Transparency	Connectivity	Interactivity	Utility	Total
Consumption	64	54.51	51.01	51.13	55.66	60.75	57.28
Financials	108	54.10	51.58	47.68	45.71	50.79	52.36
Healthcare	28	63.36	43.65	50.89	60.42	64.00	59.45
Infrastructure	43	41.57	42.96	43.14	40.04	31.93	39.98
Nonrenewable Resources	100	43.20	49.54	46.66	41.95	45.30	46.28
Resource Transformation	41	54.53	52.08	48.19	55.35	59.42	58.02
Services	14	50.25	44.04	41.65	47.88	55.08	48.45
Technology & Communications	51	58.90	62.97	47.48	55.36	58.66	60.57
Transportation	51	49.10	52.30	44.15	50.95	42.98	49.76
Average score		52.17	50.01	46.77	50.37	52.10	52.46

"Most major industry classification systems use revenue as their basis for classifying companies into specific sectors and industries. However, a company's market value is determined by more than financial performance: in many industries as much as 80 percent of market capitalization is made up of intangibles. To address this shortcoming, SASB developed the Sustainable Industry Classification System™ (SICS™), which categorizes industries based on resource intensity and sustainability innovation potential. The system is tied back to traditional classification systems such as Global Industry Classification Standard (GICS) and Bloomberg Industry Classification System (BICS). SICS is structured in three levels. The lowest level, industry, is comprised of the 80+ industries for which SASB is developing standards. The middle level, industry working groups, groups industries based on sustainability impact similarities. The highest level, sector, is comprised of ten sectors that reflect the ultimate purpose given to these resources." Sustainability Accounting Standards Board. Industry Classification, http://www.sasb.org/industryclassification/, accessed April 2014.

TABLE 8.2 Global 500 Reporting Website Categories by Region

Region	Number of Companies	Financial Transparency	Sustainability Transparency	Connectivity	Interactivity	Utility	Total
Asia	187	34.08	44.06	41.81	30.58	31.33	35.25
Europe	150	68.68	64.09	56.21	62.89	55.51	66.78
Latin America and the Caribbean	13	41.77	54.30	48.08	42.43	46.03	51.09
North America	141	56.58	45.04	44.11	59.39	72.30	58.23
Oceania	9	51.60	64.52	56.19	43.61	53.43	59.27
Average score		50.54	54.40	49.28	47.78	51.72	54.12

Note: For the definition of regions, Global Reporting Initiative's (GRI's) Sustainability Disclosure Database was used. https://www.globalreporting.org/reporting/report-services/sustainability-disclosure-database/Pages/default.aspx artificial since it is possible that the native language version of Asian company websites would receive a higher score. While it is easy for companies based in non-English-speaking countries to translate an integrated report document into English, creating a fully functional English corporate reporting website is more challenging. How much a company should invest in doing so largely depends upon how important its foreign investors and other stakeholders are to it.

Table 8.3 contains data for the six countries with the largest number of Global 500 companies. The variation across each category is even greater than that by region due to the extremely low scores of China, which ranged from 18 to 25 across all categories. The European countries of Germany, France, and the United Kingdom mostly score higher than U.S. or Japanese companies. After China, U.S. companies have the lowest Sustainability Transparency and Connectivity scores. Yet on Interactivity, their score is in the same range as the European countries, and they have the highest Utility score by a wide margin.

The variation in Total Score by size range is the same as it is for the sector differences (Table 8.4). On balance, these data confirm our use of size as a proxy for sophistication. There is a clear relationship between Total Score and size of company, following a rank order aside from the last two size ranges, in which the order is reversed. Yet even the 100 largest companies in the world only received a Total Score of 61. The lowest variation was seen in Connectivity: the 100 largest companies actually received a score virtually identical to that of the companies ranked 200–300 in size. Although these differences are not large, the greatest variation occurred in Interactivity and Utility, suggesting that only the very largest companies see the benefit in making these important features of their reporting website. The least variation occurred in Financial Transparency and Sustainability Transparency.

Since listed companies have more reporting requirements than State-Owned Enterprises (SOEs) or private companies, we correctly expected them to have higher scores for their reporting websites. We compared the scores of the 415 listed companies to the remaining 85 unlisted ones (Table 8.5), most of which are SOEs, with a few private family-owned companies. Our expectations were confirmed. Reflecting the fact that they have no obligations to outside shareholders, the unlisted companies rank much lower, with scores of one-quarter to one-half of the listed companies and especially low scores on Financial Transparency and Utility. However, unlisted companies are still subject to scrutiny and pressures from civil society, perhaps explaining their higher but still modest Sustainability Transparency score and comparable scores on Connectivity and Interactivity.

TABLE 8.3 Global 500 Reporting Website Categories by Country

Country	Number of Companies	Financial Transparency	Sustainability Transparency	Connectivity	Interactivity	Utility	Total
United States	131	55.83	44.92	44.06	60.00	73.83	58.53
China	84	18.71	24.22	25.45	20.42	13.34	15.03
Japan	61	50.84	66.26	60.92	38.30	50.00	57.83
France	31	67.46	58.87	52.50	67.57	43.60	62.36
United Kingdom	30	63.84	62.27	58.92	63.41	64.15	66.49
Germany	29	76.78	66.24	54.99	63.22	54.90	70.17
Average score		55.58	53.80	49.47	52.15	49.97	55.07

Note: Information on the country location for each company was from *Fortune*, "Global 500."

TABLE 8.4 Global 500 Reporting Website Categories by Company Size in Revenues

Rank	Number of Companies	Financial Transparency	Sustainability Transparency	Connectivity	Interactivity	Utility	Total
1–100	100	60.52	57.46	49.99	57.67	62.58	61.46
101–200	100	54.00	56.10	47.25	58.13	55.00	56.45
201–300	100	53.13	51.30	51.09	48.72	51.02	53.43
301–400	100	43.21	42.27	41.27	38.25	40.28	41.34
401–500	100	45.74	47.77	46.40	41.93	45.71	47.48

Note: Information on the revenue for each company was from *Fortune,* "Global 500."

TABLE 8.5   Global 500 Reporting Website Categories by Type of Company

	Number of Companies	Financial Transparency	Sustainability Transparency	Connectivity	Interactivity	Utility	Total
Listed	415	58.11	55.55	50.97	53.53	58.17	58.84
Unlisted	85	18.16	28.64	28.81	26.52	15.52	18.82

Note: We used Bloomberg LP's market status coding to classify each company as Active, Private, and Unlisted.

TABLE 8.6   Website Categories of Integrated Reporting Companies

Region	Number of Companies	Financial Transparency	Sustainability Transparency	Connectivity	Interactivity	Utility	Total
Non-South Africa	42	55.71	54.20	49.56	53.49	54.31	53.17
South Africa	10	32.29	43.40	73.93	31.19	32.45	40.92

Finally, we compared the websites of a subset of the integrated reporting companies (Table 8.6) discussed in the previous chapter to the Global 500. Using the same methodology, we analyzed the top 40 non-South African companies in terms of their total score on their integrated report and the same for the top 10 South African companies.[13] The websites of the South African companies rank distinctly lower in every category except Connectivity, an ostensible artifact of their integrated report production. These results clearly indicate that having a high-quality integrated report and a high-quality corporate reporting website are completely independent of each other.

WEBSITE FEATURE ANALYSIS

The aggregate category scores analyzed above do not reveal some important differences in the individual features comprising each category. Since it is through these features that companies create effective reporting websites, we examined them in order to gain insights into exactly what a company needs to do to improve its corporate reporting website. These data are shown in Tables 8.7 (by SASB sector), 8.8 (by region), 8.9 (by country), 8.10 (by size),

TABLE 8.7 Global 500 Reporting Website Features by Sector

SASB Industry	Number of Companies	Social Media (%)	Videos (%)	Feedback (%)	Account (%)	Games (%)	Webcasts (%)	Contact (%)	Tools (%)	Excel (%)	Custom (%)	XBRL (%)
Consumption	64	78	36	3	3	0	70	36	61	48	0	41
Financials	108	62	26	5	1	1	54	33	52	31	6	19
Healthcare	28	86	46	7	0	0	79	61	71	54	4	50
Infrastructure	43	53	21	0	5	0	40	23	30	14	0	5
Nonrenewable Resources	100	53	26	4	0	0	42	29	48	32	3	15
Resource Transformation	41	71	34	12	5	2	66	34	56	49	2	41
Services	14	71	29	0	0	0	57	36	71	43	14	21
Technology and Communication	51	78	33	14	0	0	63	35	63	43	2	24
Transportation	51	63	37	8	10	0	41	25	41	24	0	18
Average score		66	31	6	2	0	54	33	52	36	3	24

TABLE 8.8 Global 500 Reporting Website Features by Region

Region	Number of Companies	Social Media (%)	Videos (%)	Feedback (%)	Account (%)	Games (%)	Webcasts (%)	Contact (%)	Tools (%)	Excel (%)	Custom (%)	XBRL (%)
Asia	187	34	14	3	0	0	19	9	25	13	2	4
Europe	150	83	47	10	6	0	71	63	67	31	4	5
Latin America and the Caribbean	13	62	15	0	0	8	38	8	54	38	0	0
North America	141	88	38	6	2	1	84	35	72	72	4	73
Oceania	9	78	11	0	0	0	89	44	78	11	0	0
Average score		66	31	6	2	0	54	33	52	36	3	24

TABLE 8.9 Global 500 Reporting Website Features by Country

Country	Number of Companies	Social Media (%)	Videos (%)	Feedback (%)	Account (%)	Games (%)	Webcasts (%)	Contact (%)	Tools (%)	Excel (%)	Custom (%)	XBRL (%)
United States	131	89	38	7	2	1	83	36	71	76	3	78
China	84	12	10	0	0	0	5	6	5	0	0	0
Japan	61	48	21	5	0	0	34	0	41	26	5	10
France	31	87	48	19	6	0	61	45	45	13	3	0
United Kingdom	30	80	60	7	0	0	80	60	90	43	0	10
Germany	29	76	52	10	21	0	66	76	62	38	7	0
Average score		62	33	6	3	0	54	29	49	39	3	30

TABLE 8.10 Global 500 Reporting Website Features by Size

Ranking	Number of Companies	Social Media (%)	Videos (%)	Feedback (%)	Account (%)	Games (%)	Webcasts (%)	Contact (%)	Tools (%)	Excel (%)	Custom (%)	XBRL (%)
1–100	100	76	41	10	5	0	74	41	62	50	4	39
101–200	100	72	49	7	5	1	52	29	57	41	4	21
201–300	100	74	23	5	1	0	59	30	53	31	4	19
301–400	100	53	16	3	0	1	39	30	41	25	1	18
401–500	100	53	24	4	1	0	48	35	49	31	1	22
Average score		66	31	6	2	0	54	33	52	36	3	24

8.11 (by type), and 8.12 (for companies publishing an integrated report). As expected, much of the variation in these specific features matches the patterns discussed above, since these categories are comprised of the items shown in these tables. While some features, such as social media, are used by most of the Global 500, others, like providing data in the Extensible Business Reporting Language (XBRL) format, are used by very few. Most companies could dramatically improve the quality of their corporate reporting website with relatively little effort.

Two-thirds of these companies use social media; one-half use webcasts and provide tools for users to help analyze data; one-third provide videos, the name of a specific contact person at the company (vs. a general "Investor Relations" email address); and one-quarter provide data in XBRL. Very few companies ask for feedback on their website (29 companies), ask the user to create an account so they can analyze website usage by type of person (12 companies), enable the user to create a "custom report," or provide interactive games to help the audience understand the trade-offs the company is grappling with (two companies). The larger companies, especially the largest 100, are more likely to have taken advantage of most of these features. The exception lies in asking for the user to register an account, to participate in instructive games, or create a custom report; even for the very largest companies, only an extremely small percentage have this functionality on their website. This raises the question of whether these are simply not important features or whether even the largest companies are only beginning to tap into the power of the Internet. The private companies, as expected, have extremely low scores: 0% on 4 of the 11 factors and less than 5% on 8. One-quarter use social media and a little more than 1 in 10 had videos.

Unlike financial reporting, integrated reporting can perform a transformation function. With this in mind, we looked for evidence of companies trying to do so by comparing the integrated reporting companies to the Global 500. For the entire sample of integrated reporting companies, they score noticeably higher on providing the name of a specific contact (67% vs. 33%) and tools for analysis (77% vs. 52%). Both features contribute to the transformation function. The latter enables the user to better understand the meaning of what the company is reporting. Perhaps indicative of a desire for greater engagement that comes with integrated reporting, the former gives the user an accessible channel through which he or she can ask the company questions. The latter indicates a desire to foster integrated thinking on the part of the audience. On all other features, this group looks about the same as the Global 500. However, again we found a few areas in which the South African

TABLE 8.11 Global 500 Reporting Website Features by Type of Company

Ranking	Number of Companies	Social Media (%)	Videos (%)	Feedback (%)	Account (%)	Games (%)	Webcasts (%)	Contact (%)	Tools (%)	Excel (%)	Custom (%)	XBRL (%)
Listed	415	74	34	7	3	0	65	38	63	42	3	29
Unlisted	85	26	13	0	0	0	4	11	2	2	1	0
Average score		66	31	6	2	0	54	33	52	36	3	24

TABLE 8.12 Website Features of Integrated Reporting Companies

Region	Number of Companies	Social Media (%)	Videos (%)	Feedback (%)	Account (%)	Games (%)	Webcasts (%)	Contact (%)	Tools (%)	Excel (%)	Custom (%)	XBRL (%)
Non-South Africa	42	83	38	5	0	5	60	67	76	60	21	5
South Africa	10	70	0	0	0	0	70	70	80	20	0	0
Average score		81	31	4	0	4	62	67	77	52	17	4

companies are notably weaker: videos (0% vs. 38%) and providing data in Excel spreadsheets (20% vs. 60%).

 THREE EXAMPLES

We will conclude this chapter by looking at the reporting website use of three leading integrated reporting companies previously mentioned in this book: Novo Nordisk, Philips, and SAP.[14] In highlighting their websites, we simply wish to illustrate some of the interesting and useful things being done today that could be replicated with modest effort by any company of significant size. Each company scored high on its integrated report and corporate reporting website.[15] Novo Nordisk uses its website to supplement the PDF version of its integrated report with rich detail and interactive games. The approach to website use at Philips is similar to Novo Nordisk's; however, unlike Novo Nordisk's site, Philips engages the website visitor with video presentations. SAP is distinctive in that it places much greater emphasis on making the site itself, rather than a document, the basis of its integrated reporting.

Novo Nordisk

While Novo Nordisk's primary communication vehicle for the company's integrated report on financial, social, and environmental performance is a PDF document that can be viewed online or downloaded, information supplementing the annual report, as on materiality and stakeholder engagement, is available via the Home Page with a single click on the "Sustainability" tab.[16] Materiality is covered at a very high level in the integrated report. Using the path, Home; Sustainability; Our Priorities, brings the reader to six topics: Access to health, Responsible business practices, Our people, Environment and climate change, and Communities and Bioethics. Each topic, in turn, has links to as many as six subtopics, each of which can be explored further. "Our positions," a subsection of Sustainability, also provides position papers on issues of relevance to Novo Nordisk and insights into how the company views its role as a global corporate citizen. In addition, the website also presents interactive games[17] that simulate business ethics, climate change, and economics and health dilemmas illustrative of the trade-offs the company might encounter among its stakeholders. Finally, the company recently introduced a publication called "TBL Quarterly" (for Triple Bottom Line) which "tells the actions, challenges and opportunities of conducting a sustainable business. Each quarterly issue offers articles, photos, videos and infographics that demonstrate how responsibility supports long-term value creation."[18]

Like materiality, stakeholder engagement is not covered in depth in the PDF report. Rather, the "Sustainability" page links to a discussion of stakeholder engagement that identifies several key stakeholders and makes clear that patients are the ultimate stakeholder to which the company must hold itself accountable.[19] In addition to consulting with employees, investors, suppliers, and other business partners and neighbors, the company considers memberships in industry and business associations, advocacy organizations, and affiliation with think tanks to be integral parts of stakeholder engagement.

Insofar as "behind the scenes" website user tracking features are concerned, Novo Nordisk tracks content areas by interest to the company's stakeholders (seen in Table 8.13) via the number of downloads. Few users downloaded quarterly financial figures for 2011 and 2012, most likely because this information is readily available elsewhere, but they expressed a high level of interest in how much of the company's shares are held by management, management's interpretation of accomplishments and results in 2012,

TABLE 8.13 Most Viewed Sections of Novo Nordisk Annual Report 2012

Section	Views
Management's holdings of Novo Nordisk shares	1086
Accomplishments and Results 2012	402
Consolidated financial, social and environmental statements	286
Assurance	246
Our business	149
Quarterly financial figures 2011 and 2012	79
Additional Information	36
Outlook 2013	24
Governance leadership and shares	23

Note: Special thanks to Novo Nordisk for providing this data, especially Susanne Stormer, Vice President, Corporate Sustainability; Christina Salomon, Project Manager, Corporate Sustainability; and Scott Dille, Team Leader, Insights and Outreach. Specific sections of Novo Nordisk's 2011 and 2012 annual reports can be downloaded and viewed from Novo Nordisk's reporting website. Although only overall count data is provided on the number of downloads, we surmise that those visiting and downloading information from the annual report are an accurate reflection of the company's stakeholders.

the consolidated statements of all types of performance,[20] and what assurance has been given on the report.[21]

Philips

While Philips uses its website to supplement information in its integrated report,[22] the company does much more than provide additional information. It weaves interactive elements throughout the site to connect with visitors in a more visceral way than narrative and numbers can accomplish alone, while simultaneously gathering data about the kinds of people using the site. Visitors to the Philips annual report website are greeted by a request to identify which constituency they represent. The selections include customer, shareholder, financial analyst, sustainability analyst, employee, supplier, nongovernmental organization (NGO), portfolio manager, journalist, job seeker, or student. Philips also provides an "other" category with space to enter a brief description.

The use of video to engage a visitor has been a humanizing feature on the Philips website since it published its first integrated report in 2008. The 2012 website includes video commentary from the chief executive officer (CEO), chief financial officer (CFO), and Chief Human Resources Officer. The Message from the CEO brings the traditional CEO Letter to life; a visitor can hear the CEO's passion and commitment. The CFO's review of financial performance provides texture that the corporate Balance Sheet and Statement of Income cannot offer. Similarly, the Chief Human Resources Officer delivers remarks on how Philips is driving structural and cultural change.

An example of using animation creatively, "Interactive charts" encourage visitors to design their own presentations of Philips' performance. Seven charts are available—Balance Sheet, Statement of income, Profitability, Cash flow, Key figures per share, Employees, and Sustainability. Each allows manipulation based on several different properties. For example, the Statement of income charts provide sales and different computations of earnings for five years for the Group or individual business segments.

The report download center[23] offers a visitor several choices for accessing report information. While one may download the entire annual report, the visitor can also compile a personalized report by selecting individual sections. Philips also provides three prefabricated reports: Analyst selection, Sustainability selection, and Employee highlights.

SAP [24]

Containing the only report available exclusively online, SAP's website does an excellent job of organizing integrated reporting content (Table 8.14). Because

TABLE 8.14 "The International <IR> Framework" and SAP's Corporate Reporting Website

"The International <IR> Framework" Content Element	Path on SAP website
Business model	Performance; Business Activity
Strategy and resource allocation	Performance; Vision, Mission and Strategy
Risks and opportunities	Performance; Risk Report
Outlook	Performance; Outlook

of its logical structure, for example, "The International <IR> Framework" Content Elements related to the Guiding Principles of Strategic focus and future orientation are relatively easy to find.

Materiality is a separate section accessed from the "About This Report" tab. The materiality discussion provides a link to Stakeholder Engagement, an integral part of the process to determine materiality.

One of the most significant features of SAP's 2012 Integrated Report[25] is the interactive graphic connecting financial and nonfinancial performance. The graphic depicts three economic indicators, four environmental indicators, and seven social indicators (Table 8.15) and shows the relationships between them.

SAP's approach allows the reader to click on an indicator to display its relationship to other factors. For example, clicking on the environmental indicator, total energy consumed, displays a link to an economic indicator,

TABLE 8.15 SAP Connecting Financial and Nonfinancial Performance

Economic Indicators	Environmental Indicators	Social Indicators
Revenue	GHG Footprint	Employee Engagement
Operating Margin	Total Energy Consumed	Business Health Culture Index
Customer Success	Data Center Energy	Employee Retention
	Renewable Resources	Women in Management
		Social Investment
		Capability Building
		Employer Ranking

Data Source: SAP Integrated Report 2012. "Key Facts: Connecting financial and non-financial performance," http://www.sapintegratedreport.com/2012/en/key-facts/connecting-financial-and-non-financial-performance.html, accessed April 2014 (site discontinued).

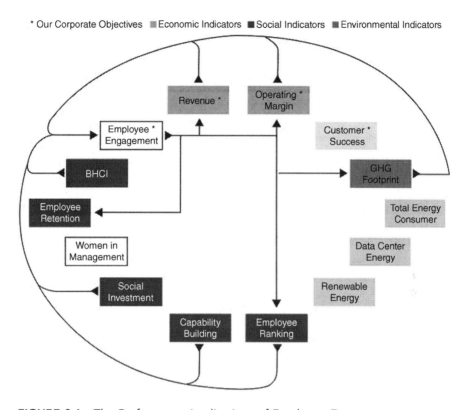

* Our Corporate Objectives ■ Economic Indicators ■ Social Indicators ■ Environmental Indicators

FIGURE 8.1 The Performance Implications of Employee Engagement
Source: SAP *Integrated Report 2012,* "Connecting Financial and Non-Financial Performance," (site discontinued).

operating margin, and to an environmental indicator, greenhouse gas (GHG) footprint. The environmental indicator, data center energy, is identified as the direct driver of total energy consumed. Similarly, Figure 8.1 illustrates this for employee engagement. No other company website we studied illustrated its interdependencies between financial and nonfinancial factors to the same degree.[26]

A first step in a process toward quantitative valuation of the relationships between financial and nonfinancial performance as contemplated by the International <IR> Framework,[27] this graphic representation demonstrates SAP's understanding of how different dimensions of financial and nonfinancial information are related to each other.[28]

Further, the SAP Integrated Report 2012 includes an Independent Auditors Report[29] and an Independent Assurance Report.[30] The Independent

Auditors Report provides a traditional opinion on the company's consolidated financial statements. The Independent Assurance Report provides both limited and reasonable assurance on selected sustainability information.[31] Limited assurance is provided on SAP's application of the AA1000 AccountAbility Principle Standard (2008) and on selected qualitative claims and quantitative indicators on sustainability performance. Reasonable assurance is provided on the indicators for Business Health Culture Index, employee engagement, employee retention, women in management, GHG footprint (Scope 1 and 2 as well as selected Scope 3 emissions including business flights and employee commuting), renewable energy, total energy consumed, and customer success.

The fact that SAP's reporting website is one of the most sophisticated we studied is not surprising given that it is a technology company. Yet its website features are based more on the exercise of integrated thinking than sophisticated technologies, and virtually everything their website contains could be easily replicated by any company of significant size. Important as a reporting website is, however, it is only one way information technology can be used to improve integrated reporting and in the process, foster integrated thinking.

 ## NOTES

1. From the *Fortune* magazine methodology: Companies are ranked by total revenues for their respective fiscal years ended on or before March 31, 2013. All companies on the list must publish financial data and report part or all of their figures to a government agency. Figures are as reported, and comparisons are with the prior year's figures as originally reported for that year. *Fortune* does not restate the prior year's figures for changes in accounting. (Source: *Fortune*, July 8, 2013) Procedure: Using the Global 500 rankings as the data set, we created a checklist of items to look for and record. The websites were viewed over a period of time (Oct. 2013-Feb. 2014) and the data was recorded on paper and entered into an Excel spreadsheet for later analysis.
2. Revenues and market capitalization downloaded from Bloomberg LP and calculated in U.S. dollars as of December 31, 2012.
3. Revenues were summed to produce a total aggregate revenue and world market capitalization downloaded from Bloomberg LP and calculated in USD as December 31, 2012. Market capitalization is in trillions.
4. Preliminary data gathering was done with over 100 sites, including known integrated reporters, the big pharmaceuticals, and a sample of the *Fortune* 500 before we settled on the *Fortune* Global 500 as our target population.

5. This chapter would not have been possible without the indefatigable efforts of Barbara Esty, Senior Information Research Specialist in the Knowledge and Library Services Department at Harvard Business School. Over many months of hard work, starting in October 2013 and ending in February 2014, she single-handedly coded up the Global 500 websites, spending hundreds of hours immersed in this effort. Barbara was also deeply involved in the analysis and interpretation of the data. To this day she remains, in our view, the world's foremost expert on corporate reporting websites. After preliminary data gathering to determine which website features we wanted to collect and the Global 500 was selected as our company set, we developed a score sheet to record the findings. The score sheet was created to maintain consistency when looking at a site. For each feature, the score sheet identified the feature, how the feature would be scored, a place to record the score, and any additional comments. While recording these on paper knowing that they would need to be entered into a spreadsheet may seem redundant, this provided an extra check for items which were missed or required a second look due to website complexity. Further, the flexibility of the form allowed for the recording of textual data that we were unsure of how to score at the onset of data collection. Each website was approached in the same way, starting at the home page, looking at the general attributes of the site, which include treatments of multiple languages, use of social media, videos, etc. We then clicked to the investor relations section and sustainability pages. The appearance of a feature was recorded if clearly visible on the site or through a simple search of the site. The feature needed to be part of the text on the webpage, not in documents found through links on the webpage.

6. eMarketer. "MOBILE SOCIAL PLATFORMS IN CHINA: Marketing Challenges and Opportunities, December 2013, http://d1vumxoj4hmk29.cloudfront.net/system/attachables/main/MuLOylpwdFtw6WpVw4U/original/Mobile_Social_Plateforms_in_China.pdf?1389666464, accessed May 2014.

7. Very few Global 500 companies do not have an English version of their website. However, for those who do not, Google's Chrome browser provides a transla-tion feature that allows for basic navigation and understanding of the website's contents.

8. Ideally for a dataset of this size we would aim to automate the process, both for time and for consistency. However, successful web scrapping relies on seeking specific items that we did not know at the onset. Rendering a complete copy of a website is difficult due to not only the sheer volume of pages of text and images but also the complex arrangement of files that comprise the site. Lastly, we wanted to be respectful of each company's website's terms of use, which in most cases limited the amount of material that can be copied and stored for future use. While there are no doubt some individual coding errors given the number of websites reviewed (a careful eye only goes so far and items can be

missed), given the aggregate way in which we are analyzing the data, we do not believe any errors have a material effect on the analysis. A double check occurred when transferring data from paper to spreadsheet—if something was missing or appeared odd, it was rechecked.

9. Ideally, we would have had these categories defined in the beginning, but it took the process of manually gathering the data from the websites to have them emerge. Due to the variety of website features, category labels, and functionality, the data elements the categories grew organically through observation. To base the list of data collection points from a small sample would have biased the set. To determine the final list of categories to inventory, a preliminary list of data points was created and through viewing a set of integrated reporting companies, large pharmaceutical companies, and a subset of the *Fortune* 500 list. Items were added based on the frequency or uniqueness of when items appeared, such as the years of an annual report archive or games.

10. By "connectivity" we are referring to a website property, not "connectivity of information" as defined by "The International <IR> Framework."

11. Detail on the meanings of each category is included in Appendix 8A.

12. We generally follow the scoring framework employed in Thomson Reuter's Asset 4 ESG database (http://extranet.datastream.com/data/ASSET4%20ESG/documents/ASSET4_ESG_Methdology_FAQ_0612.pdf). Individual items are typically scored 1 (Yes) or 0 (No) depending on whether or not we find that item in the company's website. These individual item scores are aggregated to provide a raw score for each company in each of the 7 categories. Each company's raw score in each category is then converted into a z-score measuring the raw score as a number of standard deviations from the mean across all companies in that category. Z-scores make it easier to identify differences among companies when there is less variation of scores across companies and also give greater weight to atypical scores. In the latter case, for example, a company will typically score higher for having a particular item on its website if relatively few companies have that item than if many companies have the item. Finally, the z-scores are normalized by ranking them on a scale of 0 to 100.

13. Our website analysis was composed of the top 40 non-South African companies plus Novo Nordisk and SAP. There were 13 companies—AEGON, Banco do Brasil, BASF, CEBU Holdings, Chubu Electric Power, Eni S.P.A., Maersk, Nokia Corporation, Philips, Société Générale de Surveillance (SGS) Switzerland, Statoil ASA, UBS, and YIT OYJ—that published a self-declared integrated report and were named in the Global 500. Self-declared integrated reports were from Global Reporting Initiative, Sustainability Disclosure Database, GRI [Excel] Reports List, http://database.globalreporting.org/pages/about, accessed April 2014. See Appendix 8A for the details of website coding and our scoring criteria.

14. For more background on integrated reporting at Novo Nordisk and Philips see Eccles, Robert G. and Michael P. Krzus. "Novo Nordisk: A Commitment to Sustainability." Harvard Business School Case 412-053. (Revised January 2012). Eccles, Robert G. and Daniela Saltzman. "Integrated Assurance at Philips Electronics N. V." Harvard Business School Case 412-054, January 2012. (Revised May 2013.)

15. The website characteristics of Novo Nordisk, Philips, and SAP were evaluated using the same scoring methodology as we used for the Global 500.

	Financial Transparency	Sustainability Transparency	Connectivity	Interactivity	Utility	Total
Novo Nordisk	95.2	94.6	73.9	99.3	68.9	98.1
Philips	68.2	35.3	73.9	87.0	33.6	69.3
SAP	89.1	46.4	73.9	99.3	99.0	97.4

16. Novo Nordisk. Sustainability, *Annual Report 2012*, http://www.novonordisk .com/sustainability/online-reports/online-reports.asp, accessed March 2014.

17. Novo Nordisk. Sustainability/Interactive Challenges, http://www.novonordisk .com/sustainability/games/interactive-challenges.asp, accessed April 2014.

18. http://www.novonordisk.com/sustainability/how-we-manage/tbl-quarterly. asp, accessed April 2014.

19. The importance of the patient in the Novo Nordisk culture is based on the Novo Nordisk Way, principles dating back to the 1923 founding of the company. Two of the principles are: "Our key contribution is to discover and develop innovative biological medicines and make them accessible to patients throughout the world" and "Growing our business and delivering competitive financial results is what allows us to help patients live better lives, offer an attractive return to our shareholders and contribute to our communities." Jakob Riis, executive vice president of Marketing & Medical Affairs, brings that point to life in the 2013 Annual Report saying, "Our goal is to make a difference to patients. . . ." Novo Nordisk. *Novo Nordisk Annual Report 2013*, http://www .novonordisk.com/investors/annual-report-2013/default.asp, accessed May 2014, pp. 4 and 25, respectively.

20. Consolidated financial statements refers to consolidated balance sheet, statements of income and cash flows, and notes to financials.

21. The company's shares held by management are in the report section "Shares and capital structure" beginning on p. 44. Management's interpretation of accomplishments and results in 2012 is in the report section "2013 Performance and 2013 outlook" on p. 6. The consolidated statements of all types of performance are under "Consolidated financial, social and environmental

statements," beginning on page 55. What assurance has been given on the report is described under "Assurance" on page 109. *Novo Nordisk annual report 2012*, http://www.novonordisk.com/investors/annual-report-2012/ar2012.asp, accessed April 2014.

22. Philips. *Annual Report 2012*, http://www.annualreport2012.philips.com/index.aspx, accessed March 2014.

23. Philips *Annual Report 2012*. Downloads, http://www.annualreport2012.philips.com/downloads/index.aspx, accessed April 2014.

24. Our analysis and discussion of SAP's integrated reporting content is based on the SAP Integrated Report 2012, which is no longer available. SAP's *Integrated Report 2013* may be found at http://www.sapintegratedreport.com/2013/en/, accessed May 2013.

25. SAP *Integrated Report 2012*. http://www.sapintegratedreport.com/2012/en/home.html, accessed March 2014 (site discontinued).

26. SAP *Integrated Report 2012*, "Connecting Financial and Non-Financial Performance," (site discontinued).

27. For more discussion about connecting financial and nonfinancial performance see "The International <IR> Framework", Section 3B, Connectivity of information, paragraph 3.8, Financial information and other information. For example, the implications for: expected revenue growth or market share of research and development policies, technology/know-how or investment in human resources; cost reduction or new business opportunities of environmental policies, energy efficiency, cooperation with local communities or technologies to tackle social issues and revenue and profit growth of long-term customer relationships, customer satisfaction, or reputation. International Integrated Reporting Council. "International <IR> Framework", http://www.theiirc.org/international-ir-framework/, accessed April 2014.

28. For more discussion of SAP's integrated report see Eccles, Robert G., and George Serafeim. "A Tale of Two Stories: Sustainability and the Quarterly Earnings Call." *Journal of Applied Corporate Finance* 25, no. 3 (Summer 2013): 66–77.

29. SAP *Integrated Report 2012*. Independent Auditor's Report, http://www.sapintegratedreport.com/2012/en/to-our-stakeholders/independent-auditors-report.html, accessed April 2014 (site discontinued).

30. Ibid.

31. The terms "reasonable assurance engagement" and "limited assurance engagement" distinguish between the two types of assurance engagement a practitioner is permitted to perform. The objective of a reasonable assurance engagement is a reduction in assurance engagement risk to an acceptably low level in the circumstances of the engagement as the basis for a positive form of expression of the practitioner's conclusion. The objective of a limited assurance engagement is a reduction in assurance engagement risk to a level

that is acceptable in the circumstances of the engagement, but where that risk is greater than for a reasonable assurance engagement, as the basis for a negative form of expression of the practitioner's conclusion. Source: International Auditing and Assurance Standards Board. International Standard on Assurance Engagements (ISAE) 3000, "Assurance Engagements Other Than Audits or Reviews of Historical Financial Information," http://www.ifac .org/sites/default/files/publications/files/B005%202013%20IAASB%20Hand book%20ISAE%203000_0.pdf, accessed April 2014.

Methodology for Website Coding

T HIS APPENDIX describes the scoring methodology used to evaluate the websites of the Global 500 companies. We developed a unique scoring framework and Table 8A.1 presents the selected features, why they were chosen, and how data were collected. Website features were grouped into categories for scoring. Category names and our definition of each category follow:

- **Financial transparency.** These items assess how much financial information is provided and how easy it is for the user to find.
- **Sustainability transparency.** These items measure how much sustainability information is provided and how easy it is for the user to find.
- **Interactivity.** These items assess the degree to which the user is able to engage with the website.
- **Connectivity.** These items assess the degree of integration in the reporting of the company's financial and nonfinancial performance.
- **Utility.** These items assess the availability of tools and formats provided to aid understanding and analysis of the company's data.

TABLE 8A.1 Website Coding Categories and Features

Category	Feature	Why the Feature Was Chosen	How the Data Were Collected
Financial transparency	Separate consumer and corporate site	Many companies, especially retail, put all their corporate information in an "About Us" section that is extensive or they have separate sites.	A separate site was identified by its use of a different URL, for example, www.thewaltdisneycompany.com and www.disney.com.
Financial transparency	Multiple languages or global/regional presence	Having a global web presence indicates a desire or need to reach customers or shareholders worldwide. Limitations: Entering a site from the U.S. brings up the "English" site. All effort was made to determine which languages were available. Where sites did not have an English option, Google translate through Chrome was used.	Site provides an option to "change languages" or choose a regional or country-specific site. Most regional sites are in English and most investor sites of the other language sites are in English.
Financial transparency	Other formats	Users access websites from multiple devices.	Does the site identify other formats such as mobile websites, iPad, iPhone, Android, and apps? Scoring was based on whether one of these other formats was available or not.
Financial transparency	Webcasts	Webcasts are popular ways for companies to include shareholders and stakeholders in earnings calls, analyst presentations, and other events.	A "yes" was recorded if the company provided links to webcasts, audio casts or podcasts of presentations, earnings calls, etc.

Financial transparency	Investor relations—individual contacts	How easy it is to contact company investor relations' departments varies. Some companies are more transparent than others.	A "yes" was recorded if the company provided names, pictures, email addresses, or phone numbers of the members of the investor relations' team.
Financial transparency	Investor relations—general mailbox	How easily one can contact the investor relations departments varies. Some companies are more transparent than others.	A "yes" was recorded if there was a link to a phone number, email form, or general email address.
Financial transparency	Investor relations FAQs	Companies vary in providing shareholders with self-service information.	A "yes" was recorded if there were FAQs located on the "Information for Shareholders" pages, Investors sections, or investor-related FAQs on the site.
Financial transparency	Annual report archive	The web allows for the ability to post many years of information in a cost-effective manner.	The number of years for which annual reports were available was determined by subtracting the start year from 2012.
Financial transparency	Path to investor relations' section	Websites are designed with a specific strategy in mind for the location of all content. Location of content on a website is intentional. We compare the location of the investor relations information to that of sustainability information.	The path to investor information was scored by taking the inverse of the number of steps from the homepage. For example, home/investors is two steps and was scored as .5. Companies with fewer steps received a higher score.

(Continued)

TABLE 8A.1 (Continued)

Category	Feature	Why the Feature Was Chosen	How the Data Were Collected
Financial transparency	Annual reports in other languages	Much like language use across the entire site, companies can offer documents in multiple languages.	A "yes" was recorded if there were non-English versions available on the site.
Sustainability transparency	Path to sustainability section	Location of content on a website is intentional. We compared the location of the investor relations information to that of sustainability.	The path to sustainability was scored by taking the inverse of the number of steps from the homepage. For example, home/ investors is two steps and was scored as .5. Companies with fewer steps received a higher score
Sustainability transparency	Substantive information provided on sustainability webpage	Information provided about sustainability effort varies in substance and volume.	A "yes" was recorded if the site provided data on key performance indicators (KPIs), information on initiatives, reports, etc. Sites with just a CSR report or public relations' information about philanthropy or marketing were not counted.
Sustainability transparency	Path to sustainability report	Companies vary in the location of their sustainability reporting. It is not always clearly visible on the sustainability or investor sections. The location of the Annual report is typically visible on the top investor relations page. The variability of the sustainability report warranted measuring.	The path to the sustainability report was scored by taking the inverse of the number of steps from the homepage. For example, home/CSR/CSR report is three steps and is scored as .33. Companies with fewer steps received a higher score.

Sustainability transparency	Sustainability report in other languages	Much like annual reports, we wanted to see if reports were produced in other languages.	A "yes" was recorded if non-English version available.
Sustainability transparency	Sustainability archive	The web allows for the ability to post many years of information in a cost-effective manner.	The number of years for which sustainability reports were available was determined by subtracting the start year from 2012.
Sustainability transparency	Sustainability standards/ guidelines	Companies can use the webpage to inform the user about which standard or guidelines they follow. For example, Global Reporting Initiative, UN Global Compact, and CDP.	A "yes" was recorded if the standards or guidelines were mentioned in the sustainability section or through a search of the site.
Interactivity	Social media	Social media has spread as a corporate communication to reach customers and shareholders. Limitations: Some countries limit social media use or the company has made a choice not to participate.	All prominently displayed links to various social media platforms were recorded. The number and type of social media outlets varied greatly. The ones noted were mostly located on the home page, investor relations page, or prominently displayed on the site. While major individual services were recorded, the number of services/outlet provided did not add to the score.

(Continued)

TABLE 8A.1 *(Continued)*

Category	Feature	Why the Feature Was Chosen	How the Data Were Collected
Interactivity	Video	Video enables a company to communicate to the user in a more "human voice."	A "yes" was recorded if the site prominently displayed one or more videos on the site on the home page, media page, or through a quick site search.
Interactivity	Visitor type (survey of who the user is)	Sites can deliver custom content based on the identity of the user.	A "yes" was recorded if there was a mechanism on the site to identify the user. For example, "Are you a shareholder, student, journalist, etc.?"
Interactivity	Feedback	Site has the ability to gather feedback from the users about content and their experience using the website in order to make improvements.	A "yes" was recorded if a pop-up survey appeared on the site or the site provided a prominent link for feedback. We did not consider the general "contact us" link as a feedback mechanism.
Interactivity	Registration/Account	Site asks the user to register for custom content or to access areas of a website.	A "yes" was recorded if the site asked the user to register for content-newsletter, custom feeds of articles, etc. RSS feeds were not considered part of this category.
Connectivity	Link from sustainability to investor relations	We wanted to understand how the website links the two sections.	A "yes" was recorded if there was a clear link from the sustainability page to the investor page.

Connectivity	Link from investor relations to sustainability	We wanted to understand how websites link the two sections.	A "yes" was recorded if there was a clear link from the investor page to the sustainability page.
Connectivity	Integrated report	Does the company produce an integrated report?	A "yes" was recorded if the company identified the report as an integrated report or displays "annual and sustainability report" in one document or provides language on the site that says they participate in integrated reporting.
Utility	Investor tools	There are many easy to use graphing and charting options available for companies to provide their users a way to look at data.	A "yes" was recorded if the site provided any tools allowing the user to change inputs and manipulate data to produce a table, graph, or spreadsheet.
Utility	Annual report as a .PDF	Companies provide annual information in many forms, but we feel that the .PDF format provides the user with a portable form that is universally easy to read and to use.	A "yes" was recorded if the annual report was provided in a downloadable .PDF format. 10-K fillings were not counted as .PDF annual reports as the Form 10-K in .PDF format does not add to the utility of the document.
Utility	Sustainability report as a .PDF	Companies provide sustainability information in many forms, but we feel that the .PDF format provides	A "yes" was recorded if there was a sustainability report and it was provided in a downloadable

(Continued)

TABLE 8A.1 (*Continued*)

Category	Feature	Why the Feature Was Chosen	How the Data Were Collected
		the user with a portable form that is universally easy to read and to use.	.PDF format. Many sustainability sites are microsites, but the report can be downloaded.
Utility	Spreadsheet for financials	Companies can provide multiple ways to make it easy for the user to download and manipulate financial information.	A "yes" was recorded if an export-to-spreadsheet feature was provided.
Utility	Games	Sites can provide information and education through interactive games.	A "yes" was recorded if the site contained a game that asks for a response from the user and provides information based on the response.
Utility	Custom views	The web allows for information to be parsed in custom ways. We wanted to see how companies were using these features.	A "yes" was recorded if the user could pick and choose pieces of information and create a single new document.
Utility	XBRL (Extensible Business Reporting Language)	We wanted to see if companies are using this technology to make data more usable to the user.	A "yes" was recorded if the user could download the raw XBRL data.

CHAPTER NINE

Information Technology

LTHOUGH THE USE OF information technology (IT) is not a focal point of the integrated reporting movement's conversation today, it should be. IT, which involves the "development, maintenance, and use of computer systems, software, and networks for the processing and distribution of data,"[1] poses a major challenge for integrated reporting. Yet it is also an opportunity. Not only can IT dramatically improve the process and quality of integrated reporting to the benefit of both the company and its audience, it can also improve both parties' integrated thinking.

To understand how this can be accomplished, corporate reporting in general and integrated reporting in particular must be considered in the context of four technological trends sweeping the business world today: big data, analytics, cloud computing, and social media. Companies have rightly focused on how these technologies can support and transform their business model. Virtually no attention, however, has been given to their application in integrated reporting. We believe that should—and will—change. Until senior management gives proper consideration to how to leverage IT for corporate disclosure, the full promise of integrated reporting (<IR>) and integrated thinking (<IT>) will not be achieved. The previous two chapters' analysis supports this contention. As shown in Chapter 7, paper-based reports have severe inherent limitations and, as shown in Chapter 8, the corporate reporting websites of the 500 largest companies in the world today only scratch the surface when it comes to using currently available IT. To put IT more directly into the movement's conversation about integrated reporting, we have devoted an entire chapter of the book to this topic.[2]

We will begin by explaining how existing IT can be used to support the processes required for integrated reporting. Emphasizing the role intelligent, machine-readable data will play in the not-too-distant future, we review the four trends and how they might contribute to <IR> and <IT>, ultimately introducing the concept of "contextual reporting"—a kind of reporting in which any single piece of information is easily viewed in the context of the "big picture." The chapter concludes with a brief glimpse into the future of integrated reporting with the hypothetical company World Market Basket.

 ## INTEGRATED REPORTING PROCESSES

Used properly, IT, along with supporting internal control systems, can play a major role in the support of integrated thinking and integrated reporting. But this can only be accomplished if the company has a clear strategy for how to use IT to support its fundamental business processes. In an integrated reporting context, these processes are identification, validation, analysis, audience filtering, publishing to internal audiences, and publishing to external audiences (Figure 9.1).[3]

Identification

Integrated thinking inside a company is contingent on management's access to information about business processes, their outcomes, and the positive and negative externalities created as the company uses the International Integrated Reporting Council's (IIRC's) six capitals to create value for its shareholders. This information exists in at least three different forms: narrative or story format, structured information, and unstructured information. Given the broad scope and holistic nature of integrated reporting, the information that drives <IT> and <IR> could come from any unit in the company or outside the boundaries of the enterprise, including its suppliers, customers, business and partners, nongovernmental organizations (NGOs), and members of civil society. For this reason, it is necessary to identify relevant sources

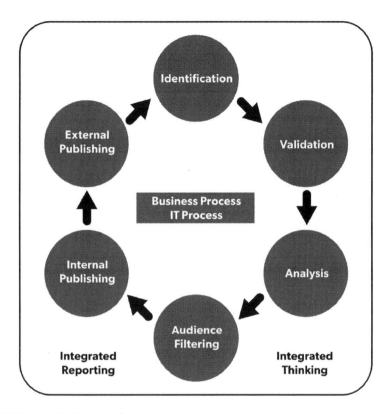

FIGURE 9.1 IT Support for Integrated Reporting Processes

of information and, when it is not available, use proxies or develop new sources.

While a company's enterprise resource planning (ERP) system[4] offers one major source of information, others include employee spreadsheets, online databases, and social media platforms like Twitter. The ERP's carefully structured information usually relates to the tracking of transactional data. As they exist now, these systems are limited in their ability to track the sort of nonfinancial information integrated reporting requires. Much of it is unstructured; it is not neatly organized within the company's ERP system or any other information system that has conventions to which the data must adhere. The challenge for IT is to pull together the structured and unstructured information that comprises the content elements in the International <IR> Framework (<IR> Framework), which, taken together through the Framework's guiding principles, create the narrative backbone of an integrated report.

Validation

While audit and validation processes for financial reporting have been in place for a very long time, they are largely still immature when it comes to nonfinancial information. As a result, report producers and consumers alike are justifiably suspicious of the reliability of the nonfinancial information they report on and use. IT can provide a greater degree of comfort regarding the quality of information being used in integrated reporting by ensuring that there is a single source of truth—that all who consume information inside the company acquire it from a single, systemic source, like a relational database, a data warehouse, or virtual cloud solution. This will reduce errors like the incorrect transposition of numbers or the loss of connection between narrative reporting and the underlying data. IT solutions that deliver a single source of truth are available, but their implementation requires a good alignment between business and IT processes inside the company.

Analysis

The key to analysis is to use information from internal and external sources to link the content elements—such as strategy and resource allocation, governance, performance, and outlook—in a meaningful way. IT tools for analysis are becoming increasingly available, many for a low cost or even free. Earlier analytical systems focused on transactional data, and subsequent ones then incorporated information tucked away in relational databases.[5] The advent of big data, however, has catalyzed the development of more sophisticated analytical tools that can use both structured and unstructured data. Discussed below, these tools can generate new insights on how different pieces of information can be understood and how they might be related to each other.

Audience Filtering

While integrated reporting is holistic by nature, not everyone needs all information all the time. As discussed in Chapter 5, what is regarded as material by each audience varies widely. Both the producer and user of information can filter it and, in both cases, numerous IT tools are available for doing so. However, filtration processes certainly need to mature as most companies using integrated reporting have not yet reached this level of sophistication in their integrated thinking processes. When availing themselves of filtering capabilities, audience members should also be conscious of the fact that information they filter out may be related to information they think is material, so users should approach the process with a certain degree of judgment.

Publishing to Internal Audiences

Once the information has gone through a "materiality filter," it needs to be published for the relevant audience. Currently, a number of potential audiences for integrated reporting information are found inside the company, including line management and the strategic planning, performance monitoring, risk, sustainability, corporate reporting, and investor relations functions. If the information needed by each audience is available in systems or formats that enable portability, then each audience can choose to view and work with the information that is delivered to them using tools appropriate for their task. The challenge for those responsible for the provision of IT is to ensure that any time the users of integrated reporting information massage it, their action does not abstract the information from the context that gives it meaning. The IT system also needs to preserve audit trails, keep track of version control, and maintain links to underlying data sources.

Publishing to External Audiences

For external audiences, the challenge for integrated reporting is to ensure that the important content elements are crafted and honed out of the process of integrated thinking before they are delivered to external consumers of the company's reports. While traditional reports are delivered on pieces of paper (or as PDFs, the digital equivalent of pieces of paper), IT enables more powerful methods of report delivery and consumption. Already, companies are using websites to deliver digital reports that enable role-based or interest-based consumption. While concision is an important guiding principle of integrated reporting, IT can be used to supplement the information in the integrated report by providing metadata (such as through Extensible Business Reporting Language (XBRL)),[6] context, and access to underlying data sets for those who are interested in more detail.

 FOUR IT TRENDS

While use of big data, analytics, cloud computing, and social media is mainstream in the IT community, it is also pervading the broader, global business world today. The terms "big data" and "analytics" are used somewhat interchangeably because they are so closely related to each other. Analytics— looking for patterns, trends, insights, and outcomes—are performed on big data sets, but it seems that the more evocative term of big data is what has caught on and is most commonly used. Little work has been done to examine the relevance of these big trends for integrated reporting, but we think that all can be relevant.[7]

Big Data

Big data is defined as a vast quantity of structured and unstructured data from traditional and digital sources inside and outside an organization that represents a source for ongoing discovery and analysis.[8] From the perspective of integrated reporting, its power lies in the ability to access sources of information ignored by traditional IT systems and to offer proxies for performance outcomes that are difficult to measure (e.g., the value of intellectual property or the benefits of employee engagement) or difficult to track (e.g., customer satisfaction or social impacts). When it comes to big data, companies are doing more than just talking about it; they are spending money on it. According to Gartner, big data investments in 2013 continue to increase. Compared with 2012, in which 58% of organizations surveyed were investing or planning to invest in big data technology, 64% of organizations had taken the plunge.[9] To date, the main areas companies have addressed through big data concern customers (enhanced customer experience, new products/new business models, and more targeted marketing) and internal operations (process efficiency, cost reduction, and improved risk management).[10]

Big data can be both structured[11] (prepared according to a well-defined convention) or unstructured[12] (not prepared according to a well-defined convention). For integrated reporting, both financial and nonfinancial data are important. While they can both be structured or unstructured, non-financial information is more likely to be the latter. Both can be delivered in terms of three different formats, ordered from least to most useful: (1) human-readable data,[13] (2) semiautomated data,[14] and (3) intelligent, machine-readable data. The type of data format a company uses for its integrated report heavily determines how quickly, accurately, and cost-effectively a company and its audience can use that information to make decisions.

The most useful, accurate, efficient, and cost-effective form of data is intelligent, machine-readable data. Intelligent data has built-in validation rules, calculations, and formulas that verify its accuracy. It can also be linked to other data or narrative information in order to illustrate its relationships and interdependencies. The latter is important for fostering integrated thinking because it makes it easy for the user to see how one piece of information is related to others. Finally, it contains tags of "metadata"[15] (data about data) that point to other useful information, such as the accounting standard on which the information is based if it is financial information, or the standard or method of calculation used if it is nonfinancial information. Intelligent, machine-readable data means that almost no human intervention is necessary to work with it: the data go directly from the entity's machine that produces it to the entity's machine that consumes it.

To enhance its utility and value while reducing the amount of manipulation and risk of error later in its life cycle, data should be created as intelligent, machine-readable from the outset. XBRL, a proven global technology for making business information machine-readable, offers one way to accomplish this. As only a handful of the world's largest companies currently provide data in this format for their annual reports on their websites, this is an area of immense opportunity for companies to improve their corporate reporting and their integrated reporting.

Analytics

Analytics helps companies identify relationships between financial and non-financial performance across functions, operating divisions, and their supply chain to provide greater understanding of the "connectivity of information" in support of integrated thinking. Broadly speaking, big data analytics has four basic types of applications: (1) descriptive analytics[16] for hindsight or understanding *what* happened, (2) diagnostic analytics[17] for insight *why* and *how* it happened, (3) predictive analytics[18] for foresight or understanding about what *could* happen, and (4) prescriptive analytics for understanding what *should* happen.[19] The extent to which they create value for the business and foster integrated thinking varies (Figure 9.2). In all cases, the greater the degree to which the input is intelligent, machine-readable data, the greater the power and flexibility of the analytics will be to support integrated thinking on the part of both the company and its audience. Companies typically begin with descriptive analytics, to which they add diagnostic analytics, and ultimately predictive and prescriptive analytics, building from one application to the next as the company gains experience with this IT. Predictive and prescriptive analytics are today's big data "frontier."

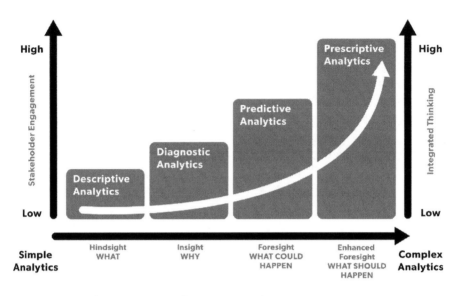

FIGURE 9.2 The Four Types of Big Data Analytics

Cloud Computing

Cloud computing, in which a wide variety of business functions are performed on dispersed servers in a secure, on-demand, capacity-sharing, and scalable manner available from wherever an Internet connection exists, is an increasingly important way to perform analytics on big data. In the Gartner study, cloud computing was cited by 41% of participants as the single most popular information technology for deriving value from big data.[20] Cloud computing is also regarded as one of the most effective ways of encouraging collaboration—which itself fosters integrated thinking—across functions, geographies, time zones, and organizational boundaries.[21]

Social Media

Social media, which enables individuals to share information and communicate with each other and the company on a real-time basis, from anywhere in the world, on platforms like LinkedIn, Facebook, Twitter, and Google+ is an increasingly important source of big data. Through it, companies can access the perspectives of employees and customers, which can be used in an integrated report. It can also help foster more robust integrated thinking, as humans have a natural tendency to see an issue through the lens of their knowledge and experience, often without the full context in which it resides. When people share these perspectives, all of them develop a more complete picture of the causes of outcomes they care about and what can be done to improve them.

Leveraging These Trends

There is no reason why companies and their audiences cannot use big data and analytics with cloud computing and social media to improve the creation, distribution, and consumption of integrated reports. Most simply have yet to do so—in our view, because compliance and filing requirements in a largely regulatory-driven corporate reporting world have reinforced a paper-based paradigm for decades. When the power and collaborative benefits of cloud computing are brought to bear on big data analytics' applications, using information generated from many different sources, companies can significantly improve their integrated reporting and integrated thinking.

The Gartner report cited above identified the types of data analyzed. Most common were transactions (cited by 70% of respondents), log data[22] (55%), machine or sensor data (42%), emails/documents (36%), social media data (32%), free-form text (26%), geospatial data (23%), images (16%), video (9%), audio (6%), and others (12%).[23] Virtually all of these types of data are or can be used in assembling an integrated report. Social media in particular offers a two-way information channel for companies; they can monitor websites to see what employees, customers, and NGOs are saying about them in order to generate data relevant to human and social and relationship capitals, as well as to communicate their integrated report to these audiences.

 CONTEXTUAL REPORTING

Connectivity, a key guiding principle in integrated reporting, comes from the mutually reinforcing relationship between integrated thinking and integrated reporting. In enabling both <IT> and <IR>, IT can help the company understand and report on the links between the content elements of the company's value creation story. IT can play a similar role for the audience of a company's integrated report. Once published, the integrated report becomes *context* for the user. Beyond simply being a report, it is a means of providing access to underlying data sets that provide more detailed information than is contained in the integrated report. Conversely, when a company has published an integrated report, users who access information from outside the report from another source can trace it back to the larger context of the integrated report. We call this technology-enabled "two-way street" between an integrated report and specific pieces of information "contextual reporting" (Figure 9.3). Without the appropriate IT, an integrated report is simply a very useful report. With the appropriate IT, it becomes a vehicle for enabling the

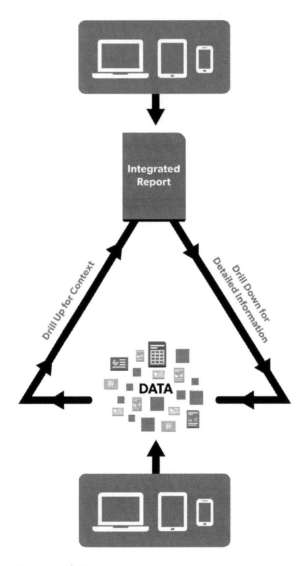

FIGURE 9.3   Contextual Reporting

user to deepen their own understanding of connectivity in terms of the topics that are of interest to them.

Corporate reporting today supplies vast volumes of information, often made available to users via online methods, such as a data terminal, but it often lacks context. These terminals offer the user news, market prices, and messages, in addition to company data. What this plethora of information typically lacks is context regarding a company's strategy, its business model, and its understanding of the risks and opportunities it faces—something an integrated report can provide. With IT embedded in the report, the user can link disparate pieces of information. Conversely, relying solely on the integrated report without the additional insight provided by the underlying data can also result in an incorrect or limited understanding.

Ideally, we need both: large and disparate sets of structured and unstructured data, with the linking apparatus of the integrated report. This way, the user who starts with the integrated report can find the data relevant to the content elements of interest to them, while the user who starts with the data can locate the context for that data via the integrated report. Such an approach would add contextual value to the typical user of the data terminal and the rigor of multiple streams of data to the typical consumer of narrative reporting.

Bringing contextual reporting into existence will require standards (e.g., in the definition of electronic reporting formats, as is being discussed in the European Union's Transparency Directive),[24] the application of big data analytical methods, and the integration of digital reporting information with other forms of corporate information. It also potentially challenges the notion that integrated reporting lacks detail because of its focus on brevity. In effect, the integrated report becomes a concise contextual map that points to a rich load of information that can be found beneath the ground for both internal and external users of the integrated report. Without the use of technology, the capability for integrated reporting to provide context and connectivity is limited.

世界市场篮 (WORLD MARKET BASKET)

We will conclude this chapter with a short scenario of the 2022 integrated reporting practices of World Market Basket (WMB), a hypothetical Chinese company based in Shanghai that has annual revenues of $225 billion. WMB is a global manufacturer and distributor of food products, both through its 8,000 retail stores—located in Asia, Europe, the Americas, and Canada—and online (from anywhere in the world). Listed on both the Shanghai and New York stock exchanges, WMB has a market cap of $165 billion due to its high margins and growth rate, making it one of the largest 50 companies in the world in terms of market cap. In its 2022 "Statement of Significant Audiences and Materiality" (found in the "Description of Business" section of the company's Form 20-F), the board notes that the company's financial objectives and executive compensation are based on five-year targets. It also notes that its most significant audiences are long-term investors (those which have held the company's stock for three years or more), the more than 100,000 farmers (both company employees and independents) located all over the world from which it sources its products, and, for the first time, its "Big Basket" customers. In its 2021 Statement, the board simply said, "customers," but it made this change when "Big Basket" customers, representing 5% of the company's 175 million customers (defined by making at least one purchase in the past year), crossed the threshold to account for 80% of the company's annual sales.

Qualification as a "Big Basket" customer is based on an algorithm that reflects the amount and range of purchases within certain time periods, adjusted for local buying habits (Chinese and European customers tend to shop more frequently than North and South American ones) and for self-declared income levels, with this declaration being a requirement for achieving "Big Basket" status. Incentives to do this are great because this status results in automatic 25% discounts on all list prices, along with periodic 50% discounts only made available to them. Incentives to be honest about self-declared income levels also exist because many of the 50% discount products are geared to particular income levels. Purchases by "Big Basket" customers are a key metric included on the company's integrated reporting website. The company's integrated report is a contextual one; users are able to drill down for more detail on individual pieces of intelligent, machine-readable information. Conversely, information on WMB accessed through other sources can be linked back to the integrated report. Detailed analytical tools are also made available to the many different internal users.

Issues that are especially important to the company's audiences are so indicated on WMB's "Sustainable Value Matrix (SVM)." For example, the SVM shows that the company perceives genetically modified food (GMO) as a societally significant issue but not something that is material to the company; it is not an issue that is important to its long-term investors, its farmers, and its "Big Basket" customers. One consequence of this is that NGOs opposed to GMO food are actively campaigning against the company to modify its stance. In response, the company actively monitors social media and includes metrics of NGO perception on its integrated reporting website, available in both Chinese and English. These metrics are updated on a weekly basis. The page on which they are reported also has links to relevant articles and is an open platform for anybody, including company employees, to share their views and debate this issue with others.

The frequency with which performance metrics are updated is determined by the cycle deemed relevant by management. For example, aggregate sales are reported on a daily basis, sales to "Big Basket" customers and farming injuries on a monthly basis, and profits on a quarterly basis. Most metrics regarding material natural, human, and social and relationship capital issues are updated annually. 您可信赖保险 (Assurance You Can Trust), the only China-headquartered member of the Big Five, provides a real-time integrated assurance opinion to individual data items (which can be accessed as such) through certificates that indicate which of five levels of assurance has been provided and when. Assurance for the entire website is done on a pass/fail basis every month. All assurance opinions are delivered quickly and inexpensively and are largely based on technology, with relatively little human intervention.

WMB has outsourced its integrated reporting website to a boutique IT service and consulting firm, London-based Integrated Reporting Solutions (IRS), that specializes in integrated reporting and helping companies build integrated thinking into their strategic planning process. IRS has contracts with cloud computing facility providers and has licensed big data and analytics applications that it uses to do descriptive, diagnostic, predictive, and prescriptive analyses under WMB's direction. Social media data are free and are gathered through IRS-proprietary search engines. Executives in functions spanning finance, procurement, supply chain management, marketing, and stores have access to these applications to do whatever analysis they want. 您可信赖保险 also provides an assurance opinion on IRS's capabilities for its clients. To the extent humans are involved in assuring WMB's reporting, most of this effort is devoted to the scope of audit and contractual terms with IRS.

Simple versions of these analytical tools are provided for free on WMB's integrated reporting website. More sophisticated ones from third-party app providers are available for a fee. Users can download any of the data the company is reporting into these tools, integrating them into their own analytical models if they so choose. For each metric, the company provides equations specifying how this metric is related to other metrics, along with supporting data. A tool is also provided for users to create their own equations to test hypotheses about connectivity. To the extent that competitors are providing similar information, WMB's provides links to their website so that the user can download this information as well for benchmarking purposes.

The SVM is also one of the main platforms for stakeholder engagement. When users connect to WMB's integrated reporting website, they are asked to identify which type of audience member they are. (Long-term investors, farmers, and "Big Basket" customers are automatically tracked.) IRS tracks the usage patterns of website visitors in order to provide data for updating the SVM on an annual basis. All of the issues above the "Societal Issue Significance Boundary" are linked to a page for stakeholder engagement, as is done for GMO foods. This is an important input for the company in developing next year's SVM, which has a page detailing the methodology that is uses for constructing it. Each issue page also has relevant reports and studies done by WMB and other parties, such as academics and consulting firms, who give permission to post them, along with relevant videos produced by the company and its stakeholders (with approval by the company).

While WMB is a hypothetical example, all of this could be done today.

In addition to better incorporating information technology into the integrated reporting movement, there are four other pressing issues that must be addressed as well. We discuss them in our next and final chapter.

 NOTES

1. *Merriam-Webster Online*, s.vv. "information technology," http://www .merriam-webster.com/dictionary/information%20technology, accessed May 2014.
2. Since we are not experts on information technology, we could not have written this chapter without an extensive amount of constructive criticism and support from Jyoti Banerjee of the International Integrated Reporting Council, Brad Monterio, and Liv Watson. We learned much from them in the process of writing this chapter. We alone, however, are responsible for any errors and omissions this chapter contains. Our hope is that this chapter will prove to be the start of an ongoing conversation about the role of information technology in supporting integrated reporting and integrated thinking.
3. Jyoti Banerjee is exploring the relationship between reporting processes and information technology through a series of workshops with leading companies practicing integrated reporting. He plans to publish the results of this study in the first half of 2015.
4. An enterprise resource planning (ERP) system serves all departments within an organization. It can include software for manufacturing, order entry, accounts

receivable and payable, general ledger, purchasing, warehousing, transportation, and human resources. For more information see, Shehab, E.M., M.W. Sharp, L. Supramaniam, and T.A. Spedding. "Enterprise resource planning: An integrative review." *Business Process Management Journal*, Vol. 10, No. 4, 2004, pp. 359–386, http://miha.ef.uni-lj.si/_dokumenti3plus2/192008/vseoERP-BPMJ-2004-1570100401_nov.pdf, accessed May 2014.

5. "A database is a means of storing information in such a way that information can be retrieved from it. In simplest terms, a relational database is one that presents information in tables with rows and columns. A table is referred to as a relation in the sense that it is a collection of objects of the same type (rows). Data in a table can be related according to common keys or concepts, and the ability to retrieve related data from a table is the basis for the term relational database. A Database Management System (DBMS) handles the way data is stored, maintained, and retrieved. In the case of a relational database, a Relational Database Management System (RDBMS) performs these tasks. DBMS as used in this book is a general term that includes RDBMS." Oracle. The Java Tutorials, A Relational Database Overview, http://docs.oracle.com/javase/tutorial/jdbc/overview/database.html, accessed June 2014.

6. Introduced in approximately 1996, eXtensible Business Reporting Language (XBRL), is a globally adopted and freely licensed open standard for providing structure and context to information to facilitate the digital exchange of financial and nonfinancial information. "XBRL is a member of the family of languages based on eXtensible Markup Language (XML), which is also a standard for the digital exchange of information between organizations over the Internet." Under XML, a standardized set of unique "tags" is applied to information so that it can be processed efficiently and automatically by computer software. "XBRL is a powerful and flexible version of XML that has been specifically defined to meet the requirements of business information reporting. It enables unique identifying tags to be applied to individual pieces of information, such as 'net profit'" or tons of carbon that provide context and structure to the information, identifying whether it is a monetary item, percentage, fraction, or other form of measure. XBRL allows labels in any language to be applied to the information. It also links each piece to any relevant contextual information, like accounting or reporting framework references. XBRL can show how items are interconnected. It can also represent how they are calculated and validate the accuracy of that calculation. Most importantly, XBRL is easily extensible so organizations can adapt the standard to meet a variety of special reporting requirements unique to that organization. The rich, powerful structure of XBRL allows very efficient handling of business data by computer software. It supports all the standard tasks involved in compiling, storing, and using business information, which can be converted into XBRL by suitable mapping processes or generated automatically in XBRL

by software applications. It can then be searched, selected, exchanged, and analyzed by a computer or published for human viewing. For more information, visit XBRL International's website at www.xbrl.org. The above information is excerpted from "XBRL Basics, How XBRL Works" at http://www.xbrl .org/how-xbrl-works-1, accessed June 2014. For more information about XML, please visit www.w3.org/XML/.

7. Watson, Liv and Brad Monterio, "Integrated Reporting Technologies in the NOW Economy," September 2014, https://www.workiva.com/resources.

8. SAS. Insights, Big Data, What is Big Data, http://www.sas.com/en_us/ insights/big-data/what-is-big-data.html, accessed May 2014; OgilvieOne worldwide. A Day in Big Data, http://adayinbigdata.com, accessed May 2014; and Lisa Arthur, "What is Big Data," *Forbes*, August 15, 2013, http:// www.forbes.com/sites/lisaarthur/2013/08/15/what-is-big-data/, accessed June 2014.

9. Gartner. "Gartner Survey Reveals That 64 Percent of Organizations Have Invested or Plan to Invest in Big Data in 2013," press release, September 23, 2013, http://www.gartner.com/newsroom/id/2593815, accessed June 2014.

10. Ibid.

11. "Data that resides in fixed fields within a record or file. Relational databases and spreadsheets are examples of structured data. Although data in XML files are not fixed in location like traditional database records, they are nevertheless structured, because the data are tagged and can be accurately identified." *PC Magazine Encyclopedia*, s.vv. "Structured Data," http://www.pcmag.com/ encyclopedia/term/52162/structured-data, accessed June 2014.

12. "Data that does not reside in fixed locations. The term generally refers to free-form text, which is ubiquitous. Examples are word processing documents, PDF files, email messages, blogs, Web pages and social sites." *PC Magazine Encyclopedia*, s.vv. "Unstructured Data," http://www.pcmag.com/encyclopedia/term/ 53486/unstructured-data, accessed June 2014.

13. Human-readable data is information in a digital or electronic format that humans can see on a computer screen, as in a PDF document or on a website (in HTML or similar format). This is the most common way in which companies provide data today for their financial, sustainability, and integrated reports because it is an effective and inexpensive way for the company to make its report easily available to its audience. It also has its limitations, particularly when it comes to being searchable. As discussed in Chapter 7, information is typically scattered throughout the integrated report and it is difficult to locate. Although this information is easily readable by humans, it is not in an ideal form to be automatically consumed by computer software. It often requires manual manipulation, copying, and pasting into other software or spreadsheets, and this can introduce errors into the data. Typically, this information has little or no structure or context around it.

Giving it sufficient structure to make it useful and meaningful is time consuming and expensive.

14. More useful is semiautomated data. This type of data can be automatically processed and converted by software tools that use built-in automation capabilities (e.g., optical character recognition or OCR) to perform a key function (e.g., OCR uses pattern recognition and artificial intelligence to convert text into usable data), but it still requires some type of human intervention given that machine-converted information is generally seen to have a lower level of trust and credibility. Nevertheless, semiautomated data is less time consuming and more cost effective to use than human-readable data, making it more useful overall.

15. "Data that describes other data. For example, data dictionaries and repositories provide information about the data elements in a database. Digital cameras store meta-data in the image files that include the date the photo was taken along with camera settings. Digital music files contain meta-data such as song title and artist name. Meta-data are stored in an HTML page (Web page) to help search engines define the page properly, and most especially, make it rank higher in the results list. Meta-data has existed for centuries. Card catalogs and handwritten indexes are examples long before the electronic age." *PC Magazine Encyclopedia,* s.v. "Metadata," http://www.pcmag.com/encyclopedia/term/46848/metadata, accessed June 2014.

16. Companies venturing into the world of analytics typically begin with less complex, descriptive analytics that help the company summarize and present results regarding what has happened in their business operations. It is a way of condensing large volumes of data, perhaps dispersed in many different physical and virtual locations, in order to see patterns which, in hindsight, can be reported internally and externally. Because data are presented in a way that leaves more time for reflection, as opposed to spending that time preparing it for consumption, descriptive analytics lays the foundation for a modest degree of integrated thinking. It involves little internal collaboration or external stake-holder engagement because it is simply and ultimately about "reporting," rather than initiating a dialogue within and outside of the company. Descriptive analytics are explained at, Advanced Software Applications Corp. "An Introduction to Descriptive and Predictive Analytics," https://faculty.washington.edu/socha/css572winter2012/ASA_Introduction_to_Analytics.pdf, accessed May 2014.

17. Reflection on the patterns identified by descriptive analytics generates hypotheses about why and how these patterns emerged, what caused them, and relationships between them. Diagnostic analytics describe ways to test these hypotheses, enabling the company to develop insights into why things happened the way they did. Users can do the same. In both cases, insights that are obtained about cause-and-effect relationships and interdependencies

improve integrated thinking. The number and quality of these hypotheses, and the insights they can generate, is a function of the degree of internal collaboration and stakeholder engagement involved in generating them. Throughout this book we have emphasized how linkages between different kinds of information, or "connectivity of information," are essential for a company to move from a combined report to a truly integrated report. While some degree of connectivity can be obtained without diagnostic analytics, it is more difficult to do so and the possibilities are limited. For more information about diagnostic analytics see, IBM. "IBM Watson and Medical Records Text Analytics," http://www-01.ibm.com/software/ebusiness/jstart/downloads/MRTAWatsonHIMSS.pdf, accessed May 2014.

18. The insights from diagnostic analytics form the basis for the more sophisticated predictive analytics. With predictive analytics, companies gain foresight about what could happen in the future. Forward-looking, predictive analytics utilizes a variety of statistical, modeling, data mining, and machine-learning techniques to study recent and historical data, enabling companies to make predictions about the future. Predictive analytics can forecast what could happen in the future because it looks at probabilities. It does not necessarily predict just one possible future but "multiple futures" that can be proposed based on the decision-maker's choices. Because greater insight into what stakeholders care about (e.g., what is material to them, how they might respond to a new product offering, and what they think about the company's reputation) yields more context and data points to use in the modeling, predictive analytics depend upon higher levels of internal collaboration and external stakeholder engagement to source those additional data points. For more information, see Waller, M.A. and Fawcett, S.E. (2013). "Data Science, Predictive Analytics, and Big Data: A Revolution that Will Transform Supply Chain Design and Management," *Journal of Business Logistics*, Vol. 34[2], Forthcoming, http://papers.ssrn.com/sol3/papers.cfm?abstract_id=2279482, accessed May 2014.

19. The future orientation of predictive analytics provides the basis for the most advanced form of analytics, prescriptive analytics, which uses the former's predicted possible outcomes to determine what should be done to achieve the desired outcome. Prescriptive analytics requires the highest levels of internal collaboration and stakeholder engagement to provide input into optimization models for defining what are considered to be the most desirable outcomes. This type of analysis is of the greatest value to a company and its audience insofar as it intelligently prescribes future actions to achieve the desired outcomes. In terms of the <IR> Framework, prescriptive analytics can be used to assess different strategy and resource allocation decisions that will enable the company to achieve its desired level of future performance given its outlook and the risks and opportunities it is facing, adjusting its business model

as necessary. Prescriptive analytics helps companies achieve the highest level of integrated thinking by assisting internal collaboration on determining the best possible outcomes and contributing to the creation of economic value over the short-, medium- and long-term. See the following for more information. IBM Software. "Descriptive, predictive, prescriptive: Transforming asset and facilities management with analytics," http://www-01.ibm.com/common/ssi/cgi-bin/ssialias?infotype=SA&subtype=WH&htmlfid=TIW14162USEN, accessed June 2014. "Predictive analytics is the next step up in data reduction. It utilizes a variety of statistical, modeling, data mining, and machine learning techniques to study recent and historical data, thereby allowing analysts to make predictions about the future." Bertolucci, Jeff, "Big Data Analytics: Descriptive Vs. Predictive Vs. Prescriptive," *Information Week*, December 31, 2013, http://www.informationweek.com/big-data/big-data-analytics/big-data-analytics-descriptive-vs-predictive-vs-prescriptive/d/d-id/1113279, accessed June 2014. Wu, Mike, "Big Data Reduction 3: From Descriptive to Prescriptive," Lithium Technologies (Science of Social blog) http://community.lithium.com/t5/Science-of-Social-blog/Big-Data-Reduction-3-From-Descriptive-to-Prescriptive/ba-p/81556, accessed June 2014.

20. Gartner. "Survey Analysis: Big Data Adoption," September 12, 2013, Figure 10, p. 14, https://www.gartner.com/doc/2589121/survey-analysis-big-data-adoption, accessed June 2014.

21. "When it comes to the strategy and practice of collaboration, nothing can compete with next-generation cloud-delivered tools and processes." "Collaborating in the Cloud," Forbes Insights, p. 2.

22. Log data is data generated by any activity, such as by a click on a website that has a time stamp and perhaps other data associated with it, such as type or location of the person that generated the data (i.e., meta-data).

23. Gartner, "Survey Analysis: Big Data Adoption," Figure 8, p. 11.

24. Effective January 2020, publicly traded European companies will be required to prepare their annual financial reports in a single electronic reporting format. The European Securities and Markets Authority (ESMA) has been charged with the development of draft regulatory standards for adoption by the European Commission. The text of the Directive follows. "With effect from 1 January 2020 all annual financial reports shall be prepared in a single electronic reporting format provided that a cost-benefit analysis has been undertaken by the European Supervisory Authority (European Securities and Markets Authority) (ESMA) established by Regulation (EU) No 1095/2010 of the European Parliament and of the Council. ESMA shall develop draft regulatory technical standards to specify the electronic reporting format, with due reference to current and future technological options. Before the adoption of the draft regulatory technical standards, ESMA shall carry out an adequate assessment of possible electronic reporting formats and conduct

appropriate field tests. ESMA shall submit those draft regulatory technical standards to the Commission at the latest by 31 December 2016." DIRECTIVE 2013/50/EU OF THE EUROPEAN PARLIAMENT AND OF THE COUNCIL of 22 October 2013 amending Directive 2004/109/EC of the European Parliament and of the Council on the harmonisation of transparency requirements in relation to information about issuers whose securities are admitted to trading on a regulated market, Directive 2003/71/EC of the European Parliament and of the Council on the prospectus to be published when securities are offered to the public or admitted to trading and Commission Directive 2007/14/EC laying down detailed rules for the implementation of certain provisions of Directive 2004/109/EC. http://ec.europa.eu/internal_market/accounting/legal_framework/transparency_directive/index_en.ht, accessed June 2014.

CHAPTER TEN

Four Recommendations

I N THIS BOOK, WE have taken stock of the integrated reporting movement's state of affairs. Given its current level of adoption, the accelerators in place, and its present visibility, it is unlikely that the movement will disintegrate any time soon. But persistence is a necessary, not sufficient, condition for progress. Members of the integrated reporting movement want tangible, substantive changes in corporate reporting practices to influence resource allocation decisions in companies and markets. By fostering a broader, longer-term view in these decisions, they hope to help create a more sustainable society.

As discussed in Chapter 4, exactly what the movement's strategies and priorities should be in order to achieve these goals is the subject of an ongoing debate among its participants. Many necessarily pursue individual goals that do not map directly onto those of the International Integrated Reporting Council (IIRC). Participants must balance their activities—and in particular, the extent to which they should expend resources—in collaboration with each other.[1] Adding to the social movement's collective but sometimes conflicting conversation, interested observers will express their opinions about who should be doing what. As both actors in and observers of the movement, we have our own views of what should be considered the critical issues facing integrated reporting today and how to address them. To be clear, these are our personal views; the people and organizations alongside which we work are free to agree or disagree.

In this final chapter, we identify four main strategic issues, each leading to a specific suggestion, that must be addressed: (1) striking the right balance between experimentation and codification, (2) striking the right balance between market and regulatory forces to speed adoption, (3) gaining greater advocacy from the accounting community, and (4) achieving greater role clarity among the key framework and standard-setting organizations in the movement. We will conclude by sketching a possible future scenario, not with the intention of divining the future, but to suggest that imagining such scenarios is a useful exercise in addressing these strategic issues.

 ## A VERY BRIEF HISTORY OF FINANCIAL REPORTING

If history serves as an example, supporters of integrated reporting should prepare for a long march. The current institutional infrastructure supporting financial reporting and auditing took decades to build. In the United States, for example, increasing regulations regarding financial reporting and auditing evolved over the past 125 years, beginning with the formation of the American Association of Public Accountants in 1887.[2] By 1926, in an indication of market forces' potency—and potential good news for integrated reporting— over 90% of companies listed on the New York Stock Exchange issued audited financial statements despite the absence of a law requiring them to do so. Due to a prevailing belief that certain types of information would be useful to competitors, only 62% disclosed sales and 54% cost of goods sold.[3]

Following the Stock Market Crash of 1929 and the ensuing Great Depression, voluntary disclosure was replaced by mandated disclosure. The 1933 Securities Act[4] and the 1934 Securities and Exchange Act[5] ('34 Act) put a strong regulatory stamp on corporate disclosure which continues to this day, with the most recent major regulatory intervention being the Sarbanes-Oxley Act of 2002.[6] The '34 Act mandated that all public companies file annual reports certified by independent public accountants and gave the Securities and Exchange Commission (SEC) the authority to prescribe the form in which the required information should be disclosed, the items to be shown in the balance sheet and the income statement, and the methods to be followed in the preparation of reports.[7] The fact that such a step was necessary in order to ensure the comprehensive and consistent reporting of financial information raises the question of whether integrated reporting must also ultimately receive a formal "stamp of approval" from the State in order to guarantee the format and content of an integrated report.

Neither sustainability nor integrated reporting is supported by anything resembling the well-established infrastructure of standards, frameworks, and reporting requirements that exist in the United States for financial reporting. Small nongovernmental organizations (NGOs), some of which are only a few years old, are responsible for nearly all of the development in this arena thus far. With the exception of South Africa, State support for their efforts is modest, particularly in the largest capital markets. Especially for ideas largely untested in the marketplace, regulators wisely move with caution toward new disclosure requirements. As a result, integrated reporting will remain a social movement for the foreseeable future.

BALANCING EXPERIMENTATION AND CODIFICATION

Because the balance between experimentation and codification must be well managed before market and regulatory forces can be properly addressed, this strategic issue is of primary importance. In Chapter 2, we described how integrated reporting emerged through company practice, after which it was studied and codified, most recently in the "International <IR> Framework" (<IR> Framework). We also described how attempts at codification continue to be informed by practice, such as in the IIRC's "Pilot Programme Business Network," which in May of 2014 had expanded to over 100 companies.[8] Early efforts at codification should be tested in practice so that these frameworks can be improved, but eventually standards must be set in order to move from codification to institutionalization, the fourth and final stage of meaning-making.

This sensible symbiotic relationship masks an underlying tension between standardization and customization. For the audience of corporate reports, "standards beneficiaries," frameworks (like the <IR> Framework or SEC guidance on the structure of Form 10-K), and standards (for both accounting and sustainability information) have clear benefits. Standardization makes it possible to compare one company's performance to another's—an attribute of interest to shareholders, stakeholders, and even the company itself, enabling it to benchmark itself against its competitors. Standards are useful for regulators because they make it easier for them to determine if regulations are being followed; they inform decision-making. As sociologist Lawrence Busch puts it in his book *standards: recipes for reality*, "While standards and choices clearly involve different forms of action, the one virtually unconscious and automated, the other conscious and goal-oriented, both are implicated in all situations."[9]

While standards necessarily have their detractors, most commonly among those to whom the standards apply (the "standards-users"), the process by which they are created is ultimately a political negotiation. This is a common trope in the history of corporate reporting, starting with the first attempt in the United States to establish a set of accounting standards, which all companies and auditors would have to use.[10] On one side of the trade-off between comparability and a more accurate, entity-specific measure, companies tend to argue that a set of standards is a "one-size-fits-all" model that fails to consider their unique circumstances. Determining entity-specific accuracy is complicated, however, when those measurements cannot be compared across companies. In the absence of standards, companies find it easier to choose a methodology that makes their performance look as strong as possible—a problem when the interests of the standards-users must ultimately be balanced with those of the standards-beneficiaries. Standards-users will attempt to influence the standards in ways that benefit them—typically by seeking less transparency and more degrees of freedom for customization. Standards-beneficiaries favor greater transparency and comparability. That said, standards vary in terms of prescriptiveness. Corporate reporting observers commonly distinguish between "rules-based" (as many claim U.S. Generally Accepted Account Principles (GAAP) to be) and "principles-based" (as many claim International Financial Reporting Standards (IFRS) to be) standards. The more rules-based the standard, the fewer degrees of freedom a company (and its auditor) have in using their judgment on how best to report on an issue.

When standard setting occurs in a non-State context, as with the NGOs discussed in this book, the perceived validity and utility of the standard will be a function of how effectively the standard-setter manages the politics of the standard-setting process. Since companies adopt these standards on a voluntary basis, it is natural for these NGOs to use the number of companies that have adopted their standard or framework as a metric of their effectiveness. While sensible, these organizations run the risk of seeing the standard (framework) become an end in itself rather than a means to an end—the crux of the dilemma.

Being too doctrinaire too early, as by insisting that a company can only call its report an integrated report if it is substantially based on the <IR> Framework, for example, can raise the bar too high and discourage adoption. Is it better for companies to call a combined report an integrated report in order to start them on the journey, to gain their intellectual and emotional commitment to the movement? Doing so risks clouding the term's meaning, whose codification and institutionalization is important to the movement's success. Conversely, attempting to draw a hard line raises questions of whether the NGO has the necessary resources to monitor what companies are doing, let alone the enforcement mechanisms to ensure compliance. NGOs have neither the State's resources to do the former nor its authority to do the latter. This does not mean they are completely impotent, however. Mechanisms can be created for companies to submit their report to be reviewed and, if approved, put on an official list of approved adopters. Trademark protection can also be used to limit careless claims about adoption.

Recommendation Number One: The International Integrated Reporting Council should establish a process for companies to get voluntary certification of whether their integrated report and website qualify as "integrated reporting" under the brand of the IIRC.

BALANCING MARKET AND REGULATORY FORCES

Adding and changing reporting regulations is a constant source of struggle between companies and those demanding information from them. Both parties put pressures on the State based on their own concerns. Although listed companies accept reporting requirements as a prerequisite for access to the capital markets, they still decry additional reporting burdens. Virtually any additional reporting requirement being considered by a country's legislature or a regulator[11] becomes the subject of a fierce debate. Companies argue that it will be costly to implement, may be irrelevant, will put them at a competitive disadvantage, or increase litigation risk—raising the question of just where the "sweet spot" falls between the extremes of irrelevance and risk. Companies insist that a proper cost/benefit analysis be done before they are required to report and point out, with some justification, that reporting requirements are never eliminated, even for issues that are no longer salient. Those in favor of a new reporting requirement will have equally strong arguments about the benefits to a particular group of having this information. Because the struggle between these forces represents the ongoing negotiation between the Corporation and the State over what responsibilities the former has for the license to operate given to it by the latter, it is inevitable.

Any group whose mission is directly related to reporting must decide how to frame its work in the context of the existing mandatory reporting environment. At one extreme, the group can adopt a purely *regulatory strategy*. In this case, it lobbies the appropriate government bodies to get its reporting framework or standards adopted as an additional reporting requirement or more likely, to get them included in an existing reporting requirement. If successful, this strategy for the movement means the State will enforce company compliance with integrated reporting as it does with financial reporting. If the regulation is carefully crafted and well-enforced, it can also contribute to the reliability and comparability of information in an integrated report.

The success of such a strategy requires overcoming a number of barriers. Because of the resistance it will likely see from the corporate community, the State is typically slow to act in this domain, making regulation a long-term goal. Consequently, such a strategy can require substantial resources that few NGOs have. Finally, while regulation can ensure broad compliance, it can also result in just that—a tick-the-box compliance approach that meets the letter but not the spirit of the law.

At the other extreme is a purely *market-based strategy* in which the group appeals to the self-interest of companies to voluntarily adopt its framework or standards through an "it's just good business" pitch. Common arguments include the idea that doing so will help investors better understand the company's value proposition (presumably resulting in a higher stock price), that the company will enhance its reputation and credibility with stake-holders (presumably reducing the risk of being a target of some NGO's campaign), that the discipline in gathering the data for external reporting purposes and using it for internal reporting purposes will lead to a better-managed company (integrated thinking), and that the company will also be better managed as a result of the dialogue and engagement with shareholders and other stakeholders that comes with the reporting of this information (the transformation function of corporate reporting). Compared to a regulatory-driven approach, this strategy is much less threatening. Consequently, it is less likely that the corporate community will mobilize itself to slow down or stop the initiative.

When companies voluntarily decide to implement a practice, they will also attempt to adhere to the spirit of its intent rather than to treat it as a mere compliance exercise. Not surprisingly, most NGOs focused on reporting place great emphasis on the benefits of voluntary adoption, while also pointing out the risks of failing to report and falling behind peers already adopting the practice. The disadvantage of this strategy is that adoption can be slow when relying entirely upon the voluntary actions of companies. Furthermore, system-level benefits, such as the ability to compare the performance of any given set of companies and influencing resource allocation decisions at a societal level, are lost. Nevertheless, Global Reporting Initiative's (GRI's) success with sustainability reporting is evidence that a market-based strategy can be effective.

In practice, a combination of both strategies should be used, the balance shifting over time. A largely market-based strategy is most effective in the early days of a movement while it is still heavily focused on the codification stage of meaning. During this stage, the movement is creating awareness and some degree of institutional legitimacy, finding early adopter companies and an audience who cares about what these companies are reporting, and gaining testimonials from them and their stakeholders about the benefits. At this time, the movement can engage with regulators to educate them and ascertain their willingness to provide some degree of support, laying the groundwork for the institutionalization phase of meaning. The greater the degree of market uptake, the more likely regulators will provide this support. In doing so, they would be moving with the wind, rather than against it. The movement can also be opportunistic and seek to embed its work in pending legislation or regulation. The pace at which the movement increases its emphasis on a regulatory strategy must match that with which experimentation is shifting to codification. Even in the unlikely chance that a mandate is achieved early on, a strong regulatory focus while experimentation is still active can backfire if the regulation ends up being suboptimal or runs counter to the desired goal.

The balance and timing of the mix of these two pure-type strategies will also vary by country. For example, a more heavily regulatory-oriented strategy is likely to be more successful in the European Union or China than in the United States, where, at least in the short term, a more market-based strategy would be effective. Within the larger countries, and on a global basis, sector- or industry-specific strategies may also be appropriate, although it would be more relevant for mobilizing market rather than regulatory forces.

Recommendation Number Two: Members of the integrated reporting movement should engage in a dialogue to establish a global strategy for the balance and timing of market- and regulatory-based strategies to speed the adoption of integrated reporting, adapting this strategy to take account of country and sector context as necessary.

GREATER ADVOCACY FROM THE ACCOUNTING COMMUNITY

With deep expertise in financial accounting and reporting and, increasingly, sustainability reporting, accounting firms and associations have a critical role to play in the integrated reporting movement. Possessed of the capabilities and global scale to conduct audits of the world's major corporations (whose combined market cap is close to 100% of equity held by investors), the Big Four accounting firms—Deloitte, Ernst & Young (E&Y), KPMG, and PricewaterhouseCoopers (PwC)—are especially important. The integrity of the world's capital markets depends upon audits that ensure the quality of the information investors are using to make decisions. To the extent that investors—and ultimately regulators—believe that this information can be more effectively delivered through integrated reporting than separate financial and sustainability reporting, companies will depend on their auditor to help them issue reports with the appropriate level of assurance. But these firms must be less timid. They must become stronger advocates for all aspects of integrated reporting, including the necessity for integrated assurance.

While the Big Four are involved in the movement, we believe they have not been sufficiently active in their integrated reporting advocacy out of concern that their clients would perceive this to be naked self-interest. The cynic would say that the accounting firms support integrated reporting because it represents a potentially large new source of revenues from audit and advisory services. Leaving aside the obvious irony that companies unabashedly pursue their own economic self-interest, we recognize that, as a profession, accountants must be held to a higher standard of placing their clients' interests before their own. But professions are also expected to provide the best advice to their clients. This includes points of view on issues they think their client should know about—even if the client is not interested in hearing the idea or does not even like it.

When it comes to the audit function, the client situation is complex. The "real" clients for an audit are investors, yet the practical reality remains that the company they are auditing selects and pays the auditor, making the company a client as well. Consequently, if the accounting firms, in their professional judgment, firmly believe that integrated reporting is beneficial to both investors and the integrity of the capital markets—and their actions so far suggest that they do—they should not be bashful in proactively bringing this point of view to their company clients and investors. Since adopting integrated reporting is still a voluntary company decision that can be executed with varying degrees of depth, the company can decide whether to retain its accounting firm (and other advisors) to help them start the journey or not. No company is being forced to pay for a service it does not want. It is the responsibility of the company's auditor to make sure its client is sufficiently informed about integrated reporting, including its still-uncertain costs and benefits, in order for the company to make an informed decision about this new management practice.

Recommendation Number Three: The Big Four firms should work with other accounting firms and professional accounting associations to establish a proactive campaign to create awareness and understanding of integrated reporting among their clients and to develop assurance standards for integrated reporting.

 ## ACHIEVING CLARITY REGARDING THE ROLES OF KEY ORGANIZATIONS

Throughout this book, we have discussed the central role of the IIRC and the supporting roles played by GRI, the Sustainability Accounting Standards Board (SASB), and CDP. Together, these four organizations are creating the institutional infrastructure necessary for integrated reporting. They are also, however, creating confusion in the marketplace as companies, investors, and stakeholders struggle to understand their missions and how they relate to each other. Are they complementary or competitive entities? Understandably, companies, investors, and stakeholders are also often confused about what exactly they are supposed *to do* in order to effectively respond to the entreaties each organization is making of them.

Our view can be simply expressed. The IIRC has established a high-level, principles-based framework for integrated reporting. From its inception, it was clear that it had no intention of becoming a standard setter for how specific pieces of information should be measured and reported. As that is the work of the other three organizations, their missions are clearly complementary to the IIRC. Each can provide input to a company about the nonfinancial information it decides to include in its integrated report.

Like the IIRC, SASB is focused on investors. Its standards are a baseline for consideration that, since they are currently being developed in a U.S. context only, may need to be adapted for global application. Some will come from metrics established by CDP, which we see as a "subject matter expert" in greenhouse gas (GHG) emissions and increasingly, on water and forests. SASB has signed an MOU with CDP, and SASB's "open source" approach will leverage the work done by CDP. When climate issues are material, the recommended key performance indicators from SASB will likely come from the work of CDP. Similarly, GRI can leverage the work of CDP in its guidelines on climate issues.

Finally, GRI and SASB have a complementary relationship. As the former's G4 Guidelines cover sustainability reporting from a global perspective, they include information material to many stakeholders that, although not material to all investors today, could be tomorrow as the management of social and environmental issues becomes increasingly necessary for a company to create value over the long term from both a risk and opportunity perspective. We do not believe that sustainability reporting will or should go away as a result of integrated reporting. Rather, its relevance for companies to maintain their license to operate will only increase. SASB's sector-specific standards for issues material to investors, which could include GRI indicators just as they could CDP metrics, will be supplemented by sustainability reporting to meet the needs of stakeholders.

Recommendation Number Four: CDP, GRI, IIRC, and SASB should work together to clarify for companies, investors, and other stakeholders how their missions are related to each other; they should also form collaborations which are mutually beneficial in support of the movement.

 ## A POSSIBLE SCENARIO

We will conclude this book by sketching one possible way the adoption of integrated reporting could unfold in the coming years. This is most definitely *not* intended to be a prediction. It is a thought experiment to imagine the drivers of adoption of integrated reporting in different countries.

Globally, the explicit call in 2014 for integrated reporting in the Sustainable Development Goals (SDGs)[12] has become an important accelerator, since it has put the movement on the agenda of all countries that signed on to the SDGs, which were adopted in 2015. Rather than being an isolated movement, integrated reporting is now one element of a broader call by Aviva for "integrated capital markets," defined as "capital markets that finance development that meets the need of the present, without compromising the ability of future generations to meet their own needs."[13] Other elements of integrated capital markets include integrated: incentives, financial regulation, stock exchanges, financial literacy, asset ownership, investment consulting, asset management, corporate brokerage, corporate governance, proxy voting, and investment legal duties.

Western Europe continues to lead the way with a new Directive in 2019 that explicitly calls for integrated reporting. Although it does not specify any particular framework or set of reporting standards, companies are increasingly using the <IR> Framework as guidance for their annual report, even if the degree and manner that they do so varies by country. Companies also begin to use SASB's standards, which have been adapted by most countries for their local circumstances, as the basis for these reports. The G4 Guidelines, which have now evolved to G5 Guidelines, serve as the basis for sustainability reporting. They are accompanied by a clearer explanation of when they are and are not relevant to integrated reporting. Active efforts are underway to harmonize the G5 Guidelines, SASB's standards, and Version 2.0 of the <IR> Framework, published in 2018. As companies, investors, and stakeholders gain clarity about the relationship between integrated reporting and sustainability reporting, the growth of each acts as an accelerator for the other.

Brazil remains a leading country in integrated reporting and Japan becomes one. In Brazil, BM&FBOVESPA takes a further step in its "Report or Explain" Cycle and calls the initiative "Report or Explain for Integrated Reports and Supplementary Sustainability Information."[14] By 2020, approximately 80% of listed companies are doing so. In Japan, the Tokyo Stock Exchange has made integrated reporting a listing requirement. The seeds for this were laid in 2014 when the Financial Services Agency released its stewardship code which aims, on a comply or explain basis, to promote medium- to long-term sustainable corporate returns based on seven principles that guide investors on their stewardship responsibilities.[15]

China surprises the world in 2018 when, following the release of the <IR> Framework 2.0, the China Securities Regulatory Commission (CSRC) mandates integrated reporting for all listed companies. Since the Shenzhen Stock Exchange and the Shanghai Stock Exchange have been requiring sustainability reporting since 2006 and 2008, respectively, this does not come as a surprise to Chinese companies.[16] Furthermore, voluntary adoption by Chinese companies has been rapidly growing since 2016 as they seek access to foreign capital markets and business partners, so this regulatory mandate by the CSRC is simply building on strong market momentum.

The U.S. remains a distinct laggard in terms of the number of companies producing self-declared integrated reports. Reporting requirements in the U.S. continue to discourage companies from paying more than cursory attention to the <IR> Framework, although sustainability reporting based on the G4 and G5 Guidelines continues to accelerate. The biggest movement in the U.S. is the adoption of SASB's standards in an increasing number of 10-Ks. The global reaction is mixed. On the positive side, some supporters of the movement recognize what a significant step it is for companies to include nonfinancial information in the carefully scripted and heavily lawyered 10-K. On the negative side, other supporters point out that this is just one more example of "American exceptionalism"—another version of the U.S. GAAP/IFRS movie. The debate shows no sign of being resolved any time soon. Many applaud this U.S. version of integrated reporting. Others belittle it as a rules-based approach that fails to implement the real principles of integrated reporting as laid out in the <IR> Framework, which itself continues to evolve as the IIRC learns from the experiences of companies, investors, and other stakeholders.

 ## FINAL REFLECTION

If success is defined as near-universal adoption by all listed companies, will the integrated reporting movement be successful? We are cautiously optimistic. The challenges may be great, but the necessity is even greater. While integrated reporting is not a panacea that will create a sustainable society, it is an important management practice that can contribute to this goal. We are personally dedicated to this cause and we hope that this book serves as one small contribution to it.

 ## NOTES

1. Because social movements are an agglomeration of a variety of actors with different objectives, they necessitate trade-offs, particularly when it comes to resource allocation and mobilization. That is, a certain amount of disagreement is inevitable. McCarthy, John D., and Mayer N. Zald. "Resource mobilization and social movements: A partial theory." *American Journal of Sociology* (1977): 1212–1241.
2. Cary, John L. *The Rise Of The Accounting Profession*. Vol. 1: From technician to professional, 1896–1936. New York American Institute of Certified Public Accountants, 1970. p. 6. In 1916, the Institute of Public Accountants succeeded it. The following year, it became the American Institute of Accountants (AIA), which it remained until 1957 when it changed to its current name of the American Institute of Certified Public Accountants (AICPA). Acting as a federation of state societies, the American Society of Certified Public Accountants was formed in 1921. Exactly who could be considered an accountant was not always clear, and from 1916 to 1936, the accounting community strove to attain a uniform standard for the CPA certificate against an opposition that considered accounting "more art than science." (quote from page 272)

3. Voluntary disclosure flattened by 1934: 100% of companies published balance sheet information, including current assets and liabilities, 93% disclosed depreciation, and 99.6% disclosed net income. Bentson, George J. "The Value of the SEC's Accounting Disclosure Requirements," *The Accounting Review*, Vol. 44, No. 3 (Jul., 1969), pp. 515–532.

4. The 1933 Securities Act "required that investors receive financial and other significant information concerning securities being offered for public sale; and (2) prohibited deceit, misrepresentations, and other fraud in the sale of securities" U.S. Securities and Exchange Commission. Securities Act of 1933, http://www.sec.gov/about/laws.shtml#secact1933, accessed February 2014.

5. Securities and Exchange Commission. Securities Exchange Act of 1934, http://www.sec.gov/about/laws.shtml#secexact1934, accessed February 2014.

6. The Sarbanes-Oxley Act includes the famous Section 404 requiring the CFO and CEO to personally sign off on the quality of a company's internal control systems for financial reporting. Established in 2002, the Sarbanes-Oxley Act (Sarbanes-Oxley) created the Public Company Accounting Oversight Board (PCAOB), which was given authority to set and enforce auditing standards. Prior to that, auditing standards were set by the profession as represented by the American Institute of Certified Public Accountants (AICPA), and the accounting firms, especially the Big Four, reviewed each other's work as a form of self-regulation. As a result of Sarbanes-Oxley, the Financial Accounting Standards Board (FASB) was to be funded by the SEC at a substantially increased budget, and greater restrictions were placed on the consulting and tax services a company's auditor could provide. Firms also had to rotate the lead partner on the audit every 10 years.

7. The SEC delegated the primary responsibility of setting standards, but not the authority to do so, to the private sector. Today, the SEC Office of the Chief Accountant (https://www.sec.gov/about/offices/oca.htm, accessed February 2014) establishes and enforces accounting and auditing policy, and the Division of Corporation Finance (https://www.sec.gov/divisions/corpfin/cfabout.shtml, accessed February 2014) oversees financial reporting policies and practices.

8. There are 107 companies in the IIRC Pilot Programme Business Network as of April 29, 2014. International Integrated Reporting Council. IIRC Pilot Programme, IIRC Pilot Programme Business Network, http://www.theiirc.org/companies-and-investors/pilot-programme-business-network/, accessed April 2014.

9. Busch, Lawrence. *standards: recipes for reality*. Cambridge, MA: The MIT Press, c. 2011, p. 6.

10. Ramesh Ramananthan is the coordinator of a Bangalore citizens' movement for participatory democracy. He views an understanding of the evolution of corporate disclosure as critical to seeing the similarity between right to

information issues in the private sector and the current debates on the same topic in the public sector. India Together. "Right-to-information or disclosure?" http://indiatogether.org/disclose-government, accessed May 2014. An excerpt from a 2009 article on the history of corporate disclosure by Ramanathan follows. "In the United States, progress on corporate disclosure followed the standards set in England, until the early 1900s. As late as the 1920s many corporations still kept sales figures secret, some did not depreciate assets, failed to treat non-operating income consistently, did not separate retained earnings from paid-in capital and did not disclose asset write-ups. It was after the Great Depression of 1929 that substantial changes were brought in. The English Companies Act of 1929 served as the foundation for Felix Frankfurter and his team in drafting the Securities Act of 1933. Importantly, the 1929 Act was the source of two major components of the current American securities regulation regime, the concept of full disclosure and the possibility of civil liabilities of the registrant, its officers, directors, and experts. Beyond the functional value of the 1929 Act is the reflection of the vision of the nation's leadership at the time. President Roosevelt's policy, which championed full disclosure as the preferable remedy to the malaise of American financial markets at the time can best be understood by Louis Brandeis's famous maxim: 'Publicity is justly commended as a remedy for social and industrial diseases. Sunlight is said to be the best of disinfectants.' Even as late as 1932, the New York Stock Exchange expressed concern about the wide variety of accounting and reporting methods used by companies whose securities it listed. A committee of the American Institute of Accountants under the chairmanship of George May was appointed to formulate improved accounting standards which could then be enforced through listing requirements. The committee's final report contained five recommendations: (1) To promote consistency, corporations listing their stock on the exchanges were asked to adhere to certain broad accounting principles, within this framework, each firm could adopt the accounting methods it preferred. (2) Each listed company would prepare a summary of accounting methods used in its statements. This summary would be formally approved by the firm's board of directors, would be filed with the exchange, and would be available on request to any stockholder. (3) The procedures listed in this summary would be consistently followed from year to year and would not be changed without prior notice to the Stock Exchange and to the company's investors. (4) Financial statements were to be the representations of management. The auditor's task was to inform stockholders whether the methods adopted by each company were actually being used, whether they were compatible with 'generally accepted' principles of accounting, and whether they were being applied consistently. (5) The committee suggested that a qualified group of accountants, lawyers, and corporate officials draw up an authoritative list of accounting principles to help corporations in preparing their own lists of procedures. The committee had two specific tasks: to educate the public as to why a variety of accounting methods was necessary, and to suggest ways to curtail this variety and gradually make the better methods universal. In 1938 the Haskins and Sells Foundation commissioned three educators, T H Sanders (Harvard), H R Hatfield (Berkeley), and Underhill Moore (Yale Law School), to formulate a code of accounting principles which would be useful in the clarification and improvement of corporate accounting and of financial reports issued to the public. In preparing 'A Statement of Accounting Principles' they interviewed both makers and users of accounting data, reviewed the periodical literature, and studied laws, court decisions, and current corporate reports. A seminal document in the evolution of the universalisation of accounting principles was Paton and Littleton's *An Introduction to Corporate Accounting Standards* (1940), the most coherent statement of principles to emerge from this period. This document set the tone for much of the subsequent evolution of corporate financial disclosure practices in the ensuing decades. The last fifty years have seen greater flesh being added to this skeleton of financial reporting that evolved in the mid 1930s and 40s, somewhat contemporaneously in the United States as well as in Great Britain. This process of continuously raising the bar on disclosure standards is never-ending, as evidenced by the recent example being the Sarbanes-Oxley Act following the collapse of Enron. The creation of standardised financial statements is not a guaranteed safety ticket to proper institutional conduct, rather that it provides a springboard from which stakeholders can hopefully procure sufficient early warning signals about the true state of an institution. The fundamental principles behind the creation of these standards have been the guiding lights of all material and legislation: creating a level-playing field for all stakeholders by providing regular, detailed, and standardised information about the state of an institution." Ramanathan, Ramesh. "Corporate disclosure and financial statements: a brief history." *livemint & The Wall Street Journal*, http://www.livemint .com/Politics/L8c4xGGYD7GkpaLjEpidHM/Corporate-disclosure-and-finan- cial-statements-a-brief-histo.html, accessed April 2014.

11. For example, additional reporting requirements are established by the Ministry of Finance in China and by the Securities and Exchange Commission in the U.S. HSBC Global Connections. Home, Tools & data, Country Guides, https:// globalconnections.hsbc.com/united-kingdom/en/tools-data/country-guides, accessed April 2014.

12. "One of the key outcomes of the Rio+20 Conference was the agreement by Member States to launch a process to develop a set of Sustainable Develop- ment Goals (SDGs), which will build upon the Millennium Development Goals and converge with the post 2015 development agenda. It was decided establish an "*inclusive and transparent intergovernmental process open to all*

stakeholders, with a view to developing global sustainable development goals to be agreed by the General Assembly." United Nations. Sustainable Development Knowledge Platform, Topics, Sustainable Development Goals, http://sustainabledevelopment.un.org/?menu=1300, accessed April 2014. The Working Document for the May 2014 Session of Open Working Group includes a reference to the adoption of integrated reporting, "by 2030 increase by x percentage points the share of companies reporting on corporate social and environmental responsibility, including integrated reporting." United Nations. Sustainable Development Knowledge Platform, Topics, Sustainable Development Goals, Working Document, Focus area 11, Sustainable Consumption and Production, Promote sustainable consumption and production patterns, (f), http://sustainabledevelopment.un.org/focussdgs.html, accessed April 2014. "The 30-member Open Working Group of the General Assembly is mandated by the Rio+20 Outcome document to prepare a proposal on SDGs for consideration by the Assembly at its 68th session (Sept. 2013 – Sept. 2014)." Sustainable Development Knowledge Platform. Sustainable Development Goals, Topics, Open Working Group, Post-2015 process, http://sustainabledevelopment.un.org/index.php?menu=1561, accessed May 2014.

13. Aviva. "A Roadmap for Integrated Capital Markets: Aviva's proposals for how the UN Sustainable Development Goals and the UN Framework Convention on Climate Change can harness the capital markets." Unpublished paper, April 2014, p. 5.

14. On April 11, 2014, the Brazilian Stock Exchange BM&FBOVESPA announced that "BM&FBOVESPA begins the 2014 'Report or Explain' Cycle with a new development: in an evolutionary process aligned to the international trend of integrating financial and non-financial information in annual corporate reports, the initiative is now named 'Report or Explain for Sustainability or Integrated Reports' (the previous description was Report or Explain for Sustainability Reports or Similar). In this way, BM&FBOVESPA expresses support for the International Integrated Reporting Council (IIRC), whose mission is to create a globally-accepted model for integrated reporting. This support dates back to the start of the movement, when BM&FBOVESPA hosted a visit of the IRRC board to Brazil, in November 2011." The "Report or Explain for Sustainability or Integrated Reports" information can be accessed on the BM&FBOVESPA website at the following link: (http://www.bmfbovespa.com.br/en-us/markets/equities/companies/sustainability-report.aspx?Idioma=en-us). Sonia Aparecida Consiglio Favaretto, Sustainability Director, BM&FBOVESPA, email on April 16, 2014.

15. The Japan Stewardship Code is applicable to investors on a comply or explain basis. The Seven Principles of the Code are: (1) Institutional investors should have a clear and publicly disclosed policy on how they fulfill their stewardship

responsibilities, (2) Institutional investors should have a clear and publicly disclosed policy on how they manage conflicts of interest in fulfilling their stewardship responsibilities, (3) Institutional investors should monitor investee companies so that they can appropriately fulfill their stewardship responsibilities and support the sustainable growth of the companies, (4) Institutional investors should seek to arrive at an understanding in common with investee companies and work to solve problems through constructive engagement with investee companies, (5) Institutional investors should have a clear policy on voting and disclosure of voting activity. The policy on voting should not be comprised only of a mechanical checklist; it should be designed to contribute to the sustainable growth of investee companies, (6) Institutional investors should in principle report periodically on how they fulfill their stewardship responsibilities, including their voting responsibilities, to their clients and beneficiaries, and (7) To contribute positively to the sustainable growth of investee companies, institutional investors should have in-depth knowledge on the investee companies and their business environment and capabilities to appropriately engage with the companies and make proper judgments in fulfilling their stewardship activities. Financial Services Agency. News, Publication of the draft of the "Principles for Responsible Institutional Investors," http://www.fsa.go.jp/en/news/pub.html, accessed April 2014.

16. The Shenzhen Stock Exchange issued the "CSR Guidelines for Listed Companies" in September 2006. The exchange's "sustainable profitability" requirements follow. "Requirement on sustainable profitability. The issuer may not fall under any of the following circumstances that would have a significant adverse impact on its sustainable profitability: a. Its business model or its mix of products or services has undergone or will undergo a material change which has or would have a significant adverse impact on its sustainable profitability; b. Its position in the industry or the business environment for its industry has undergone or will undergo a material change which has or would have a significant adverse impact on its sustainable profitability; c. Its revenues or net profits in the most recent financial year are heavily reliant on a related party or any client susceptible to great uncertainty; d. Its net profits in the most recent year have been primarily derived from investment returns off its consolidated financial statements; e. There is a risk of material adverse change in respect of the availability or use of any important assets or technologies being used by the issuer, such as trademarks, patents, proprietary technology and franchise rights. Other circumstances that would have a significant adverse impact on its sustainable profitability." Shenzhen Stock Exchange. Listing Requirements, http://www.szse.cn/main/en/ListingatSZSE/ListingRequirements/, accessed April 2014. The Shanghai Stock Exchange issued the "Notice on Strengthening Listed Companies' Assumption of Social Responsibilities" and the "Guidelines on Listed Companies' Environmental Information Disclosure" in May

2008. "According to the two documents, Shanghai Exchange-listed companies should fulfill social responsibilities, address interests of stakeholders, and commit themselves to promoting sustainable economic and social development. These two initiatives are based on the philosophy that the SSE's listed companies are pillars of the national economy and should be encouraged to assume a leadership role in promoting sustainable development. For listed companies that promote CSR, the SSE sometimes offers incentives such as priority election into the Shanghai Corporate Governance Sector, which may benefit a company's public image, or simplified requirements for examination and verification of temporary announcements. The Shanghai notice encourages all listed companies to enhance their own CSR awareness and develop a strategic CSR plan for their operations. Listed companies may disclose the goals and achievements of their CSR activities and annual social responsibility reports through announcements posted temporarily on the SSE website. To assist with this, the SSE has also developed the concept of social contribution value per share (SCVPS) - a new method of measuring companies' value creation. SCVPS is calculated by adding the tax revenues paid to the state, salaries paid to employees, loan interest paid to creditors (including banks), and donations to - and other value for stakeholders, minus any social costs that arise from environmental pollution and other negative factors. SCVPS is intended to allow the public to understand the value companies create for their shareholders, employees, customers, creditors, communities, and society as a whole. Companies may choose to disclose their SCVPS calculation in their annual CSR reports." World Federation of Exchanges. Exchanges and Sustainable Investment, Shanghai Stock Exchange, http://www.world-exchanges.org/sustainability/m-6-7-1.php, accessed April 2014.

About the Authors

Robert G. Eccles is a Professor of Management Practice at the Harvard Business School. He joined the faculty in 1979 and received tenure in 1989. He left in 1993 to work in the private sector and rejoined the faculty in 2007. In addition to this current book, he has written three books on corporate reporting, including *One Report: Integrated Reporting for a Sustainable Strategy* (with Michael P. Krzus), which is the first book on this subject. *One Report* was the winner of the 2010 PROSE award in the category of Business, Finance, & Management. In addition, he has written over 25 articles and 20 teaching cases on integrated reporting and sustainability.

Eccles is now working on two new books. The first is *Mobilizing the Global 1000* and is being done in collaboration with Professor George Serafeim of the Harvard Business School. The second is *Materiality Matters* and is being done in collaboration with Tim Youmans, a researcher at the Harvard Business School.

Eccles is a member of the International Integrated Reporting Council (http://www.integratedreporting.org/) and is the founding Chairman of the Sustainability Accounting Standards Board (SASB) (www.sasb.org).

Eccles received an S.B. in Mathematics and an S.B. in Humanities and Social Science from the Massachusetts Institute of Technology in 1973. He received an A.M. in Sociology in 1975 and a Ph.D. in Sociology in 1979, both from Harvard University.

Michael P. Krzus is an independent integrated reporting consultant and researcher. He has provided advisory services to participants in the International Integrated Reporting Council Pilot Programme Business Network, companies exploring the adoption of integrated reporting and consulting organizations seeking to enhance integrated reporting capabilities for clients. Mike is a member of the SASB's Advisory Council, a Fellow of the Governance & Accountability Institute, and a member of KKS Advisors' LLC Expert Network.

Mike is coauthor, with Robert G. Eccles, of *The Integrated Reporting Movement: Meaning, Momentum, Motives and Materiality* and *One Report: Integrated Reporting for a Sustainable Strategy*, the first book on integrated reporting.

Mike has 38 years of industry and public accounting experience in accounting principles, assurance and auditing standards, corporate financial reporting, internal audit, and SEC rules and regulations. Prior to founding Mike Krzus Consulting, he worked for Arthur Andersen; BDO Seidman; Checkers, Simon & Rosner; Grant Thornton; and Illinois Central Railroad.

Mike earned a Bachelor of Science in Accounting from Calumet College of St. Joseph and is a Certified Public Accountant. He served three years in the Army including a tour of duty in Vietnam.

Sydney Ribot is a Research Associate at the Harvard Business School. She joined the staff in 2011, providing support to Professors Amy C. Edmondson and Robert G. Eccles in the Technology and Operations Management and General Management units, respectively. In addition to this book, she has written teaching cases on entrepreneurship, integrated reporting, and corporate governance issues.

Ribot received a B.A. in English and a minor in Asian & Middle Eastern studies from Dartmouth College in 2011. In 2013, she received a Reynolds Scholarship for Foreign Study in Istanbul, Turkey, where she is currently based as creator of a narrative web TV series about life in the developing megacity. She is committed to creating a sustainable future through dialogue and innovation—be it humor that travels or integrated reporting.

Index

The letter "f" following a page number denotes a figure, "n" denotes a note, and "t" denotes a table.

Made in the USA
Monee, IL
29 October 2020